Outside the Glow

'Sir, could you brief us on the problems of Ne temere?'

(*Church of Ireland Gazette*, 26 February 1971, p. 4)

Outside the Glow

Protestants and Irishness in Independent Ireland

HEATHER K. CRAWFORD

UNIVERSITY COLLEGE DUBLIN PRESS

Preas Choláiste Ollscoile Bhaile Átha Cliath

First published 2010
by University College Dublin Press
Newman House
86 St Stephen's Green
Dublin 2
Ireland
www.ucdpress.ie

ISBN 978-1-906359-44-7

Cataloguing in Publication data
available from the British Library

The right of Heather K. Crawford to be identified as
the author of this work has been asserted by her

Typeset in Ireland in Adobe Garamond,
Janson and Trade Gothic by
Elaine Burberry and Ryan Shiels
Text design by Lyn Davies
Printed in England on acid-free paper by
CPI Antony Rowe, Chippenham

For
Elsa, Fiona, Joshua, Chloë and Callum
with love

Contents

Abbreviations

GAA	Gaelic Athletic Association
GFS	Girls' Friendly Society
ICA	Irish Countrywomen's Association
IT	*Irish Times*
NUIM	National University of Ireland Maynooth
RCB	Representative Church Body
TCD	Trinity College Dublin
UCC	University College Cork
UCD	University College Dublin
YMCA	Young Men's Christian Association
YWCA	Young Women's Christian Association

Acknowledgements

I want to acknowledge gratefully the help and support I received from so many people throughout the long process involved in producing this book. First of all, the entire project would not, of course, have been possible without the interest and enthusiasm of the people who consented to be interviewed, all of whom gave so generously of their time and effort. Several people, clerical and lay, some of them doubling as interviewees, were also instrumental in finding others who had valuable information and insights to share. Thank you all most sincerely for both the interviews and the contacts. Also, many thanks are due to those who were most helpful in supplying further details during the process of updating the PhD thesis text for this book.

Secondly, I wish to acknowledge with deepest gratitude the invaluable help, guidance and support given by the supervisor of my PhD thesis, Professor R. V. Comerford, of the Department of History, NUI Maynooth, throughout this project. Thirdly, I also want to thank Professor Jacqueline Hill and Dr Jacinta Prunty of the Department of History, NUIM, for their help and interest, and other members of the staff of the Department of History, both academic and administrative, who were always unfailingly helpful and patient, as were the library staff at Maynooth and in the Representative Church Body Library, also at UCD, Trinity and the National Library: thank you all. Particular thanks are due to Dr Susan Hood of the RCB Library, who was instrumental in providing a reproduction of the cartoon from the *Church of Ireland Gazette*, and to the editor, the Revd Ian Ellis, who graciously gave me permission to use it. Of course, I also would like to include Barbara Mennell and her staff at UCD Press in my thanks.

Friends and family have also, of course, provided invaluable support throughout this project: Miriam Moffitt gave unstintingly of her friendship, time and hospitality and I am more than grateful to her, as I am to Vanessa and Gerry, who opened their home to me on so many occasions.

HEATHER K. CRAWFORD
August 2009

Introduction

Nationalism and religion form a potent mix. And it goes without saying that the influence of each is fundamental to how we form identities – personal, communal and national. This book is based on a study which examined how they have affected the relationship between the Protestant and Catholic communities in what is now the Republic of Ireland and their respective perceptions of 'Irishness' since independence.[1] An earlier study, based on interviews carried out in 1996, found that, amongst other things, southern Protestants had a perception that they were considered as 'not entirely' Irish by their Catholic fellow citizens,[2] and the aim of my project was to assess how this perception affected individual experience on both sides of the confessional divide. Further, I wanted to see whether, at this stage of its evolution, ordinary Protestants would be prepared to break their silence on what it has been like for them to live in the state as it struggled with its divided heritage. Of course, using the term 'ordinary Protestants' has certain implications, but I want to make it clear that my aim was to give some of the majority of the minority, those who have never, for one reason or another, spoken out before, the chance to tell their story.

So, during an 18-month period in 2004–5, I set about recording personal testimony from a hundred people. Interviewees came from a wide spectrum of Irish society, and included 64 Protestants from the Church of Ireland, Presbyterian, Methodist and Quaker communities, as well as 36 Catholics. A total of 68 women and 32 men contributed, coming from differing socio-economic backgrounds and varied geographical locations. The testimony was transcribed and assessed and broad themes identified. The issues raised were then compared with the socio-historical record of the state contained in other sources, both primary and secondary, to analyse 'Irishness', to identify the dominant construction of national identity, and to see where confession came into the picture.

It was an interdisciplinary project, in that insights from historical research and other academic disciplines – in the main sociological, political and cultural studies – were used to analyse and contextualise the evidential findings. As an exploration, however, it remained within the ambit of the humanities, and, as the oral testimony was collected from only 100 people, naturally the findings were qualitative.

Some written memoir from both Catholic and Protestants was consulted, but the oral testimony was the prime source, and it predominates in what follows. When considering Protestant experience in the state, there is, of course, a great deal of significant Protestant memoir available,[3] but it is self-evident that anyone who writes such a work would not need someone else to provide them with a voice. On the value of such works, however, Robert Tobin makes a cogent point when he says in his article, memorably entitled 'Tracing again the tiny snail track':

> Rare indeed has been the Protestant writer . . . who in recounting his or her experience has not recognised how matters of origin and group belonging have been centrally important to it. Ultimately the southern Protestant fondness for memoir is attributable to neither class nostalgia nor religious compulsion, but to a heightened appreciation for the individual's relevance in reconciling the community's various pasts with its possible futures.[4]

In this project, too, the individual's capacity to make meanings from experience is what counts.

At this juncture, I would like record the strong impact *Untold Stories*,[5] Colin Murphy and Lynne Adair's collection of short essays on Protestant experience, had on me when I was in the initial stages of thinking about this project. The sometimes-expressed, frequently implied, sense of exclusion present in the 'flavour' of those short pieces seemed to indicate a need for further examination of the ways in which Protestants see themselves and feel they are seen by their fellow-citizens, so that it would be possible to consider their relationship to Irishness. Philip Roth said: 'Identity labels have nothing to do with how anyone actually experiences life'.[6] The resulting study demonstrated the antithesis of this view, showing how, in a southern Irish context, the combination of ethnic, religious, cultural, national and personal multiple identities has influenced, perhaps even governed, lived experience.

It is acknowledged that the quotations from the interviews may be somewhat longer than is the norm and that this may exercise the patience of the reader. The reason for quoting at length is to try to demonstrate the nuance and the feeling present in the words used by the interviewees as far as this can be possible when rendering speech into writing, and the reader's forbearance is therefore hoped for.

The project was prompted not only by the motives already listed but also by the observation that, nearly 90 years after partition and independence, there remain tensions in the relationship between southern Irish Protestants and the Catholic majority population of the state. The sheer durability of this under-lying current of something that is difficult to name but which could perhaps best be described as an alienating sensation of lack of safety, a 'strangeness' – felt, as will be disclosed through the oral evidence, by both sides, but in differing forms and with differing effects – is remarkable. All the more so because, in today's Irish republic, it is supposed not to exist. Indeed, its existence is strenuously denied by both sides, publicly by churchmen and politicians keen to minimise the past and to promote ecumenical rapprochement and multiculturalism respectively; privately by individuals if any attempt is made to refer to it, especially if it is couched in the form of an exclusion. Charles Flynn encountered the phenomenon during interviews for his oral history study of Dundalk in the period 1900–60: when asking about interdenominational relationships in the community, 'on two separate occasions [he] was queried for his persistence in pursuing the subject'.[7]

'Irishness' was taken to mean the combination of qualities, characteristics, assumptions, perceptions and so on that, at any particular time, go together to result in the possibility of attaching the description 'Irish' to a person, a quality or a thing. Of course, an Irish identity, personal or national, cannot be assumed to reflect a constant set of qualities and attributes. After all, people individually and collectively fulfil different roles at different times in their lives and part of the universal experience of humanity is the potential for adaptation to changing circumstances. Accordingly, Irishness was not meant to be seen as being made up of static qualities, although it is arguable that the importance of the confessional dimension – with the inevitable cultural implications that attach to it – in Irish identity formation is inflexible. For this reason, then, it is difficult to write of the issues without appearing to indicate that Irishness is made up of unchanging and unchangeable stereotypes. Indeed, two studies of national identity construction by primary schoolchildren published in 2006 disclosed that there is a tendency, reflective of current norms in society in general, towards a construction of Irish national identity reliant on static components and on stereotypes.[8] However, by striving to take 'Irishness as a category of constantly changing content . . . one can allow for the continuities with the past',[9] as well as the exigencies of the present.

The confessional divide indicates the gaps of understanding on faith, doctrine and dogma allied to ethnicity and culture that exist between Catholics and Protestants. It operates not only in the realm of overt bigotry but also, and perhaps more influentially, within the often unconsciously held bundle of underlying attitudes and perceptions that keep sectarianism alive.

Throughout, Roman Catholics are described as Catholics, except where quotations from the transcripts or other sources use 'Roman' Catholic. The term 'Protestant' is used to denote all the main Protestant reformed churches, that is, the Church of Ireland, the Methodists and the Presbyterians as well as other sub-sects. Terence Brown's view that 'since the Protestant population is such a small proportion of the total, Church of Ireland experience has tended to be normative for the whole minority' is also relevant here.[10] Quakers are referred to both as such and as members of the Society of Friends. In instances where intra-communal difference is being emphasised, this is indicated by the use of specific terminology, as, for example, when discussing the nature of Methodist isolation. Any other religious faith stream mentioned is specifically named.

When pondering the scope of the study, it was decided to exclude the situation north of the border, because to try to incorporate analysis of the highly complex situation in that part of the island and to compare it with the equally intricate conditions in the Republic would simply have made the project too unwieldy. Anyway, as it transpired, there was relatively little reference in the oral evidence to Northern Protestantism or to differences between the two territories or the two confessions in this context. However, the experience of a noticeable difference in attitude to, or treatment of, southern Protestants when there was an exacerbation of violence in the North is referred to because it came up in the interviews.

Another decision taken was to confine detailed examination of the imagination of the nation as it applies to Protestants only, primarily because of its long history, and also because it was felt that inclusion of other minority experience would further complicate the project unduly. In any case, the ways difference operates, as distinct from the content of respective agendas, can be abstracted and applied generally.

The concepts of communal memory[11] and its outcome, the emotional legacy,[12] were fundamental to this project. Communal, or collective, memory is founded on myths created with the overall aim of sustaining the concept of nationality. In this context, the word 'myth' means that mixture of empirical reality and agenda-orientated exaggeration surrounding historical events[13] which combine in communal memory to produce beliefs which, even when they do not stand up to factual analysis, reinforce the power of myths in justifying inclusion or exclusion. They keep alive the narratives of group and personal identity which bind together members of those groups and enable them to exclude outsiders who are deemed not to belong. Importantly, they distort historical narratives to serve their own purposes, and produce an enduring set of stereotypes used as a convenient 'shorthand' when reproducing and perpetuating difference.

Paul Ricoeur argued that 'collective identity is rooted in founding events which are violent events. In a sense, collective memory is a kind of storage of such violent blows, wounds and scars.'[14] Narratives of violent beginnings – and Ireland is not unique in that both the confessional divide and the state itself began with violence – enhance group solidarity and define borders between different collectivities. One such collectivity is the imagined nation, a concept described by Benedict Anderson. He suggests that the nation is imagined because there can be no possibility that everyone in even the smallest one will ever know or meet most of their fellow members, yet in the minds of each lives the image of their communion – in this case, common membership of the category of 'Irishness'. What is more, the nation is always perceived as 'a deep horizontal comradeship',[15] which goes to the nub of this enquiry: who is included in the comradeship of 'Irishness'? Who decides its components? Given that 'Irishness' can only be imagined in opposition to 'not-Irishness', in what ways is this done to effect exclusion on the basis of difference, be it confessional, ethnic or cultural?

The emotional legacy of the confessional divide is that deep unconscious divisiveness, instilled over time, liable to irrupt and to be evoked by both sides, which serves to keep the separation between the confessions alive. It is the result of belief in the myths held in the communal memory – about origins as well as events, the latter more likely to be perceived as injuries rather than blessings or benefits – and characteristics, which are 'remembered' in order to reinforce negative emotions and the deep sense of difference between groups. Their power derives from the fact that the process of 'remembering' them is largely unconscious, in that it is the result of unexamined behaviours engaged in over time for the perpetuation of group or communal distinctiveness. If the hold those 'memories' exercise were articulated and examined, it would not stand up to logical analysis.

A central tool in the execution of this project was the identification and analysis of unthinking modes of expression disclosing reliance on underlying unexamined perceptions based on the emotional legacy, usually showing themselves in the use of stereotypes. It was decided to call them 'outcroppings', and we will examine this concept in more detail later. Joseph Ruane has argued that, for Protestants, 'for the most part, [negative stereotypes like those disclosed by "outcroppings"] are irritants rather than serious issues' before stating that there is 'one Catholic perception that generates considerable resentment among Protestants: the notion that Protestants are less "Irish" than Catholics, do not identify with Ireland to the same degree, and do not fully belong'. He goes on to say that, whilst not all Catholics hold such views and that those who do are often not aware of it, they 'also reflect a continuing reluctance to grapple with this legacy'.[16]

Assessment of the degree to which these issues, conscious or unconscious, are important in inter-communal relationships in the state can only be subjective: to some they will matter more than to others. Indeed, it might be thought that the unconscious slips which underpin stereotypes are irrelevant, that even to notice them is to betray a morbid sensitivity. However, in any situation where there is a large numerical imbalance between social, religious or ethnic collectivities within any national entity now delineated by the modern concept of 'state', any minority is bound to be at least sensitised, if not sensitive – especially where religion and politics are concerned. And in the realm of the imagined nation, such sensitivities tend to proliferate, for, by its very nature, it depends upon emotional attachment to the content of the emotional legacy for its very existence.[17]

Denial of, or refusal to recognise, another's claim to membership of the imagined nation is no small thing, however difficult it may be to articulate the concepts involved. Someone adversely affected by such an exclusion can only express it in subjective terms, describing an array of emotions which can range from irritation to anger and even encompass loss or desolation, all of which, taken together, might conveniently be labelled alienation. The interviews demonstrated that there is exclusion at work, and showed that it is significant for individuals. Vitally, the study argued for the importance of taking the subjective into account, of recording how people feel about these things and the quality of their emotional response to the stimulus of alienation, because it matters not how old or how clichéd exclusionary assumptions are, but rather that they are detrimental.

Complexities surrounding personal, confessional, ethnic and national identity are daunting. Even a cursory glance at the multiple claims to and formats of 'Irishness' over the centuries bears out the postmodern stance of 'the possibility of the adoption of multiple selves and the consequent potential of many, or at least more than one, personal identities [being] available to be assumed and performed'.[18] Despite this, however, whilst broad, and surprising, differences can be found in the idea of what made up Irishness at different times, what appears to distinguish some of the elements used for construction of an Irish identity are, as already noted, remarkably static. The durability of some of the basic components of the communal memory underpinning the emotional legacy is illustrated in the testimony, showing that 'Protestant' can still equate to land-grabbing 'planter', 'English pig' and 'Protestant bastard' as well as to someone professing an inferior faith. Stereotypes occur both as 'outcroppings' and as overt insults, which differ from 'outcroppings' in that, although they, too, rely on the emotional legacy, they are deliberate and conscious retrievals of prejudice-based myths. Either way, they speak to the undercurrent of prejudice that influences the construction of Irish national identity.

When considering the use of oral testimony in any project, there are concerns which must be addressed. One of importance is the place of memory and its inaccuracy and selectivity. Yvonne McKenna, having stated that 'oral history is . . . fundamentally about memory',[19] goes on to say that it is 'no less valuable because of this'.[20] Paul Thompson argued that 'it is generally accepted that the memory process depends on that of perception',[21] coupled with interest and willingness.[22] What is more, the act of remembering is not only a conscious one based on these elements but biochemical processes are involved as well. And psychological factors also come into play, such as, for example, distortion or suppression of disagreeable facts. This, Thompson maintains, is not necessarily 'purely negative', for 'even a lie is a form of communication'.[23] Here the comparison of oral sources with each other and with historiographical primary and secondary sources is vital in order to construct authentic arguments and a cohesive narrative. Thompson also cites Maurice Halbwachs to the effect that 'the extent to which individual recollections operate within the framework of a collective memory . . . is a very fruitful perspective for exploring group consciousness, and where collective perceptions are the issue, the accuracy of memory is no longer the main focus'.[24] In sum, oral testimony provides significant and unique information from the past by conveying the individual and collective consciousness which *is* that past, and 'it is "precisely this historical perspective which allows us to assess long-term meaning in history"'.[25]

The historical accuracy of memory was less central to the study than was the subjective picture presented by the evidence in the context within which it was offered, augmented by corroboration from other sources. Rather, memory was regarded in the sense described by Ricoeur when he stated that 'remembering is a way of *doing* things, not only with words, but with our minds; in remembering or recollecting we are exercising our memory, which is a kind of action'.[26] Thus memory is at the same time an act and a process which contains both conscious and unconscious acts that produce meaning. Joan Sangster sets out other valuable factors present in oral testimony, 'such as expression, intonation and metaphors [which] also offer clues to the construction of historical memory. . . . Also . . . silences and omissions',[27] so that it is imperative to see 'the interview [more] as a mediated source, moulded by the political and social worldview of the author and subject'[28] than as an occasion for the pursuit of 'absolute truth' or objectivity. Luisa Passerini is another who emphasises the need for 'a firm grounding of oral narratives in their material and social context, and a probing analysis of the relation between the two'.[29]

Yvonne McKenna described her study of thirty Irish women religious as 'a book about identity', as being 'about subjectivity and identity formation, about the ways in which Irish women religious have inhabited, negotiated and contested a sense of self as Irish, as women, as Catholics and as religious'.[30] She highlights the ways in which oral history integrates into scholarship the histories of those who have been 'ignored or obscured',[31] something my study sought also to do. To some, given their former position as a governing elite, the notion that southern Irish Protestants have been 'ignored or obscured' may seem novel, but, in independent Ireland, there is much to support the view that they have, indeed, been marginalised.

The main questions which the study set out to explore were: what part was and is played by concepts of 'Irishness' in the formation of southern Irish identity or identities? What is the nature and extent of perceptions held by southern Protestants of their exclusion from Irishness and the possession of an Irish identity? What, if any, is the nature and extent of southern Catholic perceptions of the exclusion of Protestants from 'Irishness' and the possession of an Irish identity? And to what, if any, extent, and for what reasons, did or do southern Protestants themselves collude in and/or use strategies of exclusion? Finally, in the context of the rapid social changes occurring in the present-day Irish Republic as it confronts multiculturalism, is there a particular exclusion for Protestants, one that focuses on confessional and cultural difference as well as the historical past with its complex resentments, or is there a current dominant construction of the category of 'Irishness' that defines itself similarly against all minorities?

CHAPTER ONE

The Background

On 18 April 1949, the 26-county Irish state founded in 1922 became a republic. In May of that year, in tune with the determined optimism of the Protestants who had decided to stay on under the new order at independence, the *Church of Ireland Gazette* reported that: 'members of the Church of Ireland were treated as Irishmen entitled to their religious and political opinions by all except a limited number of extremists'.[1] Various commentators noted how the state had set out to treat its minorities fairly from a legal point of view.[2] On the face of it, the rights of minorities in the new state were recognised. The Free State constitution of 1922 guaranteed religious freedom to all minorities.[3] Nor did the state countenance manifestations of bigotry against Protestants,[4] and the community was given preferential treatment on various aspects of education policies. However, the dynamics existing between any majority and the minorities with which it interacts can generate tensions in areas less readily accessible for examination than the legal relationship between a state and its citizens. A multitude of attitudes and perceptions govern everyday relationships between individuals and groups within a society, and the existence of disquiet at any level usually indicates that all is not well. Certainly, the findings of Mennell et al. in 1996 that some Protestants perceived that Catholics thought of them as 'not entirely' Irish indicated that facets of the inter-communal relationship contained as yet unresolved tensions.[5]

In the Republic, expressions of sectarianism *per se* are relatively rare, but they can still occasionally surface, as they did with the daubing of 'Prods out' on St Brigid's Church of Ireland church in Clara, Co. Offaly, in 2008.[6] When they do, they are condemned by all sectors of society. Other more nuanced irruptions into the public sphere of assumptions based on difference tend to engender outbursts of varying degrees of fury in the Letters to the Editor section of the *Irish Times*. One that springs immediately to mind occurred in

January 2007, with Fine Gael leader Enda Kenny's evocation of the Irish as 'a Celtic and a Christian people' in an attempt to mobilise support for his party in the general election. There was an immediate response, most of it indignant. Maurice Dockrell, an eminent member of the Protestant community who has served in public office, wrote:

> So Mr Kenny's vision of Ireland – the core Ireland, so to speak – excludes people who are of Viking, Anglo-Norman or Anglo-Irish descent. Which is bad enough, but where does it leave the million or so unionists that Fine Gael claims it would like to see as part of a United Ireland? And – this is of rather more immediate relevance – what is our burgeoning immigrant population supposed to think of this outbreak of intolerance, unthinking or otherwise?[7]

The *Irish Times*' editorial for the same day maintained that Mr Kenny was being maligned in the generally outraged response to his speech in that it contained many positive proposals for the integration of immigrants into Irish society, and was in fact 'a far cry from the intolerant reaction to it'.[8] However, two points are relevant: firstly, the demonstration of how unthinking modes of expression used by a leading Irish politician in the twenty-first century betrayed underlying assumptions based on and deriving from ethnic and cultural differences; secondly, as both these categories, in Ireland, automatically include hostilities rooted in confessional differences, the fact that strong reaction can still be produced in the community at large. We will consider the nature and source of these unthinking modes of expression in more detail later, but, having isolated one example of how the emotional legacy can ambush the unwary, the ways confessional and other related aspects of difference surface, subtly but insistently, in the private sphere, and how they are experienced by ordinary citizens, are what principally concern us in what follows.

It is not easy to get people to talk about sectarianism. However, when the reluctance of individuals to discuss confessional and other types of difference is overcome, acknowledgement of that certain something present in inter-confessional contact surfaces. It ranges from an elusive unease to distinctly uncomfortable sensations, depending on circumstance and, perhaps, personality. Not everybody senses it. When they do, they may prefer to stay silent. Its existence is often denied, sometimes forcefully, mostly from a desire not to make trouble – an outcome of the well-documented trait of staying quiet on controversial issues on the Protestant side, and a shying away from unpleasant fact on the Catholic. And it is most important to acknowledge and emphasise that the majority of Catholics are unaware that they might hold exclusionary attitudes about Protestants.

Given the nature of the Protestant perception disclosed by Mennell et al.'s study, it was clear that any investigation of these matters would centre on what people thought being Irish meant, and how that was experienced. So, in order to build a picture of Irish life, interviewees living in the Republic were asked about their lives and experience under the headings of education, segregation and integration, inter-church marriage and work. They were also asked about their views on what constituted 'Irishness'. The cohort of interviewees was assembled by the 'snowball' method: having described the project to a few people, the first interviewee 'volunteered' herself, a second did the same and introduced the third, and momentum was established by word of mouth. Clergy became involved, establishing contact with parishioners, and those parishioners involved friends and acquaintances. Hence selection was random. What interviewees said was transcribed, then analysed and contextualised against the state's cultural, political and sociological history to examine how each confession defined national identity. The testimony was also scrutinised for differences of perception between the confessions, as well as the effects of those differences.[9]

Using confession at birth as the categorising principle, 36 Catholics and 64 Protestants were interviewed. The following detailed breakdown of confession represents each interviewee's own description of their confessional situation at the time of interview: three Protestants; one Anglican (convert from Catholicism); one Canadian Anglican, now Church of Ireland, and included in that total; 44 Church of Ireland (one convert from Catholicism); eight Methodist; one Presbyterian in early life who later attended Methodist and Church of Ireland churches; two Church of England; two self-designated members of the Society of Friends, one of whom also attends the Church of Ireland and one a self-designated Quaker, a recent convert from Catholicism; 11 Roman Catholic; 23 Catholic; one who called himself an 'RC'; one atheist (raised as Church of Ireland); and one Christian (raised as Catholic, child of a mixed marriage who attended a Church of Ireland primary school).

The interviews were collected mainly in counties Wicklow, Dublin, Tipperary, Sligo, Mayo and West Cork, but many of the participants resided in places other than those where they were born and brought up, so the geographical range of the study was wider in scope than might at first appear, encompassing, in fact, the whole island of Ireland. Eight interviewees were born in England and one in Canada, coming to Ireland later in life, usually upon marriage, but all of them had lived in Ireland and experienced its systems and institutions – particularly all those involved in bringing up families – for long enough to have developed informed opinions upon the matters under scrutiny in this study.

The age range covered in the project was 17 to 102, with the greatest number, 14 women and ten men, falling in the 60–69 years of age bracket. The mean and median ages of the cohort were 63.84 and 64.5 years respectively. Thirty-two females and 24 males were or had been married and 11 were in inter-church, that is Protestant/Catholic, marriages. The latter group comprised four couples where both spouses were interviewed, one Catholic woman whose Protestant husband was not interviewed and two Protestant women whose Catholic husbands were not interviewed. One young Catholic woman was engaged to be married to a Protestant, and one Protestant woman's first marriage had been to a Catholic.

Forty-one people attained university or postgraduate level, which breaks down to approximately 40 per cent of Protestant and 42.5 per cent of Catholic interviewees, and approximately nine – 15 per cent – of the Protestants and five – 14.5 per cent – of the Catholics went no further than primary level. The Irish report of the European values and attitudes survey of 1981 found that, at that stage, 'about the same proportions of Protestants as of Catholics completed their education between ages 16 and 19, but far fewer [Protestants] (by definition, older people) stopped at 14 or earlier, and rather more are "graduates"'.[10] Statistics based on the 2006 census, which confirmed that the population of the state totalled 4,239,848,[11] show that, in the general population in 2005, almost a quarter of those aged 15-64 had a third-level qualification, which figure includes 'third-level non-degree' qualifications.[12] This indicates that, taking the 'graduate' and 'postgraduate' total of forty-one, there was a higher percentage of graduate and postgraduate interviewees than in the population overall. Also, if the 'technical' level can be added in on the basis of its providing vocational qualifications which might possibly equate to the present-day diploma-level – which, in turn, might encompass the category of 'third level non-degree' qualifications in the census statistics – a total of 63 interviewees attained this level. These figures break down to 24 Protestants and 17 Catholics in the graduate and postgraduate levels, 37.5 per cent of the Protestants and 47.2 per cent of the Catholics. If the technical category is added to the graduate and postgraduate ones, 39 Protestants and 24 Catholics attained this level, 60 per cent of the Protestants and 66.6 per cent of the Catholics.

The greatest number of interviewees were engaged in teaching – 14 women and 11 men, of whom 11 of the total were Protestant and seven were Catholic. Then came the agricultural occupations, which included nine women – some of whom self-designated as 'farmer' and others as 'farmer's wife' – and eight men. Fourteen of the total occupied on the land were Protestant, and three were Catholic. Next were the caring professions, which included different categories of nursing, counselling and so on. Of the total involved in this vocational area, all 11 were women, nine of whom were Protestant and two Catholic. The same number of women was involved in the banking, clerical and secretarial sector, with ten being Protestant and one Catholic. Three women were civil servants, and all three were Catholic. Of the self-employed, three were women and four men, four of the total being Protestant and three Catholic.

Returning to the irruption of unthinking intolerance highlighted by Maurice Dockrell in respect of Enda Kenny's words, before the project took shape the occurrence of what it was decided to call 'outcroppings' had been noted. These are assumptions, surfacing in everyday communication, that betray a *lack* of acknowledgement of, or tolerance of, difference, particularly in the confessional arena and where that links to Irishness. Tolerance, that is, in the sense of acceptance and recognition of the possibility of plurality. The following are only a few illustrations: being told, 'But you *have* to be Catholic to be Irish!' Or hearing on RTÉ Radio 1, in respect of all the citizens of the state: 'We'd *all* remember the smell of incense from when we were kids.' Or, in a newspaper questionnaire, a list of queries addressed to its entire readership of whatever faith: 'Do you go to mass every Sunday?' Or President McAleese's reference, in a speech made in 2006 and based on apparently one-sided and unconsciously held assumptions, to the inculcation in Protestant children of hatred for their Catholic counterparts in Northern Ireland which seemed to make no allowance for the fact that such conditioning might also happen in reverse. Or, during a summer downpour, when sheltering under a tree on campus with a Catholic cleric never encountered before or since, and complaining about the weather, being told: 'At least we can offer it up!' Another example was noted and recorded by Miriam Moffitt in 2006, when George Hook admonished an Irish-American for belonging to the Republican Party, saying it was 'almost worse than your forefathers taking the soup during the famine'.[13] Calling someone a 'souper' bears a portmanteau of derogatory confessional and personal inferences, which will be examined in detail later. Of course, 'outcroppings' based on religious, ethnic, historical and cultural misperceptions are, for the most part, unconscious – and thus perhaps all the more insidious – slips and are not intended deliberately to be provocative or offensive, but nevertheless they often can, and do, provoke negative reactions.

The 'outcroppings' already listed are based on Catholocentric assumptions, and that this happens is not, on many levels, surprising. J. H. Whyte documented how the Catholic ethos came to dominate the new state and how the Catholic Church's moral teaching on divorce, abortion and contraception was incorporated into the legal system, although, in his view, 'these laws were not in any sense directed "against Protestants"'.[14] Furthermore, Tom Inglis argued that 'it is necessary to understand how being a Catholic occupied the minds and hearts of Irish people'[15] – although, in this context it must be underlined, not *all* of them: some might have been just as preoccupied with being Protestant, Jewish or Muslim – in the devout Catholic society that developed. Indeed, one 47-year-old Catholic interviewee from the west commented: 'I think . . . we're very cocooned . . . as Catholics in Ireland having mainly Catholics around us'. It is hardly to be wondered at, therefore, that, quite apart from any theological or dogmatic issues, Catholicism was assumed to be central in the lives of the majority of Irish people and, for them, that centrality was automatic.

Other examples of automatic, unthinking assumptions which will be encountered in the oral evidence are sustained by the historical distortions of the emotional legacy. This, as we have seen, is a fund of myths which is, in turn, based on collective memory. To recap briefly, the term 'myth' in this context means the fact-based but essentially altered 'stories' that combine in the collective memory to produce beliefs which, even when they do not stand up to examination, reinforce the power of myths to define who belongs and who does not. Myths also keep alive the narratives of group and personal identity which bind members of those groups together and both enable and sanction 'othering'. A vital characteristic is their distortion to fit various agendas so that an enduring set of stereotypes is produced for use as a convenient 'shorthand' when reproducing and perpetuating difference. Another important factor is that there is no need for someone to 'know' the specific details of those myths for the internalisation of their messages and for exclusionary behaviours to result: they are absorbed, unexamined, from the surrounding culture.

Myths of difference are not always based on the historical past. They can also be beliefs held by one group about another which, if the myths based on the epic or historic past or on fanciful constructions of origins can be called mega- or meta-myths, might be termed 'mini-myths'. These are usually personal characteristics purported to be possessed by one group as seen, 'remembered' and related by another until they take on the form of 'truths' about personae or characteristics that 'they all' have. For instance, in the Midi region of France, Catholics demonised and 'othered' Protestants by calling them 'gorges noires', or 'black throats', based on the belief that they had black tongues. To this was sometimes added the conviction that they also had an eye in the middle of the forehead, and 'numerous tales witness, right into the nineteenth century, the strength of the Catholic belief that the Protestants had black throats'.[16]

On a more trivial level, where the intent is to distance the 'other' rather than to go all the way to demonisation, interviewees spoke of the ways in which Protestants were seen to be 'different', some expressing themselves in more quasi-complimentary, as well as some sillier, tones than others, but still exemplifying the 'mini-myth' with its disproportionate power to 'other'. A 20-year-old Catholic interviewee from Donegal, said:

> I remember . . . when I was about seven or eight, one of the girls in the playground saying to me: Do you know how to tell a Protestant from a Catholic? And I was like: No, how? They have black rings around their eyes! And then you'd go round looking for people that had dark rings around their eyes. Just ridiculous. . . . These definite ideas that these people were very different.

A young Catholic brought up in a south Dublin suburb also identified Protestants by external signifiers when she was a child:

> There was . . . one Protestant house in the road. . . . And how I used to think they were Protestants was . . . those little . . . wooden decorations for a front garden . . . an oblong of wood, with spikes sticking out of it. . . . And I thought that's because they were Protestants! . . . [T]hat's what a Protestant did, got those white things, because they were really cool! They always had a beautifully kept garden, they were also painting and stuff. They're Protestants!

Another example of how the trivialising of difference can highlight it occurred at a social gathering when the – mixed, but predominantly Catholic – company agreed that Protestants wash fruit before eating it, and Catholics do not. It can be seen, then, that myths underpinning difference do not have to be based on 'history': qualities attributable to individuals, even their appearance, can attain mythical status in the differentiating stakes.

How, then, did this all come about? In order to understand how the emotional legacy arising out of the relationship between Irish Catholics and

Protestants came into being, we have to go back a long way. As we have seen, Paul Ricoeur argued that 'collective identity is rooted in founding events which are violent events [and] collective memory is a kind of storage of such violent blows, wounds and scars'.[17] This is certainly true in this context: the repercussions of the violent beginnings not only of the centuries-old confessional divide but also of the Irish Republic itself are still working themselves out in constructions of both Irish national and confessional identities.[18]

Although the Anglo-Norman barons who invaded Ireland in the twelfth century were not, of course, Protestant, a form of myth-generated contraction came to operate within the emotional legacy, conflating them with Protestant settlers granted lands by the Tudors in sixteenth-century plantations. Over time, 'elements of long established conflict between dispossessed Irish and occupying Anglo-Irish [were transformed] into the terms of conflict between Catholic and Protestant'.[19] This fusion of Protestantism with 'usurping settler' set the scene for continuing ideological and social conflict stemming from unequal power ratios and for communal polarisation.[20] An important set of myths in the emotional legacy stems from the position in which Protestants found themselves in sixteenth-century Ireland. 'In 1641, 59 per cent of Ireland was owned by Catholics . . . the original Gaelic inhabitants and the Old English.'[21] The Catholics rebelled against the usurping 'planters', though not against the crown.[22] Exaggerated reports of brutal treatment of Protestants by Catholics became mythologised, and following the English civil war these myths were used to justify Oliver Cromwell's Irish campaign, this time focusing on Protestant brutality perpetrated upon Catholics. This, in turn, produced more powerful myths of violence and persecution, reinforced by the fact that, after Cromwell's defeat of the rebels, more confiscated Catholic lands were given to Protestants.

By the end of the seventeenth century, the minority Protestant ascendancy was firmly in control of the Irish polity. Another set of myths concerning the relative civility and barbarity of the rival confessions developed as psychological justification of the subjugation of the Catholic majority because of their lack of civility.[23] The struggle between settler and native took on connotations of the battle between good and evil: 'the Irish were barbarous not only because they were Irish, but because they were Catholics'.[24] The Protestant ascendancy's monopoly on political power excluded Catholics through enactment and operation of the penal laws, authorised, as it were, by their purported barbarity. At that time, a Protestant's Irishness was based on ownership of land, consequent economic power and self-definition as the civilising element in society. At the same time, however, whilst loyal to the crown and belonging to an Ireland that belonged to Britain, he also desired legislative independence. From an emotional legacy standpoint, the stereotype that equates all Protestants with the 'Anglo-Irish' Protestant landlord intent on oppressing poverty-stricken Catholic tenants is epitomised by the ascendancy Protestant.

The aims of the Society of United Irishmen (1791) were perhaps the first organised articulation of a desire for complete separation of Ireland from Britain. Although it failed, the 1798 rebellion inspired by the society generated another important set of myths of reciprocal brutality, redolent with echoes of the 1640s, stemming both from the rising itself and its quelling. Given the United Irishmen's ethos, a supreme irony was that the rebellion became the pivotal event which brought about, in 1800, the Act of Union with Britain.

In the meantime, the lot of Catholics had been improving: by 1793, legal disabilities directed against them had almost disappeared, and, by the 1820s, Daniel O'Connell had mobilised Catholics and was propelling them through the successful campaign for emancipation. This was granted in 1829, by which time Catholics had become a politically aware power nexus. Catholic nationalism developed as emancipation, land reform, tithe, electoral and poor law reforms all contributed to the leaching of supremacy from the ascendancy: the balance of power was inexorably shifting. After emancipation, O'Connell started campaigning for repeal of the Act of Union. Although not achieved, the campaign consolidated the process whereby Protestant excludability from the emerging Catholic nationalist construction of the imagined nation took shape: Catholicism and Irish nationalism were becoming united in a new national identity that 'disqualified' Protestants.

The great famine, 1846 to 1848, the 'great dislocation',[25] caused immense suffering principally for the Catholic poor, who, already weakened by a series of bad harvests, died in ever-increasing numbers from both starvation and disease. Emigration increased, and an overall trend of decline in population began that continued to the middle of the twentieth century. It also generated a new wave of myths for the emotional legacy based on universal oppression by the landlord class.[26] The sense of grievance borne by the poor 'was sharpened by sectarian resentment; [most] of the tenants were Roman Catholics, while the landlords were almost to a man Protestants'.[27] Even the poorest Protestant was regarded as privileged by Catholics, a perception that still infuses the emotional legacy.

The 1820s also saw the start of an intensive programme of Protestant evangelism, the impetus for which derived at least in part from a political agenda which saw Roman Catholicism as a conspiracy against liberty aimed at dominating all Christians.[28] On the purely religious front, it also stemmed, according to Alan Acheson, 'from an evangelical imperative . . . not to win converts, but to teach faith in Jesus Christ'.[29] By the start of the 1850s, myth already had it that during the famine only starving Catholics who converted – the infamous 'soupers' – were fed by the missioners, and more anti-Protestant myths, this time centred on proselytism allied to provision of famine relief, became 'facts' in the emotional legacy. However, Acheson argues that in the context of the Great Famine

> souperism is an intrusive irrelevance. The Church of Ireland can recall without distraction the unremitting efforts of her clergy and their families to save lives, and with pride the sacrifice of those men and women who in love laid down their own.[30]

Miriam Moffitt has examined the role played by the evangelising Irish Christian Mission to the Roman Catholics at the time of the famine, and, as well as concluding that the Mission's claims on the number of converts were, to say the least, over-estimates of its effectiveness, she has traced how, well into the twentieth century,

> proselytism came to be interpreted as a nation-wide occurrence to the extent that by 1937, what was, in effect, a very localised provision of mission-relief, was perceived as a national 'hurt'.[31]

The need to evangelise the Catholics of the Irish Free State was shared across the Protestant denominations. Presbyterian and Methodist colporteurs systematically covered the country in the early years of the twentieth century with the aim, as it was put, of bringing Roman Catholics to Christ. By that stage, they continued to consider their activities essential because of a perception that, although Catholics were beginning to read the scriptures and think independently, they were also in danger of becoming involved in communism.[32] Although missionary activities tailed off as the century progressed, they did continue for quite some time, and an eye-witness account of what happened to some Protestant street preachers in the early 1960s was supplied by Frank Sweeney:

> I was a newly appointed teacher in Granard, Co. Longford in 1963. One evening about 4 p.m. on the Main Street . . . a few preachers – I think three of

them – began preaching from the pavement. Very soon the fathers of the town descended upon them. These were mainly the shopkeepers of the town and they were in the process of physically removing them from the place. Anyway they were determined to not let them speak. Just then the local sergeant appeared and pointed out to the locals the rights of these people. The preachers made an effort for a while and then moved on. The police presence remained.

The good burghers of Granard were, it would appear, still influenced by the threat of proselytism as viewed through the distortions of the emotional legacy.

Fear of proselytism did not, of course, only derive from perceptions centred on the famine or in rural areas. Jacinta Prunty has catalogued the nineteenth-century denominational divisions that led to myths concerning it in areas where poverty and overcrowding existed, principally in the Dublin slums. Sectarian claim and counter-claim of the poaching of souls contingent on the doling out of charity could and did lead not only to verbal hostility but also to physical violence.[33] That the suspicion of Protestant proselytism was still prevalent following independence is further demonstrated in a paper delivered to the Maynooth Union in 1926 by the Revd Fr M. Creedon entitled 'Proselytism: its operations in Ireland'.[34] The emotive tone reads distastefully now, but it does disclose the strength of the fear of proselytism and the suspicion with which Protestant charitable work was perceived. Suffice it to say that, with the agreement of at least some of his listeners evidenced by the record of the discussion following the paper, Fr Creedon's views that the 'base' Protestant proselytiser tried to 'tamper with religious beliefs by bribery', that 'the proselytising mind is dead to the extreme spiritual dereliction of its own Protestant multitudes', and that the aim was 'to detach [the souper] from the Catholic church', were not seen as exceptional. Furthermore, he listed the means by which 'proselytisers' supposedly went about their business, listing not only street preaching but also hospitals, free meal services and hostels offering shelter and food with which, it was alleged, they cloaked their activities and which were part of the 'proselytising system'.[35]

In her study of the work of the Protestant Orphan Society in the nineteenth and early twentieth centuries, June Cooper has pinpointed the problems faced by the Church of Ireland when it came to perceptions of its charitable works. In the first two decades of the twentieth century, the society admitted children of Protestant parentage and children of mixed marriages, who then received a Church of Ireland religious education. However, she argues, evidence suggests that the committee refused specific inter-church marriage cases because they were reluctant to become embroiled in any form of inter-faith conflict that might arise between the society, Catholic relatives, and/or Catholic clergy who opposed the placement of children in the Protestant rather than the Catholic child welfare system. By refusing certain cases, the Protestant Orphan Society hoped to prevent any allegations of proselytising, but in so doing ironically they ran the risk of triggering further criticism because of their alleged sectarianism.[36]

Of course, nineteenth-century Protestant evangelical activity was bound to trigger intense resentment amongst Catholics. However, Miriam Moffitt has pinpointed the crux of the problems arising from the perceptions surrounding it with her findings: the number of conversions was exaggerated, and the means used to effect them, although there may well have been some instances of unscrupulous methods, were not in the main the nefarious activities that the emotional legacy held them out to be. All in all, a portmanteau of other socio-economic resentments became entangled with confessional ones, so that landlordism, the famine and the nineteenth-century evangelical crusade all contributed to the potent sense of Catholic grievance. In the context of nineteenth-century societal imbalances, these aspects of confessional difference did nothing to alleviate inter-communal hostility, and, in the twentieth century, they persisted to colour inimical perceptions.

From the 1860s on, Gladstone, increasingly convinced of social and legal inequities in Ireland, set out on a series of political measures in repeated efforts to ameliorate conditions. It was immediately apparent that, from a Protestant perspective, the legislative programme would appear specifically directed against the minority elite rather than against the conditions it sought to improve. Nevertheless it went ahead. In 1871 the Anglican Church of Ireland was disestablished. In 1870 a land act was passed which started the process of devolution of land from landlord to tenant proprietors. From mid-nineteenth century, the franchise had been based on occupation rather than property owning, allowing more rural Catholics into the polity. Land reforms continued through independence into the Free State. The new class of Catholic 'small farmers' became a considerable power bloc in the agriculture-based economic system of the emerging state, as, save in Belfast, industrialisation failed to develop in Ireland.[37] Some even saw themselves as descendants of the mythic Gaelic proprietors,[38] defining their identity in oppositional terms to that of their former Protestant landlords.

The politics of unionism allied to Protestantism began to combine in opposition to those of burgeoning Catholic nationalism.[39] Originally, the romantic nationalism that captured the popular imagination,[40] formulated by Thomas Davis and the Young Ireland movement in the early 1840s, was inclusive, wanting an independent nation where Catholic and Protestant could both find a place.[41] However, it also emphasised dying for Ireland, which 'helped inculcate a verbal cult of physical violence . . . inseparably part of Irish nationalism from this time on'.[42]

The end of the nineteenth century had seen an upsurge of cultural nationalism centred on romantic ideas of a mythical Gaelic past. Two organisations were particularly important: the Gaelic Athletic Association, formed in 1884 to encourage Irish sports to the express exclusion of 'foreign' – British – ones, and the Gaelic League, founded in 1893 with the aim of promoting the Irish language and literature and of 'de-anglicising' Irish culture.[43] Many of the League's numbers, members also of Sinn Féin and involved in the rising of 1916, became legislators after independence.

Paradoxically, it had been nineteenth-century Protestant interest that had kept Irish alive in the face of the British government's policy to replace it by English through the curriculum of the primary education system set up in 1831. This interest was not entirely without ulterior motive, for the language was undoubtedly seen as a tool for converting Catholics. However, it also meant that, despite efforts to eradicate it in favour of English through the primary school system from its inception, Irish was still available for the Gaelic League to promote within a culturally nationalistic agenda in the late nineteenth and early twentieth centuries. But myth insisted that Protestants were universally hostile to the language and culture because of their attachment to their 'Anglo' ethnic and cultural heritage.[44] The Free State government introduced compulsory Irish in the confessionally segregated schools, together with other curricular changes, particularly in history, designed to inculcate its vision of the new construction of national identity. Although it had vital cultural implications for them, the language policy was opposed by Protestants primarily because it caused a drop in overall educational standards due to what they saw as an overemphasis on the language.

By the second decade of the twentieth century, the ideals of the nationalists, of Sinn Féin and of the labour leader James Connolly had fused into revolutionary nationalism.[45] These developments were regarded with great apprehension by Protestant unionists, who feared what might be in store for them in a new nationalist state. Plans were made for the Easter rising in 1916. As a military operation it failed, but the summary execution of the leaders by the British turned hitherto-hostile public opinion in the rebels' favour.[46] Because of irreconcilable differences between unionist Protestants, strongest in the northern areas, and nationalist southern Catholics, partition of Ireland became inevitable. Sinn Féin had been declared illegal, but nevertheless its candidates successfully contested every constituency in the general election of 1918. They met in Dublin, proclaiming themselves the government of Ireland. The British government, afraid of alienating American opinion, delayed taking action, so that Sinn Féin was able further to consolidate its position. Eventually, the Anglo-Irish war broke out in 1919. The Irish Republican Army fought a guerrilla campaign against the British army and police, who countered with the 'Black and Tans' and the Auxiliary mercenary forces; the indiscriminate brutality exercised by all concerned reinforced the emotional legacy.

By January 1921, Britain's choice lay between military conquest and offering terms acceptable to Sinn Féin. It was a dangerous time for everyone, particularly for those who lived in the countryside, but the fear engendered among the Protestant population because of their vulnerability in the face of the anarchy surrounding them was stimulated by reports of ill treatment meted out to the scattered rural members of the community throughout the south. At the same time, the working-class Catholic minority in the north of the country also suffered at the hands of Protestants: this perceived 'cause and effect' was to continue to dog inter-confessional relationships at various times well into the twentieth century. And, in emotional legacy terms, the divisive conflict perceived as adequate reason for the sanctioning of sectarianism in both parts of the now-divided island bore echoes of the myths accruing to the rebellions of 1641 and 1798. The Anglo-Irish war ended with a bitterly contested treaty, ratified by the Dáil[47] on 7 January 1922, dividing the island into the Protestant-majority British North and the 26-county Free State with its Catholic majority. The treaty was unacceptable to republicans, who wanted an independent whole-island republic, and civil war broke out on 6 June 1922.

Southern Protestants were the target of attacks during the struggle for independence and the civil war. D. H. Akenson saw this violence as sectarian, 'mostly a rural affair [consisting] of hectoring, intimidating, burning, and murdering isolated Protestants, most, but not all, of whom were owners of small town businesses or of relatively large farms'.[48] Leigh-Ann Coffey, however, argues that the causation may have been more complex: in country areas '"Protestant" was synonymous with "planter" and "land grabber", creating an identity with both religious and agrarian elements',[49] a direct link to the emotional legacy. What is beyond doubt is that the situation was seldom clear-cut and many divisive factors, not least class and economic, were at work.

A large number of Protestants left the Free State, sometimes forced out, often having to abandon their possessions. Others stayed, locked within a need to remain muted for fear of drawing attention to themselves. Even staying silent was no guarantee: 'Neutrality and passivity could not overcome past confessional divisions and abiding ethnic and political stereotypes. In the Irish revolution, an unobtrusive unionist was still a unionist.'[50] Peter Hart found that, over the period 1911–26, the territory covered by the 'Irish Free State lost 34 per cent of [its] Protestant population'.[51] From being approximately a quarter of the population of the whole island in 1920, Protestants were no more than 7.4 per cent of the population of the new 26 county state.[52] They were largely, though not universally, unionist in political affiliation, which is to say that they would, at that stage, have preferred to remain linked to Britain. Most were Church of Ireland (Anglican), with significant subgroups of Methodists and Presbyterians and other smaller sects.

The dominant construction of national identity as Catholic, nationalist, Gaelic and centred on the Irish language was firmly in place in the new state, and Protestants who stayed on saw the maintenance of their ethos, culture and social practices threatened by Catholic numerical superiority and newly acquired political power. Public Irishness in the early years was clearly Catholic as well as culturally and politically nationalist and it ignored plurality. Along with other minorities in the Free State, Protestants 'experienced hegemonic constructions of national identity, in various ways, as ideological justifications for material, spatial or political exclusion'.[53] As a result, from independence to the end of the 1940s the community kept to itself.[54] A not inconsiderable aspect of that isolationism, and not the least important, was the community's need to recover from its experiences during the struggle for independence and to assess where it stood in the new scheme of things. They centred their lives on church and parish life[55] and socialised only with each other in both urban and rural areas as a defensive tactic against hostility and the perceived threat of assimilation. Needless to say, Protestant withdrawal reinforced lingering stereotypes of Protestant snobbishness and elitism. As with all stereotypes, this perception had some truth in it, but it needs to be realised that there was also the lingering, and marginalising, feeling that they might simply not be welcome.

Another pivotal misperception, to be developed later but which is outlined here, is that of universal Protestant prosperity and privilege. Protestant domination of the economy in Ireland originated in the seizure, occupation and exploitation of land and the elite position of the Protestant landowning elite of the eighteenth and nineteenth centuries, which lasted until the late nineteenth century. As a consequence, there is no doubt that they held the economic high ground in Ireland for a long time, although Kurt Bowen contends that 'the economic dominance of Protestants in the South had been broken by 1922, since they had lost control of the country's major productive base – namely the land'.[56] In *Protestants in a Catholic State*, he analyses the extremely complex relationship between the size of the community and the operations of class and economic advantage to show how 'the proportion of industries under [Protestant] control had fallen from approximately 50 per cent in 1966 to 24 per cent in 1973'. Similarly, he traces the decline of the Protestant firm, where owner, management and staff were co-religionists. Indeed, many employees 'had never considered looking [for employment] beyond their own community' – but neither, he thought, would Catholics. He demonstrates that, by the early 1970s in urban settings, Protestant privilege had all but died out, and, in any case, was no longer a barrier to Catholic advancement.[57] However, it will be seen from the oral evidence that there remain lingering resentments grounded in misperceptions of unfair privilege.

The perpetuation of, and aggravation at, the myth of universal Protestant wealth will be seen in the feeling and frustration apparent in a speech made by Bishop R. G. Perdue in 1975, when he indicated, from specific knowledge on the income levels disclosed by education grant applications, that many of the community suffered real economic hardship.[58] It is also significant that he went on to say that Catholics 'know surprisingly little about us, about our difficulties, and frustrations, economic, social and religious'.[59] Indeed, rather than considering Protestants to be fellow-citizens with daily concerns similar to their own, it appeared that they could still be perceived only through the distorting prism of the emotional legacy. Also, when the stereotype of the wealthy Protestant is aggregated to the fact that the community is now predominantly middle class, it will be comprehended not only how the subliminal message that *all* Protestants are privileged has been reinforced strongly, but also that things are not necessarily as they were in the past. These, and many other, aspects of difference will be considered in detail in subsequent chapters, and the oral evidence will show that a mono-dimensional view of any group, in this case the southern Irish Protestant community, can never represent the real picture or the inherent diversity it possesses.

After the isolation of the early decades, by the time the republic was declared in 1949, the community became more outward looking, and its members began to interact more with Catholics and actively to row in behind the state.[60] Inter-communal social boundaries crumbled; education became, for demographic reasons, more confessionally mixed in the schools, although the principle of denominationalism was and is still in place; inter-church marriage increased, although it still met with disapproval[61] because of the Catholic Church's insistence that children of such unions be raised as Catholics, and the confessions mixed more in the workplace. Overall, although they still worked to retain their group identity, it was then that to all intents and purposes Protestants started to become a part of mainstream southern Irish society. As we shall see, however, their position in the community of the imagined nation was, and remains, a different matter.

CHAPTER TWO

Segregation and Education

It has long been recognised that education systems can be used for more than teaching the three Rs and instilling a modicum of good behaviour into unruly youth. Ideologies and agendas, be they religious, political or cultural, are also inculcated and transmitted in the classrooms of a nation.[1] There are two prime examples of the use of Irish schools to promote particular agendas or programmes. One was the systematic attempt to erase the Irish language by the imposition of English and its culture in the curriculum of the national primary-cycle education system set up by the British in 1831. Another was the desire of the founders of the Free State to reverse this process: extensive curricular changes and a language policy designed to replace English by Irish as the day-to-day language for all purposes were brought in immediately following independence with the aim of producing, reproducing and reinforcing the dominant construction of Catholic nationalist identity around the central pivot of Irish and its culture.[2]

Originally, the British government had not only wanted to impose its cultural agenda on Irish children but had also aimed to use the primary education system to promote multidenominationalism because it recognised the potential for disharmony inherent in ongoing sectarianism. The intention was, therefore, that all children from an area were to share school premises separated only by gender and into faith streams for religious instruction. However, because of inter-confessional jockeying for advantage and the hold exercised by sectarianism in Irish society, within 20 years the system was effectively denominationalised.[3] And so it remains: despite there now being some multi- and inter-denominational schools, the Irish Republic's education system is still officially acknowledged to be *de facto* denominational.[4]

Segregation and education are dealt with together in this chapter because, for the majority of twentieth-century Irish children, their first experience of confessional difference happened at school, and this was bound to influence how they saw and behaved towards each other subsequently. And, though things have changed, elements of the effects of denominationalism are, as will be seen, still evident in present-day conditions. Moreover, in their study of a Catholic multi-ethnic primary school, Devine and Kelly found that majority-community children, reflecting the norms of the society from which they came, constructed Irishness as 'white, settled and Catholic' with those coming from outside those norms seen as 'other', and with a strong 'anti-English bias'.[5] Obviously, then, the remnants of the emotional legacy have implications not only for Protestants but also for an increasingly multicultural Ireland.

By the time the new state came into being, sectarianism had been institutionalised into the education system for generations. This, of course, had social consequences, and a striking feature of the oral testimony of older interviewees was the parallel nature of Protestant and Catholic existence. Segregation in schools, if not imposed from birth, defined their lives both inside and away from the classroom, although it appears that young children did sometimes mix 'unofficially' through neighbourhood pre-school playing. And, even though at first glance barriers seemed to disappear after communal boundaries were breached in the second half of the twentieth century, the influence of the segregationist mindset are still clearly discernable in the lives of younger interviewees in the twenty-first century.

Overall, the impression given was that experience of the national education system ranged from being at best neutral to, at worst, strongly negative. There were surprisingly few who, for one reason or another, expressed positive emotions about, or gave instances of happy memories of, their schooldays in state-run schools. On at least one level, that is to be expected, as even good schooling is schooling and has the element of coercion and limitation of personal freedom from a child's perspective. As one 59-year-old Catholic said about his school, which must have been one of the better ones because he made no mention of unduly harsh punishment: 'There was no problem with school. None whatsoever. . . . It was just something you had to do. We didn't like it, mind you, but we had to do it.' Be that as it may, the overall tone from the experience of the older interviewees who went to national schools is one which tends towards the conclusion that, at least in the first four decades or so of the new state, the school experience and learning conditions for children, certainly as they are now understood, at any rate, were far from optimum.

All the same, there were, of course, some good experiences of national schools, and one 77-year-old Protestant spoke affectionately of her first Church of Ireland national school in north Co. Dublin: '[S]chool was . . . lovely, [it]

27

wasn't private school, but it was just a school, and it was great. I had a great start.' The following two accounts are also exceptions to the less-than-positive tone of the generality. When an 85-year-old Catholic from the south-west was asked whether she was required to stay home and help out on the farm or in the house, which had been common experience for her contemporaries particularly in rural areas, she replied: 'No. I was the youngest, and I was given the opportunity of education', and provided a singularly vivid account of her primary schooldays:

> I went to primary school. . . .There was a girls' school and a boys' school. . . . The smaller children were at one end, and the bigger ones at the other end, and . . . one fire was at the bigger end. So, a few times during the day we'd be let up to the fire to warm our hands . . . they were great teachers. My teacher, Mrs McCarthy, she was a very sensitive woman, a lovely woman, and I can quite remember her now warming our hands between her own. . . . [P]rimary school at that time, my God, it was a very extensive curriculum. . . . there was the Infants and First and Second, and then we graduated on to the other school, and that Principal Teacher, she had Third, Fourth, Fifth, Sixth, Seventh, and everyone did Seventh at that time, you didn't leave school then until you were fourteen, and she had so many subjects. She had Irish, English, Arithmetic, Needlework, Geography, History, and we did a bit of Nature Study as well. . . . Such a spread of ages. . . . [The teachers nowadays] don't know about . . . being overworked!. . . And she even introduced Algebra to us now in Seventh class. . . . When I look at the hygiene . . . what we had at school in the old days, we had water, needless to say, we had to go about a mile and a half for a bucket of water in the morning. That was one of the first chores. In the winter, we had to light the fire and take bits of kindling to light the fire. We had no water except the bucket for the day. There was no such thing as hand washing or anything like that, it was only that if any of the children wanted a drink of water during the day, the bucket of water was there. And we had plenty of 'small company' [mice] in the school because it was old! I needn't tell you! Loads of them!

Overall, an issue that could not be ignored, as it stood out from all others for older interviewees, was that of corporal punishment. Little else generated as much manifest emotion in the interviews. In the glare of what has been revealed about the terrible treatment meted out to so many Irish children, this is not, with hindsight, to be wondered at. However, when the interviews for this project started, the issue of abuse, physical, psychological or sexual, was still an open secret: that is to say, whilst people 'knew', they were not openly acknowledging it. Hence, although it would now be an obvious area for enquiry from the start of any investigation into early experience, even only five years ago it was not so, and no question on the topic was included in the first draft of the guideline questionnaire used in the interview. However, after several older interviewees referred to it spontaneously, it became obvious that the issue was important, and so specific questions were added.

It has to be remembered that, in general terms, corporal punishment used to be not only tolerated but even encouraged. However, a study in 2005 found that 'little has been written, in a historical or global context, about corporal punishment in the home or school, so it is virtually impossible to know if Ireland's experience of corporal punishment policy and practice was in line with what existed elsewhere in Europe and the West'.[6] Tellingly called '"A good beating never hurt anyone": the punishment and abuse of children in twentieth century Ireland', it found that, into the early 1980s, corporal punishment was accepted practice in school and home, on the basis that 'some corporal punishment was necessary to instil respect for authority, to maintain discipline, and to rear "good citizens"'.[7]

An elderly Catholic from the rural southwest, born in the year of the Easter Rising, became noticeably angry, even at the remove of some 80 years from his primary schooldays, about the treatment he and his companions received at the hands of teachers:

> [T]here was a lot of violence with the teachers. They practised an awful lot of violence. I hated that. I, I used [to] hate it when I see a master pounding a child for next to nothing.
> Q. Made you angry.
> A. Oh, it was, it was terrible. I, I always said, even at that time, I said, they should be inside in jail for it. What they were doing to children. They shouldn't be allowed into, into a school where children were, some of them, they were, they were practising that violence.

A Catholic from an eastern seaboard county, considerably younger (47) and educated in the 1960s when in other respects changes were slowly filtering through to the classrooms, spoke of her strong dislike of the way both parents and children were maltreated both physically and psychologically by the implementers of the system, in this case nuns:

Well, I remember being in national school and then a religious order . . . and it was a very strict regime at the time. . . . [P]arents just had to do what [the nuns] said in relation to rearing children. And we had to go by what they said to our parents. . . . [W]hen I think back on it, I didn't like the way I was treated in school, and I didn't like the way other people were treated in school. Sometimes the nuns would get girls up and not just saying about the nuns, but I suppose people that were in authority at that time did that, because parents didn't have a say and if one girl forgot to do something in school she was dragged up by the head of hair and hit with a ruler and I thought it was very bad . . . looking back on it . . . all the girls in the class, I think it ruined your self-confidence as you get older and you think people in authority then should be always right, but it's not true.

A 48-year-old Catholic was born in Belfast and raised in the seaside town of Ardglass when the family moved to get away from the strife in the city after his mother had been wounded by a stray bullet. His educational experience parallels that of the last interviewee from a male point of view:

[O]ur school was run by Christian Brothers and we know all about them! . . . very sadistic. . . . Never encountered any sexual thing, or anything, you know, you hear about it now, never happened to me or never heard of it happening to anyone else, but certainly they beat you black and blue. . . . They just seemed to get a pleasure from it. . . . They were God. No one could challenge them. . . . Ach, people did: my father did . . . I got beaten up by one of them, and my pop came in and just challenged him over it. He was the headmaster. . . . He just didn't like people . . . from Belfast. He didn't like people from Ardglass. So, if you were from Belfast and moved to Ardglass . . . !

A young Catholic woman, only 31 years old, from a seaside village on the east coast, also had bad memories of primary education, but she acknowledged that bad treatment was not universal:

They'd be the kind, I think if you were any way brave enough to be a divvil in front of them . . . you could suffer for it. . . . Whereas, well, I just stayed quiet, and just – don't get in trouble! . . . It was the easier option. . . . Because, yeah, they were vicious. I'll be honest. . . . Yeah, they were hard . . . some of them were horrible. [Though] some of them were lovely ladies.

Another interviewee, a 59-year-old middle-class Catholic Dubliner, went to a city-centre all-Irish girls' primary school with a nationalist ethos, where corporal punishment and victimisation were the norm and were accepted as such:

> And in that [primary] school [there were] very poor children and they were victimised horribly. We were all beaten to within an inch of our lives in that school. I mean, until our hands bled. And it was just accepted, really. . . . But there was an incident one day, where a teacher, our sewing teacher who wasn't our class teacher, took up a big tailoring scissors and hit a girl on the head with it, and cut her.

Not only physical punishment but also the fear engendered by its threat were detrimental. A 56-year-old Catholic from Mayo recalled:

> I would have had a very strict . . . Catholic . . . education from the nuns. Too strict, really.
> Q. You look back on it in that way?
> A. Oh, yeah, I do, yeah – with terror.
> Q. Terror? It was that strong, was it?
> A. It was, yes. It was, yes. Yeah. Yeah.

So terrified was she that she could not learn Irish from them, and, instead of going on to the order's local secondary school where the teaching was through Irish, she went instead to the vocational school, where she learned Irish and all her other subjects without difficulty from lay teachers.

A Catholic from Dublin, 92 years old at time of interview, had kind words to say about the nuns who taught her, however, whilst at the same time implying that in her frame of reference 'Irish' was good, and French – 'not-Irish', 'other' – not so good:

> [My Protestant friend] said, 'my aunties always said that the nuns give the girls a much nicer education than the other schools'.. . . Because they were ladylike. Well, they did emphasise the ladylikeness. . . . These were the Sisters of Charity. And they were in Sandymount. They were the ordinary Irish Sisters of Charity. But there were French Sisters of Charity also. But these were the Irish, and our nuns, I must say, were lovely.

Another Catholic, this time from Cork city and 36 years old, also found her experience of being taught by female religious positive:

> Actually, very good. I have to say . . . none of the nuns ever, in our school, used any kind of corporal punishment. The only corporal punishment I remember was from lay teachers . . . overall, my memories of the nuns would be very good. We'd a few who were bad teachers. We'd one or two were really bad disciplinarians, they would let you away with murder. This is very contrary to a lot of the, the stereotypes now.

Tellingly, during an interview with a retired nun from the west, one question – to do with work practices – was misunderstood, and in responding to what she thought had been asked, she herself brought up the issue of discipline:

> [O]ur strictness as Sisters of Mercy, and teachers. I would have seen evidence of that, and I would have practised some of that strictness, too. Maybe not to the same extent as I saw it, especially in one or two other people, but maybe I had my own emphasis on strictness, distinct from theirs. . . . Being too strict with pupils.

Let it quickly be said that the mistreatment of children was not the sole preserve of members of Catholic religious orders. Amongst the oldest middle-class Protestants, early teaching at home or private education was more usual than state,[8] and those interviewees did not speak of corporal punishment, so it is assumed that it was not a feature of their experience. However, an elderly Protestant from the upper working/lower middle class told of his bad experiences, both physical and mental, at the hands of teachers in a north Dublin Church of Ireland national school. In particular, he was singled out when, as the youngest of a number of brothers who had preceded him through his school, he was to move into

> the boys' . . . Senior School. And we had to queue up, maybe about twelve or fifteen of us, where there was the junior teacher and the senior teacher, we were to call out our names, and walk in. [When I walked in and said my name, I heard:] 'Good heavens . . . are we to be cursed with another one?' That ruined me . . . I was finished . . . Even at that age. . . .They [my brothers] weren't misbehaving, they'd never done anything bad. They had gone to school. They didn't come out scholars, or anything – well, one, one got a, a scholarship. . . . And I never got through any scholarship, or anything. I, I was sort-of hackled at

the start . . . It's only when . . . I took up studies in the technical schools and I couldn't believe there was no cane, and there was no threats. . . . It was punishment based on psychology. To make it even worse: 'Come out here, boy, and I'll put the fear of God into your heart!' You know . . . But the worst thing about it was, there was always some who were, their parents were influential, or in big positions, they escaped.

It would seem, then, that the words of John McGahern, another victim of the system, encapsulate the experience of many others. His junior teacher, a Mrs McCann,

> kept a supply of bright yellow bamboo canes in the press, and when they splintered she used ash and sally and hazel from the hedges and plied them with zeal all through the day, for errors and mistakes, oral or written, for any straying of attention or the slightest indiscipline. The worst punishments were administered out in the corridor, away from the classroom. . . . [I]t was a descent into hell. . . . [O]nce anything is licensed it can grow monstrous and be scarcely noticed.[9]

The insight of the last point is indeed significant. All in all, the totality of this evidence concurs with Maguire and Ó Cinnéide's findings that

> the Department [of Education] . . . tolerated the extensive use of corporal punishment, even very severe corporal punishment, in breach of their own formal regulations, and provided little if any defence of children against abuse by teachers.[10]

At independence, there were some 800 schools in the Irish Free State under Protestant management, the vast majority of them managed by the Church of Ireland.[11] Such was the degree and rapidity of the fall in Protestant numbers during and after the Troubles, however, that parishes were forced to amalgamate and schools to close. By 1928, the number of schools under Church of Ireland management had shrunk to about 600. By the early 1930s, it had fallen further to 500, in which 600 state-paid Church of Ireland teachers taught about 15,000 children.[12] It is true that the state granted concessions to ameliorate the lot of Protestants. For instance, fewer Protestant children were required to constitute a recognised school, and, because of the greater distances that they had to travel to their nearest school, special transportation concessions were made for them. Nevertheless, as we shall see, educational policies still had outcomes that were less beneficial to them than to Catholics, and 'through the years, typical southern Protestant parents . . . paid a higher portion of their children's educational costs' than did Catholics.[13]

Apart from ideological concerns on religious and cultural aspects, there were many practical problems facing the minority community on the educational front. The Revd E. C. Hodges, then principal of the Church of Ireland teacher training college, highlighted two of those facing the Protestant schools: 'The money available is very small, and the problem of securing a teacher and of maintaining and equipping the schools is a very urgent one',[14] with the Church of Ireland remaining responsible for the provision and maintenance of buildings within the state scheme. For Protestant schools in general there was a constant shortfall in funding.

One of the fundamental problems of the system in the early days was that of staffing Protestant schools – or, indeed, Catholic ones – with appropriately qualified teachers when state policy on the language demanded a proficiency in Irish that few primary teachers could demonstrate. In the rural parishes, the provision and financing of transport to enable Protestant children reach their far-flung schools was a necessity, and, although state subvention for transport was granted in 1933,[15] it was not sufficient to meet the requirements of the scattered community and had to be supplemented from diocesan, parish or parental funds.

Figures supplied by the Church of Ireland's Representative Church Body confirm that in the early 1990s there were approximately 212 primary schools under Protestant patronage.[16] Department of Education figures furnished in June 2006 showed that there were 3,157 national schools in 2004–5, 2,913 of which were Catholic run. In the same period, 183 schools were run by the Church of Ireland, 14 by the Presbyterians and one by the Methodists. There was one Jewish school and two served the Muslim community. Thirty-nine schools were multi-denominational, and four were interdenominational. The decline in the number of primary schools, especially over the period 1978 to 2004–5 reflects the tendency towards amalgamation of small schools into larger ones for broadly economic reasons. This was a cause of considerable ongoing anxiety to the Protestant community, as amalgamation meant more mixing of the confessions in the classroom and therefore a dilution of the Protestant ethos for Protestant children.

An interesting feature of the current educational scene is that many Irish parents are choosing to send their children to gaelscoilleanna, that is, schools in which the teaching and all other activity is in the Irish language. Figures furnished at the beginning of 2008 indicated that there were 135 of these schools at primary and at secondary level in the state, 12 units within an existing post-primary school, three streams in an existing post-primary school and 44 all-Irish post-primary schools. In addition, An Foras Pátrúnachta, the charitable patronage body for these schools estimated that there were between 45,000 and 50,000 children at their schools.[17] A description of the manner in which these schools approach confessional matters is useful here, because, as well as dealing specifically with the patronage of gaelscoilleanna, it sets out clearly the ways in which denominationalism is dealt with in different types of school in the state system:

> The patron of a gaelscoil may be clerical or lay, or a legally-incorporated entity and recognised as such. . . . An Foras Pátrúnachta to date regards inter-denominationalism as between two denominations – Catholic/Protestant. However inter-denominationalism might involve more than two religions at a future date. The interpretation of inter-denominationalism and its practice is the responsibility of each patron. The patron is responsible for the implementation of the confessional ethos of the school. In a Catholic school the ethos and the religious education taught during official school hours is, naturally, Catholic. In an interdenominational school Catholic and Protestant religion classes and preparation for the sacraments form part of the programme taught during official school hours. The main issue is that the teaching of religion happens during official school time as laid down by the Department of Education and Science. In a multi-denominational school, a core curriculum of Religious Studies is taught during official school hours but denominational instruction and formation including preparation for the sacraments where relevant is the province of the parents, who organise this independently of the Patron.[18]

Another interesting development of recent years is formation of 'Educate Together'. Established in 1984, it is the national representative body for multi-denominational education in the state, and its schools are mainstream national schools which operate according to the rules for national schools set by the Department of Education and Science. As well as being multi-denominational, the ethos is child centred and co-educational, and the schools are democratically managed. There were 56 of these schools in the state in January 2009.[19] In line with an announcement issued in November 2007 that Educate Together intended to move into the secondary cycle, some of them are post-primary.

The intermediate, or secondary, education system was implemented more recently than the national schools, with the Intermediate Education Act 1878, introducing 'a modicum of financial support and a magnum of regulation into the intermediate educational scheme'.[20] At independence, all secondary institutions in the state were privately owned,[21] and fee paying, 'and therefore were economically and socially discriminatory'. In 1921 the Free State government authorised the striking of a penny-in-the-pound rate for scholarships to enable working-class children to acquire secondary schooling.[22] However, throughout the early years of the state, 'state funds for secondary education were extremely scanty'. Although Catholic-owned schools were affected by lack of funding, Protestant ones were more so, as they employed lay teachers who needed salaries capable of supporting themselves and, where relevant, their families, whereas government subsidies paid on behalf of 'religious' teachers were often used to underwrite the running costs of Catholic schools.[23]

The schools were, of course, almost all under confessionalised ownership and management, and the Free State government did nothing to change the principles of private and denominational control. Of the Protestant institutions, approximately half required their governors to be members of the Church of Ireland, with other Protestant sects controlling many of the remainder.[24] The Catholic secondary institutions were owned and run by religious orders, which had 'built up a series of colleges from the late eighteenth century onwards', to serve their community.[25] E. Brian Titley lists three reasons why the Catholic Church had placed so great an importance on gaining and keeping control of education: the first was to maintain steady recruitment of priests; the second, to influence and exert moral control over the future dominant class and political elite and the third was to create a loyal Catholic laity.[26]

Until the mid-1960s, when economic and social changes started, slowly, to work their way through Irish institutions, low levels of government funding, scarcity of scholarships and the overall lack of coordination of primary and secondary systems were all problems faced by secondary schools. The Irish Republic was at that stage looking towards entering the European Economic Community, and the combination of the appointments of Patrick Hillery as minister for education in 1959 and his successor Donogh O'Malley in 1965 combined to bring about major changes in state policy on education. Hillery was responsible for bringing in grants of up to 60 per cent of capital costs for expansion and new buildings, raising the school leaving age to 15, and for the opening in the early 1970s of post-primary level comprehensive schools in areas of the country where there was insufficient provision of secondary education.

To compete internationally, it was obvious that Ireland needed a better-educated workforce and more concentration on research and development, which in turn required more graduates. With the aim of bringing this about, in 1967 O'Malley announced that there would be free post-primary education up to intermediate certificate level, so many more children in the state gained access to free education in a post-primary school.[27] However, again, financial reforms did not assist Protestants as much as Catholics,[28] for their schools could not afford to forego fees in return for the proposed grant of £25 per child. Even the subsequent allocation of a special bloc grant was still not sufficient to allow the abolition of fees.[29]

Despite the denominational nature of the education system, things were beginning to change on the segregation front at classroom level. There had always been a few Catholic children at Protestant schools even in the 1920s, despite strong clerical condemnation[30] – and, indeed, that of the *Catholic Bulletin*, when all of a hundred Catholic children attended 'Protestant and godless secondary schools'.[31] By 1974, 14 per cent of pupils in such schools were Catholic and by 1978 this figure had grown to 19 per cent. The greatest increase was in the new comprehensive schools, where the 'Catholic proportion [rose] from 3 per cent in 1971 to 33 per cent in 1974'. A larger survey of 15 Protestant schools showed a Catholic presence in the student body of 19 per cent.

The desire of Catholic parents to send their children to Protestant schools occurred not only at secondary but also at primary level, probably because of 'the smaller size of Protestant classes, because they were seen to be a little less rough', and because they were thought to provide a somewhat more progressive education.[32] A Catholic primary teacher spoke of what happened in her area:

> A lot of new people who move into the area . . . go along to the school, particularly if they're Catholics and don't, don't have a clue, they'll see. . . that it's written up 'this is . . . Church of Ireland parish', but they don't read it and they go in and they, they sign up there, because it's the local school. . . . [W]eeks later, they suddenly realise their children are going to the Church of Ireland school. But they're happy there, and they say: That's fine. . . . it doesn't tend to work the other way, we don't tend to get Church of Ireland making the same mistake, coming to us. . . . The Church of Ireland people always seem to know which school they, their own community is serviced by.

This is interesting from several aspects. The lack of Catholic concern could be read either as no longer caring about confessional difference or church directives, or as achievement of confidence and consequent loss of fear of proselytism. The Protestant approach, on the other hand, may indicate a lingering perception of a need for caution. It could also be, of course, because the Protestant community is so small and so tight-knit that the relevant information is readily accessible from family or friends. A Canadian Anglican commented on the cohesion and connectedness of the Church of Ireland community: '[I]t's such a little community. They all say: Oh, I know your sister, and you're so-and-so, and so-and-so! . . . Because they're so connected.'

Up to the 1970s, although Protestant parents wanting their children to go to a Protestant school were generally still able to find such a place in the Dublin area, there was an increasing breakdown of confessional barriers both at student and staff levels in the state's schools in rural areas. Protestants who could not afford boarding fees had no choice but to turn to vocational schools and later to Catholic secondary schools. As Protestants outside Dublin increased their attendance at secondary level from 63 per cent in 1961 to 94 per cent in 1970, those at Catholic schools almost doubled from 26 to 45 per cent. There was also a new, and increasing, reliance on Catholic teachers, particularly in the comprehensive schools, where, by 1978, 19 per cent of the pupils were Catholics. However, most Protestant schools, including comprehensives, were not prepared to open their rolls fully to Catholics because they saw their first responsibility as being to Protestants.[33]

At the turn of the nineteenth century, the only arm of the post-primary education system in Ireland both apparently independent from overt religious control and democratic in the sense of the involvement of the community it served,[34] had been the parallel secondary-level system of vocational training delivered through the technical colleges. Post-independence, improvements in funding to local civic bodies was effected by the Vocational Education Act 1930, which also renamed the technical schools 'vocational schools'. Despite the system's apparent freedom from denominationalism, however, 'in practice the demography of the country and the pervasive influence of the Catholic church ensured that they had an almost equally Catholic ethos'.[35] At the end of the 1950s, as a civil servant in the Department of Education wrote, 'because of its predominant position at both primary and secondary levels the Catholic church was, by far . . . the greatest influence in the Irish educational sphere'.[36]

Any real degree of community involvement in mainstream secondary education had to wait for the development of a new type of secondary school which was to happen in the last quarter of the twentieth century. In 1970, community schools were brought into being to replace both secondary and vocational schools in localities where these were unable, for one reason or another, to provide a full range of courses, and also to provide facilities for adult education. Most of the secondary schools were run by religious orders, and the Catholic Church opposed initial proposals for community school management because they threatened the extent of its control. Counter-proposals were produced, stipulating that it would agree to the scheme provided it retained the power to nominate a majority of the board of management and that the other members be nominated by the vocational education committee. There was opposition both at national political level and from the vocational education authorities as well as from Protestants, for the scheme would obviously have resulted in even more control by the Catholic Church. Parents would no longer have had a choice, such as it was, between denominational secondary schools and supposedly non-denominational vocational education. The scheme was eventually modified, and the current situation is that there are 77 community schools in the state, managed by ten-member boards of management comprising three members from local religious communities, three from the Vocational Education Committee, two representing parental interests and two those of the teachers.[37]

At third level, the oldest university in Ireland, and one of the oldest in the British Isles, is Trinity College, Dublin, founded in 1592. From 1794, Catholics could graduate from it, and the founding of St Patrick's College, Maynooth, in 1795 provided Irish Catholic candidates for the priesthood with a seminary. However, given Trinity's Anglican ethos and the lessening of discrimination against Catholics, a demand soon arose for an institution to serve Catholics and other non-Anglicans. In 1845 the Queen's University, with colleges in Belfast, Cork and Galway, was established by the government. These colleges were, astoundingly, 'thoroughly undenominational',[38] so in 1854 the Catholic bishops founded the Catholic University for its flock. Apart from its medical school, this institution did not receive the expected support from the community. Trinity, already enabling Catholics to graduate, opened to all-comers by 1873,[39] but it remained firmly associated with elitist Anglicanism for many more decades.

The denominational situation generally remained at an unsatisfactory impasse until eventually, in 1879, the Royal University was instituted as an examining body, through which the Catholic University and the Queen's Colleges' students could compete for prizes and fellowships. The Catholic University became University College in 1882, and catered for students coming up through the Catholic secondary schools. Again, matters rested for some time until 1908 when the system was overhauled and reformed. Queen's College Belfast became the formally nondenominational Queen's University, but its ethos was mainly Presbyterian; the Queen's Colleges in Cork, Galway and Dublin became the new National University of Ireland, which soon fulfilled expectations by becoming almost exclusively Catholic at both faculty and student-body levels.[40]

Trinity, not compelled at that stage further to change formally, remained distinctly Anglican in flavour, and, as F. S. L. Lyons put it, 'in the generation before the treaty . . . made practically every political mistake it could make'.[41] Few Catholics attended it, for their church strongly opposed their doing so. In 1944 John Charles McQuaid, the Catholic archbishop of Dublin, forbade the laity of his diocese to attend Trinity without his special permission, and in 1956 the ambit of this decree was extended throughout Ireland.[42] In 1970, however, 'the prohibition was quite suddenly repealed'.[43]

The evidence of an 85-year-old Protestant on her time at Trinity in the 1930s is a fascinating insight on cocooned Protestant student life in the period between the two world wars:

> I'd decided I was tired of doing all the school subjects that . . . I would like to do something new, something different, so I decided I would do Natural Science. And it was quite the, wonderful thing for me. And we had wonderful people in college, H. H. Dixon and J. W. Biggar and Kenneth Claude Bailey and they were just huge people . . . we did three subjects each term for three terms, that was nine subjects, and the end of the year, you just chose three. . . . I didn't . . . do any work, because there was . . . too much going on. I never, never worked. . . . I was sorry afterwards, but, it was my brother's fault. He . . . said: . . . there's no point in working . . . don't ever miss the year, or miss an exam or anything, but don't work all the time . . . because there's so much more to life than working!. . . [S]o I go into college and do no work . . . I was sorry afterwards, when I got married, that I hadn't done something like domestic economy, or something. . . . [more] useful. . . . Trinity was good.

The Commission on Higher Education convened in 1960 took until 1967 to report. It concluded that the problems the universities faced included over-crowding, an excessive absorption with university politics, a staff appointments procedure that inhibited recruitment, a need for regional universities, and an almost total absence of working-class students. The introduction of third-level grants at that time did, however, help to alter the social composition of some of the colleges, notably University College Cork. It also mooted the amalgamation of Trinity and University College Dublin, a proposal that ultimately came to nothing.[44]

In 1984 the government published the *Programme for Action in Education 1984–87*. It showed a desire to 'secure greater productivity and economies in higher education'. Hardly any of its proposals on improved access were implemented, but the focus was shifted onto technological studies with consequent links to industry and the provision of funding to enable this. The combination of changes in the social and economic climate in the late 1960s and the partially executed initiatives of the 1980s resulted in the number of third-level students increasing from 16,327 in the mid-1960s to 50,945 in the mid-1980s. The percentage of women rose from 30 to 46 per cent and the number of postgraduates rose from 650 to 3,094 over the same period. Despite the changes, however, significant socio-economic inequalities remained. There were some advances over the same 20-year period, including improvements to buildings, resources and equipment, a more democratic approach to government and more professional administration.[45]

The 1967 report of the Commission on Higher Education criticised Trinity 'for expanding beyond the demand of its Irish constituency'. This had come about because of the decline in the numbers of Protestants in the state, from whom their student body traditionally came, and the lack of Catholic admissions, so that it needed to admit students from the North and overseas. In the early 1960s, 39 per cent of the college's students were from the Republic, another 14 per cent were Northerners and the remaining 47 per cent were foreigners, of whom 34 per cent were British. Trinity's dearth of Irish students was not only due to the diminution in their Protestant student reservoir, but also to the restrictions on Catholic entry imposed by the Catholic hierarchy. The Provost replied to the accusations of the Commission by stressing Trinity's desire to be part of national life, and not to be seen as an exclusively Protestant enclave. The Catholic hierarchy responded in turn by stating that they no longer opposed Catholic attendance on ethnic, religious or class grounds, but that they now objected to Trinity's increasingly 'neutral and secular' climate in which opposition to Catholicism could gain ground. In tune with the times, however, more Catholics applied to Trinity, and, from 16 per cent in 1961, their numbers rose to 66 per cent in 1978.[46] Furthermore, by 1970, only 11 per cent of the student body was composed of overseas students.

As can be seen, then, denominationalism was a basic tenet of the education system, strongly so at primary level and secondary levels at least up to the end of the twentieth century, less so at third level – where, indeed, it no longer features. And, although, mostly for demographic reasons, there have been increasing degrees of mixing in the state's classrooms with consequent social effects, there remains, reaching into the twenty-first century, a strong consciousness of denominationalism and of the desire for confessionalised control.

The results of early and lasting segregation are bound to have repercussions for individuals and for societies. For one thing, as one commentator said in the early 1980s, at the school gates on their first day at school, Irish children went 'their separate ways . . . [to be] imbued with the unthinking prejudices and historical memories of their own tradition, and [as a result] not a few found that they could never be completely comfortable with "the other side"'.[47] In Protestants, this uneasiness was all-too-easily construed as aloofness, as a desire to retain an elitist place in Irish society, as a manifestation of the emotional legacy component that saw Catholics and their faith as inferior. That there was some snobbishness alongside the self-protection was inevitable and is undeniable, but fear of loss of communal identity, rather than hankering after lost status, was more of a driving force towards isolationism. Whatever the motivation, however, withdrawal had its negative consequences for Protestants themselves. Perceiving themselves to be surrounded by ideologies that to a greater or a lesser extent viewed them as outsiders in their homeland, by isolating themselves they helped bring this perception into being and ensured its continuation. At the same time, Catholics were living in a visibly Catholic environment with the validation that the dominant construction of Irishness reflected the ethos of the state and the imagination of a nation in which they felt they were entitled to claim unquestioned centrality.

What was it like for Protestants in the early days of the state? A south-western Protestant, born in 1914 to a Church of Ireland farming family, described a typical Sunday scene during the Troubles: 'I can see them coming out of church and then standing around in groups . . . they could talk about things [there] that they couldn't in any other gathering'. When asked about the nature of the family's relationship with neighbouring Catholics, she confirmed their social as well as geographical isolation. Although, as was the custom in farming communities, they helped each other out with hay-making and harvesting, that was as far as it went: 'We didn't have any socialising with the Catholics, you see. Absolutely none'.

A decade later in the same area, another interviewee said that whilst children were mixing outside school, both schooling and parish activities were separate:

But then they had table tennis in [the primary] school, and it was only Protestants went to it, and our Catholic friends, we had plenty of Catholic neighbours, you see, our own age, they'd be peeping in the windows, and I often thought it was very sad to think that it couldn't be all in one. You see. But we couldn't go to [their] school, it was a Catholic school, they were going to that school, and right in front of our Protestant school when it was opened there was a family, no matter how it rained, they'd be walked down to [their] school because they were Catholics, to their own school.

Two Methodist sisters, aged 81 and 82, also from a farming family in the southwest,

went to a private school first. It was in the hall next to the Methodist church and then we went to school, secondary type school . . . it's across from the old technical school.
Q. Was that also a private school?
A. It was, yes.
Q. And were there only Methodists or –
A. Oh, no.
Q. No?
A. It would have been Methodist, Church of Ireland, I suppose.
Q. OK. But no Catholics?
A. No.

They gave evidence that differed in tone on the point of mixing with Catholics outside school in early childhood. The elder said, hesitantly:

[All] the near neighbours would have been Catholic. . . . [T]here was the only family, we played with them, but then there weren't, others wouldn't have had young children our age. . . . there were five of us girls we sort-of played amongst each other.

The younger sister, however, maintained that they had mixed freely with many Catholic children:

We grew up amongst them and we, all our friends, we'd lots of friends and we played with them. And all our neighbours were Catholics, we were the only

Protestants in our neighbourhood, and we were welcomed in their homes and
we played together with the children, and, you know, whether they were poor
or rich, we got on well with them all.

On balance, taken with the experience of other members of that community,
the evidence of the older sister on the limitations on contact in early childhood
was more persuasive. She had married a Methodist farmer, and so went from
helping on the home farm straight into marriage in a similar situation,
consequently staying within the confines of her gender and her community.
The younger one, who never married, left home at the age of 17 to take a
secretarial course in Cork city, then worked in the bank in Cork and Athlone.
She had wanted to join the British Armed Forces during the Second World
War, 'but, of course, my father wouldn't allow me to, but he was quite willing
for me to go into the bank, so I went into the bank as a second choice, really'.
That she lived away from parental control and mixed with both Protestants
and Catholics on her own terms from her late teens may have influenced her
answer about early childhood and put more of a de-segregated gloss on
contemporary conditions. Also, subjectively, her answers carried a note of
wishing to give what she perceived as the desirable, that is the more liberal or
'ecumenical', answer.

A picture of segregation and isolation for rural Methodists is confirmed by
the evidence of a now-elderly family of the 'large' farmer socio-economic level
in the west. Although they sporadically attended a local national school in
between periods of home schooling and left home for varying short periods to
attend secondary boarding school in Dublin, they spent the greater part by far
of their childhood days at home with teachers coming in to give them lessons.
One sister told of her childhood isolation, marooned up one of those long
avenues that formerly featured so much in Protestant lives, separating them
from the rest of Irish society both literally and metaphorically:

Q. [I]n your youth, did you have any Roman Catholic pals, at all, that you
played with?
A. Just one, just one, that came to the house. Our house was a quarter of a mile
up an avenue, so we were virtually isolated.

Her brother's evidence corroborated their social segregation, but he recalled
that they had *no* Catholic playmates. He made an interesting comment on the
nature of their sequestered childhood:

A. Protected. Probably . . . being brought up in a Methodist household of those days was very strait-laced and . . . you weren't encouraged to mix.

Q . . . did you have any friends from, from the Roman Catholic community?

A. No.

Q. Right. Simply 'No'?

A. No. Just simply 'No'.

Upon noting the contradiction between these two accounts, the discrepancy was queried and it appears that the visitor in question was, in fact, Church of Ireland, so segregation was confirmed.

Apparently exceptionally, another Methodist had, at first glance, a rural childhood which differed from the customary one. She was brought up in the midlands, and recalled:

I'm the second youngest of seven. . . . [I]t was quite a big house that my grandfather had bought. And we lived in one side of this big house, when my Dad got married, and then my grandparents moved out and my uncle married, and he lived in the other end. And they were two children. So, we had a wonderful childhood. Plenty of children to play with. . . . And within walking distance, easy walking distance, of Sunday School, church, Christian Endeavour, school.

Although she had plenty of company during her childhood and did not experience isolation, it was Methodist company, mostly closely related to her, and therefore it remained firmly within Methodist parameters and boundaries, both physical and ideological.

In general, it appears that rural Methodist isolation was more pronounced than that of other Protestants. One elderly Methodist said:

I always think that the Methodist church had us out on a limb, and never looked after us socially. . . . Totally isolated us, and never put anything in place. . . . And, and also keeping us apart, in that . . . alcohol, smoking, mixing with anybody like that, was totally out. . . . I blame that really on the fact that I never married . . . That we were so isolated, and because . . . 'oh, she doesn't smoke or drink', so . . . totally cut off.

Another, much younger, Methodist, who was a schoolgirl and a young woman in the 1960s/early 1970s, when barriers were beginning to break down for others in the face of the changes of those times, also felt isolated. She recognised the damage caused by segregation, and her words also support the view that Methodists segregated themselves to a greater degree and for longer than did other Protestants:

> I always regretted, I felt the loss of Catholic friends, and I always felt that I would have wished my parents had sent me to the local convent school so that I could have grown relationship with people in the area, in the community. And I still have never actually managed to grow that kind of community thing with my Catholic friends really to any great extent. I would still feel very much Protestant.

However, perhaps the most extreme case of Protestant childhood isolation, on its face value at any rate, was that of a 65-year-old, who said:

> I didn't go to school until I was eight and a half because I was taught by my father up on the farm. In those days, one wouldn't have gone to a Catholic national school. The nearest one, anyway, was three miles away, and so my father started to teach me when I was about five and a half. At eight and a half I went to a small [school] . . . with a small group of children, and we were taught by a retired Protestant national school teacher. I think there was eight of us. At eleven and a half I was sent to boarding school in Waterford, which was the nearest Protestant boarding school available.

Her earliest years were spent far from contact with any children at all:

> Q. What early childhood events can you remember?
> A. Probably just in general, wandering around a farm talking to the old men . . . because it was a hill farm . . . and there were no children to play with, except later my siblings.

The closest sibling was three years younger, so she had several solitary years before she had company in her wanderings. Her evidence epitomises the isolation experienced by the children of rural Protestants.

In the early days of the new state, if there was no confessionally suitable school nearby, most Protestants simply would not have attended a Catholic national school, preferring private education instead. Before 1945 'dire necessity was considered to be the only legitimate grounds for such deviant behaviour, and even then it was regarded with much suspicion by many Protestants'.[48] The disapproval was engendered by general anxieties over the spiritual welfare of Protestant children being exposed to Catholicism whether by association or from indirect influence through the content of texts in use in the schools.[49] However, a 75-year-old Protestant from a farming family in the south-west, attended the closest, Catholic, school, as her father would not harness the pony to take them to the Protestant school three miles away because to do so would clash with morning milking. A north-western Protestant family also attended the local Catholic national school in the 1950s because, amongst other factors, the interviewee's father had views that were decidedly *not* ghettoised, and he wanted to demonstrate his desire to be seen as being part of the local community as a whole. However, many rural Protestant families stayed within the norms of behaviour for their group.

A sharp contrast to the picture of rural isolation for the older age groups is that painted by members of the Protestant urban shopkeeper and working classes in Dublin and in other smaller urban areas in the country. Obviously, isolation *per se* was not an issue in cities and towns, but the contiguity of the confessions meant that the presence of denominational boundaries and the ways they were maintained were all the more important. An 81-year-old Protestant, daughter of a dairy proprietor, described relationships within the locality where she grew up near the North Circular Road in Dublin, and went on to relate an incident when she and her sister were set upon by Catholic children:

Q. Did you have any Roman Catholic friends?
A. Oh, yeah. They were, sure they were all the types. Yeah.
Q. Did you visit in Roman Catholic houses?
A. Yeah.
Q. And did they come to your house?
A. Yeah.
Q. Right. So it was free and easy among the people who lived around here?
A. Oh, yeah. Yeah. No difference.
Q. Right. Was there any, ever name-calling or anything like that?
A. Oh, well, we had a bit of that now, like . . . my sister . . . she just sit down and let them pull her hair, and the screaming of her. . . . But my father said: you have to learn to take your part in life, and that's all there's to it. And my brother Willie . . . said: 'I'll go and sort them out!' 'You won't do such a thing, you'll let them alone!'

She also said that her father told her and her siblings: 'politics and religion don't mix. You serve your milk and that's all there's to it', indicating that discretion was mandatory in order to preserve the peace and hence that Protestants were apprehensive, not to say downright afraid, of causing trouble. This was muting of the Protestant community at a local level.

The issue of name-calling arose frequently in the testimony, sometimes accompanied by physical violence. For most of the age groups in the study, even the younger ones, the interviews contain evidence of inter-communal harassment. Because there were more Protestants than Catholics interviewed, there are more instances of Catholic hostility in the study, and it does appear that Protestants were more likely to avoid than to attract trouble, but there are also some incidents of Protestants perpetrating confessional hostility.

The most sinister instance, with its indications of the far-reaching implications of sectarianism at times of crisis, occurred in the evidence of a 90-year-old Protestant from the southwest. During the Troubles,

> children from the local Catholic school, would be lying in wait and they'd pelt us with stones . . . we told my mother, but I don't think she ever told my father, because of she'd be frightened that my father would go and complain, and you see you didn't want even, you wouldn't complain. Because you were frightened of what might happen.

For them, fear was real and constant, and she also recalled being sent home from school early one day because the father of schoolmates had been shot dead by the IRA. Also during that period, a 92-year-old Protestant born in Limerick recalled that

> as things weren't so good [in Limerick], my father used to take me to school every morning, and I can remember hopping along beside him . . . they used to shout at us, 'Proddy-woddy, go to hell', was one thing.

The evidence of a 59-year-old Protestant from another small community in north Dublin corroborates evidence of habitual communal muting long after the Troubles were over:

> [M]y father always told us, never antagonise anybody . . . because he said it only adds fuel to the fire, as he put it, makes things worse. Just play and be as normal

as possible. . . . Because, he said, there's no point, he said, in starting rows unnecessarily.

In general, there appears to have been more name-calling in urban locations, but this may simply be because there were more people concentrated in smaller areas. It is clear, however, that Protestants both were and felt vulnerable, whether they lived in town or countryside. A 79-year-old middle-class Protestant – one of the few older interviewees whose parents were in an inter-faith marriage in which, atypically, the children were not raised as Catholics – was brought up in the north inner city of Dublin. Ironically, her particular memory of name-calling concerned another family with parents from different confessions:

> There was always name-calling . . . Proddy-woddy, you'd be, and all that sort of stuff . . . One family particularly in the national school, where there was a mixed marriage, and . . . if you wore your poppy in on the Armistice day, they would snatch it and stand on it and that sort of thing.

This raises the question of whether the children concerned were in fact Catholic, and, if so, it is surprising that they attended a Methodist-managed national school, or whether they were, against the norm, also being raised as Protestants and were reflecting in their anti-Protestant behaviour what they had 'picked up' from the Catholic part of their heritage and/or the sector of society they inhabited.

An 81-year-old Protestant from the working classes recalled what happened as a matter of course on the streets of Dublin in his youth:

> When we used to go down to Boys' Brigade we used to go down with fear and trepidation because . . . we used to get jeered going down and in, and then when we came out of Boys' Brigade, you used to have to . . . run like hell, because we used to be chased. Or there'd be gangs waiting for us to come out. . . . I couldn't understand, at that age . . . what it was all about, but now I can. . . . But they used to jeer . . . Proddy, Proddy on the wall! Who's the . . . chase us like hell, and we used to run.

His 77-year-old wife, identifying an important point when it came to being targeted, found that community relations were quite good between herself and the children in the lower-middle-class area in north Dublin where she grew up, except when leaving the Girls' Brigade, you probably would get heckling from other children because you had a uniform on.

Q. So they could pick you out.

A. Coming home, and they'd identify in that way.

Q. But . . . if they knew you anyway, they might have known you were a Protestant, but it wasn't 'til you put the uniform on that they'd start heckling, I suppose?

A. Yes. It made a division then.

Harassment was not always contingent upon the sight of a uniform, however. A 79-year-old Protestant brought up in the Coombe area of inner Dublin was still affected by what happened to her:

> [W]e were always called 'Proddy-oddy on the wall', and all these sort of things, and . . . it used to be dangerous, like, at times, and I can remember coming home from my Christian Endeavour meeting one night . . . going up Hanover Lane, which is still there, but every time I see that place I don't go near [it] . . . there was tenement houses there, and these kids came out and they used to call us 'Proddy-oddy on the wall', for they all knew who we were, like . . . and I got a bang on the mouth, and when I went home . . . my mouth was bleeding, I was in an awful state.

A 64-year-old Protestant from the west described another form of harassment, non-physical but institutionalised and unpleasant. She went to a convent in Sligo to sit a state examination

> and . . . some of the children sort-of turning on me . . . when they asked me which school [I went to] and saying: Well, you know that your religion is wrong? And that Henry VIII brought it in, and this sort of thing. And I was getting very, very nervous and anxious and one girl . . . said: you shouldn't say that, you know. Whether she picked up my anxiety or not, I don't know, and [the first girl] said: Well, the priest tells us that we should always say that . . . to Protestants!

The evidence of a 46-year-old Catholic from an eastern county illustrates the durability of emotions engendered by such incidents and the fact that they were also perpetrated by Protestants on Catholics. She told of her sister's reaction to the news that she was going out with the Protestant she later married:

'Do you not remember,' she said, 'when we went to national school and coming down along the wall all the Protestants used to be sitting outside their school, outside on the wall, and they used to throw stones at us.' Now, I don't remember that, but she said she used to grab a bag and she used to fire it at them and they would fire stones back at her. So, I said, 'No, I don't remember that,' but she had that feeling inside her and she remembered that from when she was younger, and me telling her I was going out with a Protestant, she kind of, as if to say to me, don't do that, don't do it!

A 59-year-old Protestant recalled his middle-class upbringing and another instance of Protestant sectarian bullying of Catholics:

I think there was the odd, you know, if you were getting at each other . . . Proddy dogs, and that sort of thing, but no, we were in a very nice area . . . it was middle class. . . . I hate to use the term, but . . . people were not deprived, they were well brought up, they went to good schools. . . . I remember there were people . . . a load of girls from . . . Sligo. . . . And they were very, they were 'Catholic' wouldn't be the term, but very, very strict about their religion and the girls dressed in a very, in a very, almost like young nuns . . . and I suppose we would tease them because of the fact that they were so [religious].

A 40-year-old Protestant did not, however, think that the childhood name-calling was based on confessional difference:

People used to point the finger at us when we were going to school and 'Proddy-woddy' taunts that were levelled at us . . . I don't think it was even sectarian, I think it was just different schools, and . . . if we'd been mixed between the schools, there'd still have been rivalry between the two schools.

A 70-year-old Protestant from the west had a robust attitude to confessional rivalry, petty or otherwise, and told how he and his pals gave as good as they got:

[W]e walked from here . . . we had a Protestant school . . . they'd have to go into their own school further in the town. And we connected in the morning and in, out. . . . We visited, we kicked football, we were always pals. . . . Oh, we'd have a slagging match coming out the road, all right . . . Catholic, Catholic, quack, quack, quack, Go to the divvil . . . and never come back! . . . Protestant, Protestant – they had some other rhyme! That's all. And go away laughing. . . . Meant nothing.

This would appear to bear out the point that the rivalry might be between schools rather than confessions, but the counter-argument – that schools are identifiably aligned with one confession or the other, so that, *au fond,* the issue remains confessional – is demonstrated by the fact that sectarianism is at the root of interschool rivalry in present-day Wicklow. A 20-year-old Protestant was very clear about the continuation of name-calling for her generation and on the relationship between schooling and sectarian behaviour:

> [T]here's an awful lot of scraps between our school because they were Protestants and then there was the de la Salle, you know. If, for example, somebody had talked to someone's boyfriend, you know, they'd come up and say, you know, a lot of the abuse would be focused on 'you Proddy bastard', or whatever. . . . But . . . sometimes people can be very . . . Oh, where did you go to school, and it's more to do with the schools and all . . . comes back down to . . . the religion. . . . [I]t starts off, Where did you go to school?. . . therefore you know if they go to that school they must be a certain religion.

A 51-year-old Protestant, brought up in a small midland village in the mid-1950s, said she had not experienced problems with hostility or name-calling herself, but that her children, from the same generation as the young Protestant from Wicklow, had.

> A. No. Funnily enough, because my own kids often ask me [about] that, because . . . [they've] had experience of it all right, but . . . I was lucky. . . . [T]hey were called a few choice names when they went out when they were teenagers. You know.
> Q. [W]ould you mind saying what that kind of thing was?
> A. Black bastard.

A 23-year-old Catholic from the border area did not suffer name-calling herself, but was aware of the existence of another form of discriminatory behaviour:

> The only kind of thing like that would have been, there was a few families in the area who returned from England, and it would have been, you know, that kind of national racism, like. Not really bigotry, as such.

A 23-year-old Catholic of mixed Irish and Welsh heritage had unpleasant experiences of exclusionary intolerant behaviour apparently based on similar criteria in a Co. Dublin primary school:

> It was just that there was, because of my background and the fact that my mother was Welsh, and that every school holiday I would go back over to Cardiff . . . it was always a big deal with my classmates.
> Q. You were made feel excluded because of that?
> A. Yes. Not so much excluded but that I was different and that I didn't fit in. And when I was younger, First, Second class . . . it was a case of: You don't belong here. Go back to where you do belong. And . . . yeah, I never really felt I fitted in at all, and I never really got over it.

The last two instances demonstrate that for some of the younger age group the focus of differentiation includes not only the confessional element but also that of overt, as opposed to unconscious, perceived ethnic and/or cultural difference.

The evidence of another 19-year-old woman from Co. Wicklow was an exception, however. Her father was Irish Catholic, her mother English Anglican, and she herself attended a Protestant national school and a Catholic secondary school.

> Q. So . . . people's religion just doesn't matter?
> A. Not at all! . . . I wouldn't know . . . there's a girl I grew up with down the road . . . I didn't even know if she was Catholic or Protestant [until recently]. . . . So, that's like nineteen years we've known each other, and we never knew if we were Catholic or Protestant!

Her experience is atypical of the rest of the evidence, and may simply be the result of a combination of the confessional composition of her family and her own and her parents' extrovert personalities.

One 59-year-old urban interviewee told of an interesting incident from her early years which illustrates the stances adopted by urban working-class Protestants both on religious observance and in relation to the society in which they lived. When asked what it was like to be a Protestant in the midst of a Catholic community, she said:

Well, you would feel out of place sometimes, you know. . . . one Sunday, my friend Vera . . . said to me: try and get a shilling. . . . [There's] a grand picture on. My uncle's after giving me two shillings. And I said: Vera, I won't be let go to the pictures, and I daren't ask. She said: I'll ask. So, of course, she come over. Well, my father nearly hit the roof when she mentioned it. '[My children will] never stand in a picture house or anywhere like that on a Sunday. . . . 'Vera, never ask again. Sunday is the Sabbath day, and it will be kept in this house as long as I'm alive. Nothing untoward will ever be done on a Sunday. . . . [Y]ou have your Bible class to go to . . . we'll sort this problem out when you come back.' So, never asked again. . . . I was kept in for a week.. . . He went over and he said it to Vera's mother and father. . . . 'As long,' he said, 'as I'm alive . . . never, tell Vera to ever think of asking for [my daughter] to get money to go to the pictures.' So [they] apologised. . . . Her mother and father spoke to her, and told her that every family . . . doesn't matter what church you have, you have your own way of keeping to your religion, and . . . you don't go asking other people to do something. . . . But that was one thing my father was very strict on when we were young, was Sunday.

According to Martin Maguire, in the early decades of the state, 'parochialism became a way of opting out of a world that was probably hostile [and tending] towards a closed, introspective familial society'.[50] This, in turn, created a responsibility for the Protestant churches to provide not only doctrinal instruction but also opportunities for social intercourse and leisure activity for their communities with the aim of preventing inter-church marriage. This last reason was, as we shall see, the main purpose of segregation, and of central importance in Protestant perceptions of their need to police group boundaries to enhance their likelihood of surviving as a community by avoiding assimilation. But, as far as Catholics were concerned, it also led to confirmation of the perception that Protestants saw themselves as superior,[51] which played into the stereotypes generated and maintained by the emotional legacy.

CHAPTER THREE

Education, Irish Language and Identity

The early years, both inside and away from the classroom, are generally acknowledged to be the most formative in the development of the individual, and Devine and Kelly's study of children in an urban multicultural primary school argued that analysing how children engage with identity formation 'should be an essential part of understanding identity, because . . . identity is a social construction that develops over time'. One of their arguments was based on the premise that the ways children learn to 'place' themselves socially, culturally and politically grant insights into the nature of the society in which they live.[1] Hence, examining early experience of the interviewees during their school years not only illuminates the education system but also gives insights into the society they inhabited and how they formed different aspects of their identities

The language policy was only one of the curricular changes put in place by the Free State government as a means of promoting and developing a Catholic/nationalist national identity that repudiated all things 'Anglo'. During the nineteenth century, the combination of the part played by the Catholic Church in modernising Irish society and reaction to a perceived loss of culture and language as 'Anglicisation' progressed[2] succeeded in indivisibly allying Catholicism – by that stage already inseparable from nationalism – with the Irish language as integral parts of the cultural nationalist construction of an authentic Irish identity. So, given the links between the language revival of the late nineteenth century and the developing nationalist movement, it was inevitable that the founders of the Free State would see the revival of Irish as one of its duties.[3]

A fundamental problem with state education policies was the lack of consultation with parents regarding the education of their children, and the imposition of the language policy was no exception. For various and complicated reasons, the Catholic Church and the state were already allies in running the education system, although there were some stresses in that relationship over perceived degrees of power and control. One example of such tension was that which arose later over reforms in school management.[4] As one commentator said: 'The [Catholic] church's control of Irish education has depended . . . on the state accepting the Church's policy on education', and the refusal of either Catholic Church or state authorities to consult with parents on any educational matter was 'reflective of the authoritarian stance assumed by the Irish state in many matters'.[5] The ultimate outcome of the alliance was that the state was able to avoid taking action when concerns began to surface. It soon became clear that overall educational standards were falling, mainly because of a combination of the time taken for Irish each day, which obviously meant less time devoted to other subjects, and because all teaching was through Irish for the first two years of the primary cycle. On these grounds alone, parents – Protestants more or less openly, with the Church of Ireland voicing their concerns, and many Catholics tacitly – came to oppose the language policy. There was an added factor for Protestants, however: an important aspect of their relationship with the state was their resentment of the authoritarian way in which compulsory Irish had been introduced, and the absence of democratic process present in foisting it on those who did not wish it. They also resented the fact that there was no fruitful enquiry into how effective the compulsory Irish programme was, and 'For forty years, the annual reports of the Church of Ireland's Board of Education repeatedly condemned the compulsory and restrictive character of the regulations.'[6] However, given the Catholic Church's attitude to censure in general and Protestant criticism in particular, as well as its alliance with the state, critiquing of the system by non-Catholics and 'outsiders' was automatically devalued,[7] so it is no surprise that no heed was paid to Protestant protests.

Eventually, the precise degree of the damage done to all Irish primary schoolchildren's English language skills by state policies was more than confirmed in 1966 when a sophisticated empirical study was published.[8] The Revd Dr John MacNamara's conclusion, based on the testing of a large sample of Irish primary schoolchildren, was that at age 12-plus Irish schoolchildren were about 17 months behind British schoolchildren of the same age and background in English language skills. He proved that the cause was the time spent on the Irish language. The same study found that they were also behind by 11 months in arithmetic.[9] This time, both on empirical grounds and arguably also because it came from someone within the majority community, the results could not be ignored.

The placing of Irish at the centre of Irish education impinged upon Protestants' cultural and ethnic identity as well as upon standards. At first, the curricular changes instituted by state policies were perceived by Protestants as a direct attack on their cultural identity[10] rather than the ideologically driven generalised desire of nationalists to de-anglicise Irish society, and thus they were bitterly resented. However, over the decades the combination of the cessation of exposure to 'the glories of empire' and the corresponding increase in knowledge of Irish history did work together to produce a new sense of cultural identity in Protestant children.[11]

The new emphasis on Irish was, indeed, culturally difficult for some Protestants, and many Catholics saw the language policy as a threat to their children's current well-being and future economic viability.[12] But the policy on Irish was not the only curricular change: reform of the ways other subjects were taught was also deemed essential. The study of English literature was to be restricted to a minimum in an attempt to put it into its 'rightful' context amongst all European literatures.[13] Irish history was to be taught as a means of instilling national pride and self-respect, and European history at first excluded all reference to England, although this absurdity was later modified. And, importantly, in taking these steps, the state was also operating, whether consciously or not, on the premise that curricular content can be 'a source of information . . . as to what identity constructions are politically constituted as legitimate'.[14]

Bowen records how national conferences of educationalists held in 1921 and 1926 called for a strengthening of '"the national fibre by giving the language, history, music and traditions of Ireland their natural place in the life of the schools"'.[15] It is interesting to note that the Department of Education's notes for teachers, in use until the early 1960s, suggested history was about articulating and illustrating '"sublime examples of patriotism in order to refute the calumnies of Ireland's enemies"'.[16] Also, the report of the Council of Education for 1931 states that 'next to the religious motive, the most powerful influence in creating and fostering [national identity] is the study of history'.[17] However, countering assertions that there were overt directives issued to teachers to deliver a particular agenda-laden interpretation of the curriculum, the report continued that, whilst tracing the nation's past, the course should also take due note of its 'ability to assimilate other ideals and other peoples . . . and finally should give due credit to the contributions made to it by men whose religion differed from that of the majority'.[18] Such aims can only be described as not only *not* anti-Protestant but also ideologically admirable.

Undoubtedly, the issue of curriculum delivery and its outcomes, intended or otherwise, was one of great complexity and not only one of 'following orders' meted out from above. As Gabriel Doherty observed, the syllabus reflected official attitudes to the subject, but the implementation 'depended on several factors, most notably the attitude of the teacher'.[19] However, there is such a prevalent view that a biased picture of the history of Ireland's relationship to its neighbouring state was delivered, a view confirmed by the oral evidence, that it tends towards the conclusion that the view is, at least in part, an accurate one. In any case, it is entirely possible that instances where the communication of the curriculum was objectionable to Protestants were more a product of inimical beliefs and ideals of teachers as individuals than as servants of the state.

Certainly, an examination of curricular materials in English from the early days of the state does not present overt examples of chauvinistic extremes. Neither does a brief overview of the notes for teachers disclose examples of religious bigotry, which again leans to the conclusion that bias was a matter of individual subjective interpretation. In the English syllabus, the table of contents of *The Higher Literary Reader* produced by the Christian Brothers in 1925[20] shows a mixture of extracts from the works of Ruskin, Shakespeare, Fénelon, Swift, Fenimore Cooper, Donne, Byron, Cowper, Macauley, Milton, Dickens, Longfellow, Gray, Sydney Smith, Shelley, Pope, Sir Walter Scott, Charles Lamb and so on. Examination of the text of one piece by a Catholic cleric discloses an elegiac piece about the place of the mother and the respect due to her, and contains no detectable religious propaganda whatever.[21] Another Catholic cleric contributed two articles on the joys of reading which are similarly devoid of religious content.[22]

It is also interesting to note that, in a poetry text of the time,[23] a Protestant churchman, the Revd Stopford A. Brooke, is quoted in a footnote to the effect that

the note of the poetry [of Ireland] is nearly always Catholic, and Catholic with the pathos, the patience, and the passion of persecution added to its religious fervour. . . . Its writers lived under the ban of Government, crushed by abominable laws; and the mercy given to the wolf was the only mercy given to men whose crime was the love of their religion.[24]

A more sympathetic view of the position of Irish Catholics is hard to imagine, one that should have been well received by Catholics. But such was the prevalent lack of logic that Brooke was apparently 'subject to scathing attack by D. P. Moran',[25] Catholic journalist, polemicist and inventor of the term 'Irish-Ireland'.[26] According to A. C. Hepburn, Moran was 'even more influential in the 1900–10 period than Douglas Hyde or Eoin MacNeill . . . [and] voiced more clearly than anyone else the developing "Irish-Ireland" ethos'.[27]

In a study of secondary-level students carried out in 2005 in Northern Ireland, the role of history teaching in the formation of identity was examined in the context of religious group identity. It was found that initially children 'identify with a wide range of historical themes', but that later 'they draw selectively from the formal curriculum in order to support their developing identification with the history of their own political/religious community'.[28] Thus the combination of an anti-British emphasis in history with what is drawn from the communal myth-making that forms the emotional legacy accessed through respective cultures reinforced confessional, cultural and social differences in Irish society.

A 72-year-old Catholic had a clear view on the link between the teaching of history and the perpetuation of the emotional legacy. Speaking from the perspective of both pupil and teacher, she said:

> I think back on the plantations . . . where land was taken from Irish people, and . . . placed in the hands of . . . Presbyterians or Protestants . . . and I think that the history . . . as we learned it . . . there was something negative about . . . this religion that did that and took over what was ours . . . the plantations, they left . . . an awful taste.

She continued: 'And then the way the history was taught, too. We weren't helped in that. You know, because . . . this was the focus, if you like.' Bias in the delivery of the new curriculum was something that perturbed the doctor father of a 53-year-old Catholic brought up in a midland town:

> I went to the local national school . . . which was the normal Irish national school. . . . it was a very good academic grounding. . . . lots of Irish language, and lots of religion. And I know my father had, interestingly, some difficulties because he felt some of the biases we were getting in history, he didn't agree with. . . . I remember him talking about maybe sending us to somewhere else privately. But that . . . there wasn't any other option, really. But I know . . . at the time, the flavour I got was there was certainly anti-English sort-of bias in the . . . schooling, which . . . he would not have agreed with.

A 45-year-old Catholic, daughter of two primary teachers, had an interesting view of learning Irish history:

I remember being very distressed about Irish history when I was about thirteen or fourteen, and thinking: Oh, God, not another rebellion where somebody betrayed everybody else. . . . [T]hat's why I didn't like Irish history. I was much happier with European history, because I felt it was more straightforward.

Memoirs of those who experienced the education system are also illuminating. In Peter Sheridan's experience of a Dublin city Christian Brothers' school in the early 1960s, he relates how he was taught by 'The Mongrel', who

hated Lloyd George because he tricked Michael Collins into signing the Treaty. He hated Michael Collins because he signed the Treaty. He hated de Valera for signing the oath of allegiance. He hated Hitler for losing the Second World War. He hated America for joining up with Britain against Germany. He hated all foreign games, especially soccer. He loved some things just as much as he hated the other things. He loved Gaelic football, the Irish language, the Gaelic league, anything with the word Gaelic in it, Connemara, Mayo, the Ring of Kerry, Sinn Fein, the IRA.[29]

John McGahern was another exposed to similar extremes:

Master Kelly . . . was tall, good-looking in a dark way, nationalistic, a Fianna Fáil member of the County Council, intellectually conceited and brutal. . . . [H]e saw the Rockingham estate, with its high walls and gatehouses and the great white house . . . as a surviving symbol of British rule and dominance. . . . Most of the children from the estate were kept from school for the great Rockingham shoot. The boys acted as beaters and the girls helped their mothers with the cleaning and catering, and this threw Kelly into a rage. 'The peasants are still beating the pheasants out of the bushes for Milords.' When the Rockingham children returned to school at the end of the shoot, Kelly would set them tests for which they were unprepared. Then he would line them up against the wall and administer an unmerciful beating, a blow for every error or unanswered question, fulminating all the time against the whole sordid, brutal history of British rule in Ireland. . . . One of the ironies was that he expected us to climb on the grass margins and to salute him when he passed in his car as if he was a member of a new aristocracy.[30]

Such forceful role models in the formative days of young citizens can have left only very negative impressions.

In the early days of the state, there was Protestant concern regarding the religious content of some of the set texts in Irish, which went so far as the seemingly paranoid fear that the Irish language inevitably led to Catholicism and the eradication of Protestantism by indirect means. Some of this irrationality may have reflected views similar to the widely disseminated opinions of the controversial professor of ancient history at Trinity College Dublin, Sir John Mahaffy, who maintained that it was 'almost impossible to get hold of a text in Irish which is not religious or which is not silly or indecent'.[31] The authorities conceded that, where there was material 'offensive to Protestant sensibilities', they were permitted to omit it when teaching, but they could not delete it from the texts concerned. But even if the state permitted some latitude for Protestants, this did not get away from their objection to the amount of time taken for learning Irish and its corollary of the neglect of other curricular areas. Indeed, so strong was the objection of some that, when they could afford it, they sent their children to be educated outside Ireland.[32] The implications of this for identity formation will be explored later.

Of course, the effects on the general educational standard of Protestant and Catholic children in the state system were similar, but the vital difference was cultural. Catholics could at least say they were learning something which was part of their national heritage, whilst generally Protestants perceived that they could not – on confessional, cultural or ethnic grounds, despite having their own ways of constructing Irishness. As a result of the drop in standards, firstly, during the period 1920–60, no body of Catholic parents of any significance came out against the language revival programme; secondly, the only group composed chiefly of Catholics to lodge a protest was the Irish National Teachers' Organisation, and its objections were those of professional educators opposing the educational limitation and retardation caused by the revival programme; thirdly, despite the efforts of the Church of Ireland, which continued to articulate and document the community's disenchantment with the entire range of effects of the language revival programme, in the face of the evidence state regulations became ever more stringent.[33]

The weighting of marks with bonuses awarded for answering in Irish was another problem. It disadvantaged Protestant pupils from poor families, whose home language was less likely to be Irish, and who needed to win a scholarship based on one of the certificate examinations in order to continue their schooling. Also, bonus grants introduced in 1924 for secondary schools teaching through Irish discriminated against Protestant schools. All in all, those in charge 'were unable to perceive what the Protestants had at stake in the language issue and that the survival of the minority depended not merely upon religious toleration but upon cultural toleration as well'.[34]

The compulsion even took a direction that was abusive of citizens' rights as well as of legislative powers and the courts when, in 1934, another effort to impose the state's identity agenda upon minorities occurred. The then Minister for Education, Thomas Derrig, brought an initially successful prosecution against parents sending children to a private, English-language school. He wanted to obtain a judicial ruling that 'educational suitability' automatically implied compulsory Irish. On appeal, Judge Devitt stated that nowhere in the 1926 attendance act was Irish made compulsory and that the constitution of the Free State expressly recognised English as an official language on equal terms with Irish. Derrig, supported by de Valera, proceeded arbitrarily to try to change the law to say that all children of Irish parents, whether educated inside the 26 counties or elsewhere, in private or state-aided schools, could be compelled to study the same curriculum, which was an obvious breach of civil rights. Moreover, it also infringed the clauses regarding parental rights in respect of their children's education in the 1937 constitution, which had been enacted by the time the bill came to the attention of the Supreme Court, having been referred there by President Hyde in 1942. The Supreme Court found it repugnant to the constitution, so the matter was dropped. The net result of this disturbing episode was to make it clear that 'Irish nationality and cultural pluralism were incompatible concepts'.[35]

It cannot be denied that some Protestant opposition to the Irish language revival was based on prejudice, condescension and snobbishness. Adrian Kelly gives some examples of this,[36] but for each bit of snobbery indulged in by Protestants, Akenson said that 'one could quote a nasty bit of barracking from the language revivalists'.[37] In Kelly's view: 'To an extent Protestants were unable to understand the nationalist psyche which demanded that the Irish language at the very least deserved an honorary status in Irish life'.[38] By the same token, the revivalists demonstrated they did not want to understand what compulsory Irish meant in cultural terms to Protestants. The state of affairs continued in which Protestants, some of whom in fact fostered Irish with enthusiasm – certainly with at least as much keenness as their Catholic fellow-citizens – were assumed, under the 'rules' for the expression of cultural nationalism, to be universally hostile to the language and other aspects of Irish culture by virtue of their confessional and ethnic identity, so that their location in relation to the imagined nation was made even more precarious.

Despite state obduracy and strong lobbying on the part of supporters, Irish has not taken back the ground it lost to English in the nineteenth century, due, mainly, to the 'failure of adults to make the language a part of their daily lives, which had much to do with the grim and stern manner in which the issue was presented'.[39] However, learning Irish and the ability to speak Irish remain a central component both of Irish education and of the formation of an Irish identity, and, as we have seen, not a few parents choose to send their children to gaelscoileanna, where all teaching and interactions are through the medium of Irish. Despite this, the main aim of former state policy, to make Irish the everyday language of the Republic, remains unrealised, and, despite the removal of the compulsory element of state policy in the early 1970s, stresses and ambiguities still attach to the language question.

In 2006, following intensive lobbying on the part of the government, Irish became the first official language of the state,[40] and has been recognised as such by the European Union.[41] This, as very few people outside the state – save in Northern Ireland – have a working knowledge of Irish, is the triumph of ideology over logic and testifies to the persistence of the 'ethnic language validates nationality' mindset: it certainly needs to be acknowledged that ideology still exerts a strong influence. Ironically, also in 2006, a TV programme presenter, 'a fanatical gaelgeoir', tried to make his way around the Republic speaking exclusively in Irish. He demonstrated that, despite census figures showing that a quarter of the population claimed to speak Irish regularly, only a tiny minority of people were able to communicate in that language. Furthermore, he experienced not only a degree of disbelief but even overt and robust hostility when he attempted to communicate in the language.[42]

Subjectively, in line with the generalised caution already noted, Protestant interviewees were careful about expressing opinions about curricular issues, particularly Irish, and there was a reserve in some of their answers. However, several can only be said to have been unenthusiastic about their experiences with Irish, as the following three samples show. The first extract was from the evidence of a 59-year-old, the second from that of a 76-year-old, and the third from that of a 77-year-old, all from urban working- and lower-middle-class Dublin backgrounds:

How did you get on in the Irish?
A. I never really liked it.

Q. What did you feel about learning Irish?
A. . . . oh, it was just another subject. . . . Just another subject. We had to do it,
and that was it.

A. I learned Irish there.. . . A smattering of it. I think [my] school didn't go in
for it that very much.

It is interesting to speculate whether their lack of keenness was at least in part
because of their urban location, for Protestant interest in Irish was more likely
to be found in rural areas amongst the 'strong' farmer class or those whose
forebears would have been tenant farmers. As well as 'loving' Irish, a 76-year-
old Protestant from the rural southwest also had interesting information
illustrating how Irish had died out in the area in her mother's time:

> [W]e got a lot of Irish. But he [the teacher] . . . wasn't Irish-speaking at first at
> all, but he went away to learn Irish, and before we ever went to school, my
> grandfather . . . could talk Irish, because he used to learn Johnny and I, he died
> in 1937 . . . so he had some old Irish that we don't know where it came from, but
> then my mother couldn't speak Irish, it was gone in that much time. But it
> returned then.. . . We had to learn it when we went to school . . . in 1932, I
> think. . . . I love Irish. . . . I love Irish.

Another interviewee from her region, an 88-year-old Catholic, told of the early
problems of poor teaching from teachers who knew little more than their pupils:

> We had Irish as a subject, but I'm afraid I didn't learn much of it. . . . our
> teacher was not very good at it himself and he wasn't able to teach, to, to convey
> his knowledge to us, either, much.

A 59-year-old Protestant lamented the class and familial pressures that caused
her to lose her ability to speak Irish:

> I went to national school first . . . I learned everything through Irish.. . . my
> grandparents thought this wasn't a terribly posh school, and that I should be
> moved to Bandon Grammar School . . . when I was eight . . . where they did

everything through English, and so I had, for about the first six months I had to sit there and translate things into Irish in my head and then translate them back into English for the answers. And then I forgot all my Irish! And I regret it ever since. I would love now to be able to speak Irish.

An 81-year-old Methodist from the southwest had the following to say about learning Irish:

We learned Irish. . . . I [enjoyed it] yes . . . I loved to write in Irish because they had a lovely script, but they changed that then as we grew older, and it took the pleasure [out] of Irish. . . . I was quite annoyed when they changed it!

One 70-year-old, who might appear to represent the quintessential middle class – if not, indeed, 'Anglo-Irish', although he did not describe himself as such – Protestant in background and upbringing, went against that stereotype by learning Irish. The way he went about it pinned down a truth that policy makers would have done well to note: he did not spurn Irish because he had decided voluntarily to learn it. His preparatory school

did not teach Irish . . . but I learned Irish voluntarily. There was a member of staff . . . who discovered that I'd been to a national school and that I . . . had learned Irish, and he sort-of brought me on a little. And in fact for . . . many years later, I was the only boy from an Irish prep school who took Irish in the Columba's scholarship exam. Mind you, I didn't know much Irish, but I put down what little I did, because I'd learned it voluntarily. And so I had no antipathy to Irish.

However, one suburban Dubliner, 58 years old, who described himself as a 'West Brit', did express the supposedly typical Protestant of lack of enthusiasm:

Q. And you learned Irish there, did you?
A. Right through, yeah. Reluctantly. Sadly, when I look back now. . . . And I suspect, too, because we were Prod . . . we probably were even more anti it. . . . anyway . . . it was badly taught, the whole ethos, the whole way they went about it, of course, it was just . . . grammar and . . . we never tried to converse in it.

A 68-year-old rural Protestant who attended a Catholic national school expressed the following opinion about learning through Irish:

I was quite good at the Irish. One thing I didn't like, we were taught history and geography through Irish, which was really stupid and it didn't give you much of a grasp of, of what was trying to be conveyed. But the structures and the grammar and the language itself . . . I think I was reasonably good at it until I got to the grammar school, and we had a diabolical Irish teacher there and she . . . undid nearly all . . . the good that had been done to me.

A 44-year-old Protestant from the south-east told of the pride her Church of Ireland national school felt in their grasp of Irish in the late 1960s:

[T]he thing about the Church of Ireland national schools was, because a lot of the teachers . . . went to Coláiste Moibhí[43] and did the Leaving Cert . . . through Irish, so Irish was a big feature of our school life, and . . . I remember the Inspector coming in once and telling the teacher in Irish that we were one of the best Irish-speaking schools in the county. And we all understood what he said, and we were very proud of ourselves.

A 51-year-old Protestant from the midlands was another who emphasised the centrality of the teacher's role in her contribution:

But she was a very Irish-orientated school teacher. . . . And we hated her, as usual. She was very cross. But you'd come in to school in the morning and you would have to greet her in Irish, and what kind of a day it was outside, through Irish, and then you'd have to say I'm going to go to my desk and I'm going to be good all day and to what I'm told to do and then you were allowed to go and sit in your chair.

A 69-year-old English Anglican, who accompanied her Irish Catholic husband to Ireland when their three children – raised as Catholics – were young in the 1970s, echoed the importance of the role of the teacher in general and the lack of sensitivity of one in particular when she described the problems, not least of which was that of personal identity, faced by the eldest of the family, a girl:

[She] went to the local national school, which was a very good school and still is, but unfortunately they put her into a class with a teacher who spoke a lot of Irish and insisted on speaking Irish all the time, and immediately changed her name to the Irish version of her name, which upset her. She was, she's a very bright girl, and has turned out to be very good at languages, but she just got a block about

Irish, and in fact we had to get a teacher for her outside of school eventually to teach, because she had to do Irish, because all the national school insist that the children do Irish, because they get a capitation fee for them. In fact, as it transpired, because they weren't born here, none of them needed to do Irish at all . . . to go to university, because they were exempt, but I didn't know that at the time.

Turning to Catholic views on Irish, some interviewees, countering the expected stereotype and negating the intentions of state policy, expressed strongly negative attitudes to learning the language. A 59-year-old Catholic from a nationalist background unexpectedly said:

A. I hated [Irish]. Hated it with a vengeance.
Q. What were you good at, at school?
A. . . . let me see: history. I loved history.
Q. Did you?
A. I did, yeah. Very interesting, history. It was all mythical history, Cú Chulainn and this sort of thing.

Although unsuccessful with him on the Irish front, his teacher had obviously taken to heart the mission of teaching history in a manner that reflected Ireland's past glories.

A 69-year-old Catholic farmer from the west, who completed his formal education at primary level because he was needed to help work the land, expressed views that both go against the accepted stereotype and confirm the difficulties imposed upon children by the state policies:

Q. [C]an you speak [Irish]?
A. No. . . . No, I think it's a waste of time. . . . We had to learn everything through Irish when I was going to school. . . . We had to do our maths, we had to, to do our everything through Irish, even, even catechism was in Irish. . . . I found Irish difficult. . . . And even the books we got were very uninteresting. . . . A child wouldn't be interested in reading them. . . . And I'd say it put me off, as such. . . . up 'til this last few years we had to go to England or somewhere for to make a living, or America, and Irish was of no use to us. And I felt that after spending so long learning Irish and all of that, it was money down the drain. You had to go and make a living somewhere else. . . . I think this forced language that was in it in our time should never have been. That's what I think. And I think it was a waste of time up 'til recently, anyway.

And it was not only the older people who recalled having difficulties: a 47-year-old western Catholic, later to become a national schoolteacher herself, remembered her early, though transitory, problems with the language:

> And the interesting thing about that was, it was all Irish . . . walking in to a school where everybody spoke Irish and everything was taught through Irish except English and religion! And I, I can remember crying and saying, 'I hate Irish!' when I was about six! And then I remember being able to speak it . . . I don't remember the transition . . . it just happened.

Then there were those who expressed their affection for Irish and its teaching. A 75-year-old north-western Catholic expressed his feelings for the language and told of an exceptional teacher:

> I loved Irish, actually, loved the Irish language. It wasn't that I was particularly given to Irish, or that, but I liked the language, I always liked it, I thought it was a very easy language to learn, if you got the hang of it, you know. . . . We'd a very good teacher. . . . He had a system that . . . we would have half an hour in the day at school, and we'd talk Irish. . . . if they, any word you didn't know, you put in English for it, but somebody in the class would have the word. . . . It was fantastic. . . . It was absolutely ingenious. . . . And the next thing, everyone was talking Irish, because . . . if you're stuck for a word, and you hesitated, someone had the word, or else you'd put the English word on the teacher. . . . I can still read Irish, kind-of understand it, I suppose I couldn't really speak it, but I can put a whole lot of words together.

The views of one of the older Catholic-born interviewees, a former member of a religious order and a teacher for all her professional life, on the perceived relationship between Protestants and the language, are notable in that her amazement epitomises the majority's view that Protestantism and a love of Irish must be mutually exclusive:

> I have only very recently . . . in the last year or two, found out how very closely Anglicans in Ireland were connected with the whole development of the Irish language. I'm just absolutely amazed at that . . . just amazed. And very touched by it. Very touched at one level. To think that they went to so much trouble to learn the language, to understand it, and to be creative with it . . . For example, it was Protestants who first translated the New Testament . . . that one came

out in 1970. It was much later that Maynooth came out with the translation of the Bible . . . in the mid-1980s, as far as I can remember.

Apart from emphasising the negative side of Protestant interest in the language, her words show that, for her, the gulf of understanding between the two confessions remained reified until 'very recently' despite changes in Protestant attitude.[44] No credit is given, as it were, for the fact that Protestants had developed a broader, more inclusive, cultural identity, even as they held on to a communal identity centred on their religious one.

From the point of view of the Protestant community in twentieth-century Ireland, the possibility of education abroad for the middle and upper middle classes was a facet of resistance to state policy in the early years of the state and is important mainly because of its implications for issues of identity. Whilst being *ad idem* with Catholics on the subject of confessional segregation, Protestants were originally alienated from the poorly constituted state system by the changes in the curriculum brought in by the government soon after independence, and, in particular, the question of the imposition of compulsory Irish and the resulting worsening of general educational standards. These facts, together with their fears on the cultural front, meant the many of those who could afford it sent their children out of the state for secondary education. This scarcely helped to develop or foster a strong sense of identification with the nation in at least some of the young Protestant citizens of the state, severing them as it did from their families and peer groups.

A 40-year-old Protestant, proud of being able to trace his direct descent from a 'planter', related how he, like many of his class 'was born here, went to national school here', but was 'exported . . . I did my secondary schooling [in England]'. He continued:

[W]e were taught as children that we were Irish . . . [identity] became very much more important when we moved to England, where other people saw us . . . as Irish . . . often in a negative sort of way . . . most of the English people that we met thought that Irish meant being Roman Catholic and going to Mass on a Sunday, and . . . any other day as well, they really couldn't cope with the idea that we weren't members of the IRA . . . and that we didn't support Bobby Sands. And yet we still claimed to be Irish. . . . We used to spend Christmases and Easters and all of our summer holidays back home, because . . . that's where we belonged, I suppose. England was a place where my father earned money, and where Latin teachers were cross with me. And really that was the extent of it.

The manner in which he couched his memories reveals residual automatic assumptions of the incompatibility of Protestantism with a nationalistic Irishness. On not having to learn Irish at secondary level, he also said it was a

> merciful release . . . I swapped my native language for Latin and French and all sorts of exciting romantic things like that, and I was never any good at any of them . . . there was a Roman Catholic school near where I was living in England and they offered O level Irish, which must be the most perverse form of educational torture ever, an English qualification in Irish – isn't that marvellous?

Overall, this evidence displays interesting conflicts in the light of his unequivocal claiming of Irish national identity 'by virtue of the passport, if nothing else', rather than identification with it through ethnicity and lineage. It also combines ambivalent attitudes to being Irish with a typical rejection of the place of the Irish language in his anglicised cultural identity. However, given that his parents had taught him he was Irish, an English education together with the negative picture of Irishness reflected back to him by English people appear to have combined to reinforce the ethnic rather than the cultural facet of his identity.

A 65-year-old Protestant, son of an Irish father and an English mother, described his religious identity as being 'basically, Church of Ireland, but I also do in fact attend the Society of Friends'. He was educated in typical English mode as well as according to middle-class Protestant norms of the time:

> I spent three years at [a preparatory school in south Co. Dublin], and I think I can honestly say I hated every moment of it. . . . [It] must have been one of the last places in Ireland still to fly the union jack and sing God Save the Queen on the King's birthday . . . all the boys there were clearly designed to be sent to British public schools . . . [I was] transferred to [an Irish secondary school] which . . . I left at thirteen to be sent to an English public school . . . for three years. . . . I had to learn Irish [at the first secondary school] for the first two years. The third year I was being groomed . . . for Common Entrance to be sent to an English public school, and my parents . . . paid a small amount . . . for me not to learn Irish, really so that I could concentrate on Latin.

He certainly exhibits alienation from the unabashed Anglophilia of his prep school. However, public school also proved problematic for him, a situation continuing on from his unease with the ethos of the prep school coupled with his anxieties on the identity front when confronted with the negative version of Irishness reflected back from his public schoolmates:

> [G]oing to an English school . . . made me terribly conscious of being Irish, much more conscious of being Irish than I'd ever been before. . . . And one was constantly exposed to silly jokes about the Irish and then to even worse prejudiced statements about the Irish being disloyal in the war [This made me feel]. . . . Different. Also . . . I was always being told I had a brogue . . . I think somebody who is really good at language can . . . catch that I come from Ireland, but beyond that, no. My mother was English, she taught Speech and I was certainly taught to speak 'proper' by her . . . but what made it particularly ironic was that most of the boys in the school . . . had good Yorkshire accents and were sons of Yorkshire manufacturers! . . . I think probably I spoke something rather closer to RP than they did! . . . my first two years I found total hell, I don't think I was cut out for boarding school anyhow, and there was this sort-of bizarre thing that happened with a lot of middle-class particularly Protestant Irish families at the time, where their children were seen as somehow people to be sent off to these institutions in Britain . . . with an assumption they'd probably go on to a British university and eventually go out and run a colony somewhere. And I just didn't fit into this pattern at all.

So, for these two interviewees at least, the experience of being sent away to school put them in the position of being even more uncomfortable with their 'Irishness' than if they, as Protestants, had remained in Ireland all along. That they both, after some years away, eventually pursued careers in Ireland rather than choosing to stay away as their education was designed to effect, seems to underscore their ambivalence. In an interesting footnote, the second interviewee telephoned after the interview to say that, in or about 1958–60, in his early twenties, he surrendered his British passport and took out an Irish one, which was a conscious action on his part to claim 'Irishness'. It caused his mother consternation.

The 65-year-old Protestant from the midlands who had a very isolated childhood also refers to the practice of sending children out of the country for secondary education. When it came to secondary school for her, there were

> two Protestant [boarding] schools, one was Church of Ireland and the other was the Quaker one . . . I was actually sent to the Church of Ireland one, but I think really because my mother swayed it that way because she was afraid of the

liberalism of the Quaker school. Ostensibly it was because the kitchen floors were dirty. . . . [Confessional segregation] was automatic and complete because there was no need [to mix]. My father afterwards I think would have sent us to a Catholic school . . . if it had been years later. We might have even been sent to the Ursulines . . . because he hated boarding school. . . . He was sent away to England, he hated it, and he saw no reason for people to be brought up away from their homes or in another country.

Thus, whilst confirming the alienating effects of being sent from home and community to England to school, her evidence shows that her parents adhered to the communal rules and, choosing what appears to have been the lesser of two evils, sent her to Protestant boarding school within the state rather than to Catholic day school near home.

Although there has been acknowledgement of southern Irish Protestants as a *religious* minority in that, as such, they 'were treated with great generosity . . . [in other ways] they were hectored, bullied, or ignored'.[45] Through the denominationalism of the education system, they were able to protect their religious ethos in their schools, albeit whilst having to grapple with difficulties both at individual and at communal levels. However, that did not prevent the imposition of the dominant Catholic nationalist construction of national identity, inculcated through the state education system, on Irish society, so that on both the ethnic[46] and the cultural[47] fronts, Protestants continued to be irredeemably 'other'. Despite this, Protestants went from being a fearful minority immured in a 'shell of embittered marginality'[48] after independence, to one which, after the Second World War, was prepared to take its place alongside the majority in the state,[49] and which allowed community boundaries to become 'increasingly porous'.[50]

This came about mainly because, after the social and economic changes of the 1960s and 1970s, there was increased mixing of children in schools: denominationalism was the overarching principle, but confessional segregation inevitably broke down for demographic reasons. Increased mixing in the classrooms was due not only to societal changes but also to the shrinkage of the Protestant population which saw a reduction in provision of Protestant-only educational facilities and the consequent amalgamation of schools. As a result, although the older generation tended still to see Catholicism and its ethos as a threat and were sensitive to the point of paranoia over what they perceived as any attempt to put forward the Catholic nationalistic message, as *de facto* segregation broke down younger Protestants began to row back from this position. To be sure, they did not always agree with state education policies old or new, and in this, as individuals were often fearful of voicing opposition, the Church of Ireland continued to act as mouthpiece of the community. Traces of that private muting still showed in the circumspection individual interviewees demonstrated when discussing what they deemed to be controversial aspects of their experience.

To sum up, the aim of the state education system was to foster the basic construction of an authentic Irish national identity as Catholic, Gaelic and nationalist, with the national language as a necessary component. As the majority community was and is centrally placed in the dominant construction of Irishness, as its members are numerically overwhelming and as that construction was reinforced, one way or another, in the state's schools and in society in general, Catholics generally are not faced with questions about their own religious, ethnic or national identities and so are, as it were, 'identity-issue blind'. The links between the Catholic Church and the state through its administrative and educational bureaucracy – always, it must be remembered, implemented by individuals many of whose identities had been distilled in the crucible of nationalistic fervour and/or in the classrooms of the developing state – resulted in educational policies that were, whether consciously or otherwise, mediated through the confessional, ethnic and cultural strands of the emotional legacy and were consequently inimical to Protestants.

Protestants adapted themselves slowly to the conditions in the state and grew to accept facets of its culture that had formerly been anathema – perhaps by unconsciously taking on board the aphorism 'adapt or die'. In doing so, they have moved themselves towards a situation of integration into the mainstream of Irish society, rather than succumbing to any imperative to remain separate to stave off the assimilation and destruction of their community they saw threatening them.[51] However, despite the shifts in communal and self-perception, as will be seen in the next chapter, fear of assimilation is still a part of Protestant perception.

Finally, on the current state of the Republic's education system, it is interesting to note Kevin Williams's argument that, with a stultifying circularity, the hi-jacking of it by vested interests continues. In 1999 he saw it as the locus of ongoing dynamics of church/state relationship:

> The attempt to reconcile the claim of religious and secular versions of human self-understanding in modern Ireland remain a feature of educational debate. Educational policy is one aspect of a general attempt to determine the relationship between church and state in contemporary Ireland.[52]

He is referring to the relationship between the Catholic Church and the state, but it has to be acknowledged that Protestant churches also now participate in the consultation process. However, the Catholic influence, church and lay, still dominates, and it is to be hoped that continuing debate on education and identity will come to give more consideration to the effects of education policy decisions on any and all of the minority communities which now comprise Irish society.

CHAPTER FOUR

Protestants and Society

The importance of the parish to the minority community at independence cannot be underestimated, especially in remote rural areas. Of course, parish life was also important to the Catholic community, but it was not perceived as central to communal survival in the same way that it was for Protestants. And in the early decades of the state the central position of the various Protestant denominations' churches in the lives of their congregations was maintained, even as the need for a refuge in times of trouble diminished. As well as religious activities like Sunday schools and bible study fellowships, there were a host of organisations geared towards the funding of overseas missionary and charitable work together with sporting and social clubs. Because of their number and variety, however, it is possible only to give an outline in the following review, and to indicate the occasional incidence of cross-confessional membership of organisations.

At and after independence, attendance at Sunday worship was an important part of Protestant communal solidarity as well as of religious life in both town and country. A 90-year-old Protestant from the southwest gave a picture of life in a rural area during the unrest surrounding independence and of the vital role of the church:

> [O]f course we went to church, my father was a great church man . . . it was the only time the Protestants could get together . . .. That they could talk . . . they'd come out of church and stand around.. . . I can see them coming out of church and then standing around in groups . . . because they were all of a kind . . . they could talk about things that they couldn't in any other gathering.

A Protestant from the southeast recalled the prime place still held by Sunday worship in community life in the 1960s to the 1970s:

[W]e were forced to go to church every single Sunday, and it was a big event. It was a major event. You put on your hat and you put on your best frock and you went out to church and you had to behave really, really well. And all the neighbours went out, and I think it was really, I suppose, it was a show of solidarity. There was no way you would have been allowed to miss a Sunday. You would have had to be really ill not to go to church. . . . [L]ooking back now, I see it as kind-of a frontier mentality.

To take a short digression, the wearing of a hat to divine worship was a feature of the experience of nigh-on every women of a certain age, and one 65-year-old Protestant recalled that, when she

was about . . . ten, eleven . . . [I was] very sceptical of authority when they pronounced this is the only interpretation of something. . . . I . . . always lost everything, still do, but I couldn't find my hat for church and my mother said I had to go to church and I had to have a hat. Problem! Anyway, I asked her why I had to have a hat for church, because the boys didn't and she said, Oh, because St Paul said and it's religion, you have to have it, and I said well . . . why did St Paul say it? And she said, Oh, because it's for modesty and it's so that women look modest and inconspicuous. So I said, Well, why does Mrs Smith wear that amazing wedding hat? I said that's actually . . . anything but modesty. And . . . that made me suspicious of St Paul at about ten.

The Protestant minority slowly learned to negotiate inter-communal life in the 'Gaelic and Catholic ethos'[1] of the new state as it developed. In the early days, keeping its distance from the rest of Irish society was in the interests, as it saw it, of maintaining communal integrity by the strictest of policing of group boundaries. There was more at stake than religious dogma, cultural identity or boundary definition for its own sake, however. It was perceived that inter-church marriages resulted in the inevitable loss of the next generation to the Protestant community because of the requirement imposed on the non-Catholic partner to raise any children as Catholics, which all but guaranteed that the children would move beyond the ambit of the Protestant familial and social group. The ultimate consequence of this would, it was feared, be the extinction of the community.

Protestant withdrawal in itself ensured the community's 'social and psychological'[2] marginalisation, and thereby reinforced perceptions that they hankered back to their previous elite position in Irish society. Even while this was disadvantageously interpreted when seen from a Catholic perspective, from a Protestant point of view it was paramount to be separate, even at a cost. In any event, Protestant self-marginalisation did not last beyond the end of the 1950s, although the degree to which they were integrated into the society that surrounded them is quite another matter.

Following on the nineteenth-century erosion of their position as a dominant elite, for historical, political and social reasons the Protestant minority's communal morale was low at independence, and Bowen maintains that it remained so for quite some time due not only to their change in status but also to the disappearance from public life of all but a few Protestants. He also maintained that 'their self-confidence was further eroded by the hostility of Catholics to their colonial heritage'.[3] However, in contradiction to the view that the Protestant sense of identity was insecure, Martin Maguire argued that the Church of Ireland community, largely because of its survival after disestablishment and its democratic lay-centred mode of government, was, in fact, self-confident, and that this self-image helped 'overcome the rapid erosion of its formal status in Ireland'. However, there is still ambiguity, because self-confidence can, of course, be read as self-congratulation or as superiority, and, with another twist, these behaviours can also be symptoms of insecurity, so that ultimately differentiating negative perceptions are emphasised rather than diminished.

In Maguire's opinion, the community's status was underpinned by 'the informal networks of charitable, social and cultural organisations'.[4] Certainly, a positive outcome of the Protestant parish networks' sense of their place in the lives of its members was that, throughout the state, parish associations and clubs gave Protestants facilities for religious education, for recreation and, vitally, for young people to meet each other. The content of diocesan and parish magazines, with their notices about church and social activities, their rallying exhortations aimed at the maintenance of good community morale and their marking of births, marriages and deaths in the community, demonstrated the vigorous parish life. A representative sample comes from one middle-class suburban area, where the Church of Ireland's *Rathmines Parish Magazine* for October 1934 gives an overview of the activities and organisations available to parishioners in a suburban parish. The 'Parish Week' column tells them, in language redolent of adherence to the Protestant work ethic lest they might think that mere sociability for its own sake was the sole aim, that:

A very encouraging attendance marked the meetings held last month in connection with the opening of the winter's work in the Parish. There was a

Devotional meeting on Monday, September 17, in the Parochial Hall, a Corporate communion for Parish Workers on Tuesday, September 18, at 7.30 a.m., and a conference and discussion of plans for the winter in the Parochial Hall on Wednesday, September 19.[5]

Various committees were appointed to arrange missionary meetings, study circles and so on, 'to widen as far as possible the missionary interest in our parish'. Arrangements were put in hand for the forthcoming festival of harvest thanksgiving, and requests made for fruit, vegetables and flowers for church decoration. Two fundraising sales were planned.[6]

The parish ran the following organisations for children and young adults: Boys' Brigade; Life Boys, the junior section of the Boys' Brigade; Girls' Brigade; Mothers' Union; Rathmines Parish Sunday School Senior Boys' Bible Class; Girls' Guild; Rathmines Literary and Debating Society, for which 'all Protestant men are eligible for membership'; Rathmines Parish Badminton club; Guild of Youth and Dorcas Society.[7] Apart from the appeals for missionary societies and the national schools in the parish, there was also an appeal for subscriptions for a fund to be used to provide coal for the poor in the parish.[8]

This state of affairs continued throughout the 1940s and 1950s, and in June 1960 the need for the perpetuation of the close bonds of community in the parish was still evident, when, before proceeding to exhort all choir members to attend practice for the forthcoming choral festival, the editor of the Clogher Diocesan magazine, the Revd J. McMurray Taylor, called upon car owners in the largely rural diocese to give lifts to non-car-owners for outings. His reasoning gives an insight into how the parish unit was conceived:

> As I see it, each parish should be a family – if you like, a family of families – and not merely a collection of individual, separate, distinct households with no interest in one another's welfare or happiness. . . . In the course of time this idea could be developed so that some members of one parish would meet some members of another at an agreed place, and the idea of the Christian family would be extended.[9]

A 71-year-old Protestant from Mayo recalled a vital facet of parish life from his bachelorhood in the 1950s and 1960s, which indicates the effort required for Protestants in remote areas to meet one another at 'socials' in far-flung parishes, which, in the early days, at any rate, were segregated. The pooling of transportation resources was also a feature:

The schools had their own Church of Ireland socials. And no other one attended or wouldn't be allowed in. . . . [W]e travelled to Church of Ireland socials down to Sligo, Riverstown, Westport, Cong. . . . we'd gather up, fill the car and off! . . . Down to Sligo, Riverstown, Killooly, Tubbercurry, Enniscrone, you name it. And the local ones. . . . There's no more of that. . . . They used to be good nights, [dancing] and a bit of supper. . . . [They were policed by] the Committee . . . in the background somewhere. . . . Very few [Catholics came]. . . . [T]his area, they would. But, say, Sligo . . . none. . . . There'd be old women, old men, the children . . . everything'd be at it. . . . [T]hey'd sent out invitations . . . they'd announce it in the church. . . . [to] make sure they didn't clash. . . . I don't know how much marriages came out of it, but mine definitely did.

This was a time when the 'young consumer . . . afforded new nomenclature as the "teenager" [became, if in employment] a key economic actor'.[10] From the last interviewee's evidence, it can be seen that the Protestant teenager in rural and provincial urban areas, whether working or still in education, was amply catered for by parish activities which integrated the generations and ensured that young people from different areas had opportunities to meet. This also meant that they continued to socialise within the community. It would also appear that the care taken to keep them within the community was not replicated on the Catholic front, at least in one area: Carole Holohan cites a survey carried out on a Limerick housing estate in the mid-1960s which described the lack of leisure facilities for young Catholics whose education finished at the end of the primary cycle and who had been sent out to work at 14 or 15 years of age. Although there were GAA and soccer clubs, young people tended to hang around in groups at cafes or fish-and-chip shops.[11]

For young urban Protestants, the various organisations and the parish table-tennis, badminton and youth clubs as well as the Friday night hops in parish halls also kept them to a large extent within the fold. The approach of the Church of Ireland to youth work *per se* was, it appears, despite the imperatives involved, somewhat patchy. It was only in 1950 that the matter of co-ordinating the youth activities of the Church of Ireland was seen as worthy of investigation. It was found that councils, or guilds, of youth existed only in three dioceses and then only in some parishes. A Church of Ireland Youth Council representing all the dioceses was not formed until 1970.[12] Given the multiplicity of parish organisations already existing and designed for all ages, perhaps this state of affairs is not to be wondered at.

When considering formal organisations and their place in Protestant experience, in the years preceding independence, Martin Maguire states that 'in 1887 it was estimated that there were four thousand Orangemen in Dublin, organised in ten lodges', although even at that stage the Order was 'inert'. He continues: 'although politically impotent[,] Orangeism survived in Dublin after independence, perhaps as social and welfare centres'.[13] Kurt Bowen set out how, in the early years, the Orange order, with its strong anti-Catholic stance, maintained a presence throughout the state, but by the mid-1970s it had retreated to the border counties.[14] Jack White indicated in a footnote that 'The Orange Order has figured little in [*Minority report*] because its main activity has always been in the North'.[15]

The presence of bigotry and the power of the emotional legacy manifested itself again in February 2006 when there was an attempt to hold a march in Dublin by Northern loyalist Willie Frazer's 'Families Acting for Innocent Relatives', to be led by Orange Order brass bands. It was not, in fact, an 'Orange march', but was perceived as such by many, and some reacted with violence. The march 'failed after around 1,000 Northern unionists went home without marching after some of the worst rioting Dublin has seen broke out'.[16] Whether this was sectarian violence is, of course, a moot point, for it may merely have been opportunism on the part of a trouble-making element, but the event certainly roused sectarian feeling and intense debate at the time. Attempts to negotiate a formula by which a similar march could be held in 2007 failed.

The evidence of a 37-year-old interviewee who facilitates cross-border co-operative projects demonstrated both that the order is extant in the border counties of the state, and how communal rivalries express themselves. She

> visited a group . . . in Co Monaghan . . . they've an Orange lodge there. . . . [In] the middle of nowhere . . . hidden behind the trees . . . marching bands appearing from nowhere, and. . . this big . . . family day out.. . . the welcome was great . . . I thought the whole set-up was great, from the point of view of getting families together, with three generations, the whole community thing. They'd come from [a] thirty, forty, fifty mile radius. But down the road in the village was the local Catholic pipe band, so there was one set of bands up here, a few yards down the road, a Catholic pipe band . . . two separate functions going on on the same night! . . . Complete lack of communication! It was hilarious! . . . [Then we] . . . realised, No, it's something else going on altogether!

A 22-year-old Catholic from Donegal confirmed the existence and the relative acceptance, as she perceived it, of the order in that county. Her Protestant friend's father

> was in the Orange order . . . a lot of southern Protestants are, but I think it's a different kind-of ball-game, it's very accepted . . . there's a [local] march . . . every year, and there's never any hassle.

Freemasonry was also an important feature in the lives of many, mostly middle-class, Protestant men. Despite the fact that it does not exclude Catholics, their church's animosity towards the society militated against their joining, and Bowen did not find any Protestants who knew of Catholic members. Anyway, in the 1970s, membership – in suburban areas around Dublin, at any rate – was declining.[17] In this study, however, two Protestant farmers from the west gave evidence of being keen and committed current members of their local lodge and of the presence of Catholics in it. The first one told of how he had become interested in the society and, incidentally, of how masons were perceived:

> I'm a staunch member of the Masonic Order . . . since 1968. . . . I queried my own way into it. . . . Curiosity . . . I heard it being spoken about a lot in, in England. . . . Oh, the bloody Freemasons! . . . [Y]ou'd hear nothing good said about them. . . . [T]he first time I ever heard the word 'Freemason' spoken, I'd be 14, 15 or 16 years of age. . . . [A] man would come with his . . . mackerel or herring. . . . [He'd say:] 'Don't be handling them, now, Mr Rogers, they're all the same.' [My uncle would say:] 'They're not, you have the big ones in the bottom.' '. . . How do you know they're in the bottom?' 'I'm a Freemason – I know everything!' . . . 'You're too decent a man, Mr Rogers, to be a Freemason', . . . I says to him: '[Uncle] James, what is a Freemason?' He wasn't able to tell me! He didn't know. . . . But it got a lot of bad press. . . . There'd be 40, 45, 50 members [in our Lodge at present]. . . . Freemasonry is non-religious, non-political. . . . We have Roman Catholics.

The second confirmed that there were a number of Catholics amongst the members of the same lodge and indicated that, although there was the possibility of membership for Jews, it was limited because of the respective faiths' beliefs on scriptural issues:

That the Masonic Order is non-sectarian and we can . . . back that up by the
fact that we have a number of Roman Catholics, and . . . one man who may be
Jewish in our Lodge. . . . But the only shortcoming is, the Jews can only go [so
far because] . . . Masonry . . . gets Christian. . . . I think in Northern Ireland
that . . . Presbyterians gravitate towards to Orangeism and that the Church of
Ireland people are Masonic. . . . That might be a little bit of an overview. . . . I
would imagine there's cross membership, as well, people members of both.

The only subgroup which did not participate in Protestant parish life was
that of the 'West Brits' or 'Anglo-Irish', terms which are often inaccurately
used or conflated. Here, we are considering class, rather than pedigree, implications. In the early days of the state, the middle, upper and 'Anglo-Irish'
classes pursued their recreation in strictly segregated golf, yacht and tennis
clubs, the last of which could be parochial or secular. By the 1970s, however,
many of the clubs, for economic if not for ecumenical reasons, were mixing the
confessions.[18] The smallest sub-group of the Protestant community, the class
saw itself as separate not only from all Catholics save those in the 'Castle'
category but also from the rest of the Protestants. Their distinctively English
culture and accent, maintained and ensured by English public-school education,
and tortuous 'rules' governing membership of the class ensured their doubly
isolated locus in Irish society, at least until barriers generally became more
porous in the decades following the end of the Second World War and as the
generation who lived through independence died out. For the rest of the
Protestant community, however, 'from cradle to grave, this constant round of
parish activities was well able to satisfy the social inclinations of even the most
socially energetic of parishioners'.[19]

We have already encountered the 58-year-old Protestant interviewee, a
business proprietor, who described his mother's family and himself as 'West
Brit'. If Bowen's description of the anachronistic and now-absurd 'rules' of
self-delineation of the caste loosely supposed to be the remnants of the
Ascendancy holds true, which dictate that anyone 'in trade' – retailing as
opposed to wholesaling – was emphatically disqualified from membership,[20]
this interviewee might not 'qualify'. He was educated in the state and is
involved in the retail area of commerce as well as the wholesale. However, it is
interesting that he still used that descriptor to locate himself in the Protestant
community in the Republic in the twenty-first century.

Historically, among Protestant groups, the identity of the 'Anglo-Irish'
relied more on ethno-cultural factors than on the confessional one alone, and

there was a degree of interaction between them and Catholics of the same social status, class mattering more than confession.[21] The Knight of Glin, descendant of the Fitzgeralds, Earls of Desmond and an indisputable member of this diminishing caste, encompassed both his own sense of marginalisation and the precariousness of his position when he said:

> I feel totally Irish. . . . Am I accepted here? I feel part of Ireland but I'm not sure that Ireland knows what to do with me and my tribe. . . . As one of the last survivors of the old landowning caste in Ireland, I see my stewardship of [Glin Castle], and of Georgian Ireland, as a voyage of discovery. . . . We live with the spectre of the auctioneer's tent going up in the garden and seeing everything scattered in a couple of days.[22]

Bowen found variations in the forms taken by segregation based on the urban/rural divide, and on religious, ethnic and class differences,[23] but most Protestant parishes, whether urban or rural, appeared to work especially hard one way or another at providing parish activities designed ultimately to prevent inter-church marriage. It is interesting to note the existence of a considerable Protestant working class in the Dublin area at the beginning of the twentieth century, of which most Catholics as well as middle-class Protestants appeared to be ignorant. Its members certainly countered the stereotype of the prosperous, snooty Protestant. Martin Maguire maintained that, keen to promote their own respectability and elitist middle-class image, Protestants further up the social scale themselves often refused to acknowledge their 'own' poor.[24] He quoted C. S. Andrews's perception that all Protestants were middle class, then continued that it was not only Catholic nationalists who saw all Protestants as a middle-class elite. In fact, there were a number of Church of Ireland parishes in which a substantial proportion of the members were lower middle class or working class in origin[25] – which, of course, is not to say that to be working class was also automatically to be poor. However, as we have seen, in at least one middle-class parish in the Dublin suburbs in 1934 there was a parish coal fund for the aid of the poor of the parish, so it was not that Protestant poverty did not exist, but more that it was played down for the sake of image. However, an interesting present-day perception from the evidence of a 22-year-old border-county Catholic both indicates cross-confessional co-operation and also points to the continued existence of the phenomenon described by Maguire:

[T]here was one or two Protestant ladies worked in the St Vincent de Paul with [my mother] but they would have been seen as different to the other ladies of their class. . . . The kind-of golf set. . . . And there was this one Protestant family that were being given a lot of help by the St Vincent de Paul, and I remember one day my mother making the remark that their church didn't want to know about them, because they were so badly-off. And there was a lot of stuff going on in that house, really bad things. And my mother making some comments: Oh, their own don't want to know about them, like.

In the second half of the nineteenth century, as the middle classes migrated to the new suburbs to the north and south of the city, there had been a diminution in the number of city-centre Protestants, but 'by 1901 there was still a sizeable Church of Ireland city borough population of 41,663, or 14 per cent of the city population, residing in twenty-two parishes'. The distribution of the population in the twentieth century in the Dublin area was marked by class, rather than by confession, with working-class areas in the city whilst the middle classes inhabited the suburbs. Hence, 'in Dublin a person's address would give no clue to religion but could reveal much about socio-economic class'.[26] However, while segregation maintained its hold, there was little social mingling and more hostility, especially for the working and lower middle-class children, in urban areas. For them, attendance at parish activities had its risks when travelling to and fro. This did not, in the main, deter participation.

In common with others of the urban working and lower middle classes, a 59-year-old Protestant from north central Dublin, still living in the family home where she was born and raised, told of how her social life was bounded by church activities:

[B]efore we went to work, we were all in the Girls' Brigade . . . .. And we used to have to go to Bible class on the Sunday, and like my father insisted. You were in the Girls' Brigade, you went to Bible class, you went to everything that was attached to it. . . . And we had to go.
Q. So . . . particularly as you grew a bit older, did you find that your social life was geared more towards the Protestants than towards Catholics?
A. More or less, yes.

An 81-year-old Protestant north Dubliner was still, at the time of interview, running the small shop started as a dairy by her father. She spoke of the relationship between the two confessions when she was young, and confirmed the Sunday observance rules that did not permit her go to the pictures on Sundays, adding that she and her sisters often entertained themselves at home around the piano. She also told of belonging to two parish organisations, one of which had the express aim of making sure that young Protestant girls coming up to the city to work had a social network upon which to depend as well as segregated events to attend:

> Q. Now, did you belong to any of the societies attached to the church, like Girls' Brigade?
> A. Ah, yes, Girls' Brigade, and GFS.[27] My . . . sister Sarah was great at the GFS. . . . She used to take the girls out from the Oak House, and bring them over. . . . The girls used to come up to work . . . up here [from the country], and, like, they'd nowhere to go. . . . And in the summer time . . . she used to take them out. . . . They used to come over to the house to us.

One 81-year-old Protestant who had lived all his life in north Dublin and worked as a shop assistant in the city centre, recalled meeting his wife in another particularly Protestant manner:

> I met [her] . . . [in] a place called the YMCA in Abbey Street, and we used to go there, you know, the boys used to go and the girls used to go, and we were hoping to meet.

Despite all efforts to keep the youth of the two communities apart in the period between independence and the Second World War, inevitably there was some breaching of group barriers, particularly in urban areas where the communities lived in close proximity. Of course, there were inter-church marriages, although not many and sometimes with extreme consequences for those who did not conform. However, association was not something to which it was easy to admit. A 79-year-old Protestant, still living in the north Dublin city house situated in the middle-class area where she was born and her mother and grandmother also had lived, said at first that she had no Catholic friends when she was young. Then, seeming surprised at her own words as she realised she had contradicted herself, she indicated that she had, indeed, socialised with Catholics as a young adult:

[I had] All, all Church of Ireland friends.

Q. At that stage [teenage years], did you have any Roman Catholic friends?

A. No.

Q. No. And where and how did you meet your husband?

A. I met him through a Roman Catholic chemist! We were all very friendly. . . . Well, at that stage, being teenagers . . . we were friendly . . . where I go to [on holidays] and this chemist was the chemist in the shop there. And everybody thought he was lovely, and it was through him, that he invited me to the chemists' dance and invited another fellow as well, and the other fellow was my husband.

Q. So, in fact, did, you did have a little bit of association then.

A. Yes. Then. Yes. Yes.

Indeed, for someone of her generation, it was somewhat atypical that she socialised with Catholics to the extent that she did when of marriageable age, but it is possible to speculate that the contradiction in her testimony in fact disclosed that there was more inter-group mixing than Protestants like to acknowledge. Her evidence – or, more exactly but subjectively, the tone of it – indicated the deep-rooted ambivalences resulting from segregation between communities living alongside one another: she wished to register her adherence to Protestant community precepts, and yet betrayed the impossibility of maintaining strict segregation on a daily basis.

An 81-year-old Protestant, who had worked as a retail manager, a salesman and a designer, was born in the North Strand, and described himself as 'a true Dub, from Mud Island!' He talked of the working-class area in which he grew up as 'a mixed community, but pretty well balanced', and remembered how he accompanied his Catholic pals when they were fulfilling their religious duties: 'on occasions when the lads had to go to do the Seven Churches, the mothers were always delighted when I was with them, and I'd map out where they were to go and bring them back'. Then, as he grew older, he became involved in some of the usual activities attached to Protestant churches, which, in common with others, meant that he became distanced from his early childhood friends:

So, anyway, as I got older, the lads who were Church of Ireland in the neighbourhood joined what was called the Life Boys. . . . They were a junior organisation to the Boys' Brigade. . . . [T]he captain of the Boys' Brigade company of St Barnabas came around to the house to get me to join Barnabas's Boys' Brigade, which I did. But that sort-of formed a little gang of these lads who were in the Boys' Brigade. If you were going for a walk, you went out with about five or six of them. If you were going on a Sunday to the YM, you went with about a dozen of them.

Indeed, he was another of the older generation who did mix with Catholics but the difference was that he was not afraid to acknowledge it. However, in spite of his good relations and high profile with Catholics in his community, he experienced an episode of intimidation when he was a young man:

> Lady Ardilaun had presented an ex-war nissen hut as a tennis pavilion and she gave two tennis courts for the children . . . to learn to play tennis, and, as they grew up into teenagers they'd have their dances in the pavilion, and . . . it was there . . . I met this [Roman Catholic] girl . . . Anna, she was the belle of the neighbourhood, everyone was chasing [her]. So, we got very friendly and then in time, I got a letter telling me not to see her any more, from her father, or he would have me charged. . . . That's the only thing, I've never had anything else.

In the end, though, he said, things worked out for him, and in common with so many of his generation, later he and his future wife met at a parish dance.

Another 65-year-old unmarried Protestant from north inner Dublin spoke of being the only Protestants in the area when she was small: 'No matter where we lived . . . we were the only Protestants'. In common with other interviewees, she did play with Catholic children when she was small, though this changed as she grew older, when her social life was completely centred on the church:

> I was in the Girls' Brigade and I was in the Girl Guides, and I was in the Junior CE, that's the Christian Endeavour. . . . And Sunday School, and Children's Services.
> Q. Did you teach Sunday School at any stage?
> A. I did. . . . [And] I played table tennis . . . in the Parochial Hall. And then I went down to the YMCA in Abbey Street and I played there for a number of years.

In rural areas, although there were fewer parish organisations, for 'rural Protestants generally tended to be less associationally minded',[28] the 1960s did see the beginning of a movement away from Protestant-only organisations to those with mixed membership – which logically had to mean more Catholics than Protestants in the ranks. Macra na Feirme and its junior branch, Macra na Tuaithe (1952), were examples of this. Formed as educational and social clubs for young people involved in agriculture, they were modelled on the American 4H clubs and the Young Farmers Clubs in the United Kingdom. By 1946 there were 25 branches of Macra in existence in the state. By 1951 it had almost 15,000 members in 400 clubs. In line with its non-denominational ethos, Protestants were active in the clubs, particularly in Donegal and West Cork. In the 1970s, Declan Martin, a Protestant from Blarney, Co Cork, was elected President, and another President from the minority community, Dr Fergus O'Ferrall, served during the period 1985–8.[29] However, no one interviewed for this project spoke of belonging to the organisation, although one farmer from the west, when questioned specifically later, thought that there had been some Protestant involvement in his area.

Another organisation which provided opportunities for cross-confessional social contact and educational activities in rural areas was the Irish Country-women's Association, the membership of which was, for demographic reasons, predominantly Catholic, whilst the Mothers' Union provided social and educational facilities for both urban and rural women from the Protestant community. A 65-year-old rural Protestant member of the ICA – who demonstrated practical community-mindedness in providing transport for her co-members in a manner that the Revd McMurray-Taylor could only have applauded – said:

> You attended anything they had, like plays and all that sort of thing . . . you bought tickets for this, that and the other, even though you couldn't afford it. . . . [W]e organised with another Presbyterian woman the ICA, and we had a ball until it got to the stage where the rules and regulations . . . got in the way. . . . To us, ICA was where . . . a group of women came together and they had a speaker and they had a good giggle over a cup of tea, but then . . . there was all these rules, you had to do this, and you had to do that, and you had to attend this meeting, you had to attend that meeting. . . . It just fell away then. [I was also a member of] The Mothers' Union . . . my perception of that was that it was only for . . . grannies, but I was the only one in the church that could drive, and therefore, the meetings were always in Ballina, and I went along . . . to bring them.

Another elderly south-western Protestant remains an involved member of the ICA, however. In response to a question about whether she had ever witnessed religious discrimination, she replied:

[N]one at all. . . . I'm fifty years in the ICA. . . . I was six years in the ICA in Rosscarberry and then [here, after I married]. . . . [W]e've very few Church of Ireland members because they're just not joining the ICA and I'm the only one here except two Methodist friends.

Her response appeared to indicate by implication that other members of the local Protestant community held themselves somewhat aloof from the association.

The suburban middle class of Dublin which emerged in the 1960s was made up of upwardly mobile working-class Protestants who had moved to the suburbs after the Second World War,[30] and were likely to work at the managerial level and in banks and businesses, and Catholics and Protestants from the professions and business-owning circles. The following extract is taken from the interview with the 58-year-old Protestant business proprietor who described himself as 'West Brit'. He had early contact with Catholics, but, as he grew older and progressed to secondary school, he described the phenomenon of having different groups of friends, one in the neighbourhood, one at school and church. As soon as he started school, he still had contact with Catholic neighbours, but tended increasingly to gravitate more to Protestants. He then speculated on the differences there might be now, and compared his situation with the circumstances pertaining for his children:

At home I would still have had friends who were Catholic, but . . . my next-door neighbour who I was very pally with . . . was Presbyterian. . . . And homes that I would visit, more often than not they were, as it happens, they were Protestant. . . . Whereas my children, absolutely different . . . yes, it's interesting now that . . . I discuss it with you, I realise how different my social involvement with Catholics was compared with what it would be now, or what my children's has been.

So, through his family and his own inter-communal contacts, he had experienced the changes in the relationship between the confessions wrought by the passing of decades, but had not articulated them to himself until the opportunity afforded by the interview, although he acknowledged that confessional orientation has always been, and still is, something which interests him and of which he is conscious:

[T]his one neighbour, one very good friend, has always felt that I was very conscious of my religion. . . . I am always interested to know what religion

people are. . . . And of course we are quite devious, aren't we? As to how we –
you love to find out, you know and you'll ask the subtle question, like 'where
were your kids at school?' or whatever. And I do have an interest in that.

A heightened level of confessional consciousness is, not surprisingly, also
apparent in the evidence of a 47-year-old Catholic from Belfast who was
absolutely sure he could identify to which community someone belonged by
picking up unconscious signals, but it is interesting that the businessman
couched it in negative terminology by labelling it as deviousness. An Anglican
interviewee who was not raised in the state described the process of discovery,
echoing in some respects that of the man from Belfast, that she uses when she
meets someone for the first time:

> I don't like to say to people: Are you Church of Ireland? But sometimes I see
> somebody and I say: I know they're Church of Ireland! Just the way they look
> and the way they talk! . . . but not being Irish, I can't pick up on that straight
> away. So, I might, if I chat to them, I might lead the conversation. Do, did you
> ever see that . . . comedian . . . Kilty? Kilty. Anyways, he said he'd be at a dance
> in Belfast. He'd be dancing with this young woman, and he'd say: Where're
> you from? And she say where she was from. And he'd say: Well, could be
> Catholic, could be Protestant. And then he'd ask another question . . . could
> be Catholic, could be Protestant [and so on].

Another interviewee, a 58-year-old Protestant, born in the Republic but
educated in Northern Ireland, referred to an abrupt dawning of confessional
consciousness resulting in a degree of alienation when she came to Dublin to
study physiotherapy in the late 1960s:

> I came down to Dublin, and of course I came to live in the YWCA, [it] was a
> terrible shock to me, when I realised . . . we were this little tiny minority. . . . In
> Dublin . . . Out of the girls' boarding school. . . . I suddenly noticed it, whereas
> I would not have been aware . . . of other people's religion [before] . . . and
> suddenly I realised . . . well, I don't know whether I was going to be a wee
> Northerner, but when I went North they said I had a brogue, and when I came
> south, they said I had a Northern accent.

Her sense of marginalisation, especially the matter of her accent, echoes the
evidence, adduced in the last chapter, of the interviewee who was sent to

English public school, where he was bullied because of his 'brogue', but it is even more ironic here, in that she was in her own country but yet was marked out as 'different' by the way she spoke. It is intriguing how often the motif of accent occurs in connection with Protestants, almost always with a negative connotation attached, and with complete lack of awareness that everybody speaks with an accent.

A 68-year-old Catholic was another who referred to different groupings of friends in his youth. He described a delightful childhood in a north Dublin seaside suburb in the late 1940s and early 1950s. Having confirmed the existence of three different groups of friends – one at school, who were Catholic, another in the neighbourhood which included Protestants, and another in the tennis and sailing clubs – he went on to reply to the question of whether these clubs were confessionally mixed in a noticeably irritated manner before continuing:

> Of course they were. . . . They were indeed. Both of those clubs, the tennis club and the, eh, and the sailing club were very much mixed. I'd say they were even about fifty–fifty. . . . Or very nearly fifty–fifty. . . . I was aware of, of those sort of [segregated] clubs. In fact . . . my first, maybe my second girlfriend . . . was a Church of Ireland girl, and she belonged to a club, a tennis club that was totally non-Catholic.

This is interesting for three reasons. Firstly, the emotional reaction to a perceived assumption of intolerance: he did not like what he interpreted as an implication that he might have belonged to a segregated club, that is, to have behaved with sectarian bias. Secondly, he clearly mixed freely if he had a Church of Ireland girlfriend, which would make him doubly sensitive to implications of intolerance. Thirdly, it confirms the existence of Protestant segregated clubs alongside those of mixed membership in middle-class enclaves.

Confirmation of the mingling of an earlier generation of the two communities in such clubs was provided by an 81-year-old middle-class Protestant, who also commented on the place of sport in minimising segregation, a topic to which we will return later:

> [M]y father and mother were members of Drumcondra Tennis Club, which is long since gone . . . it was a mixed club, and we were dragged down there every Saturday, so we mixed with Catholics down there, and then, when I was about fourteen, I joined Glasnevin Tennis Club, which had a very flourishing junior

section, and it was a mixed club, so I was immediately involved with Catholic young people, and became very friendly with a lot of them . . . and went to their houses and they came here, and we all got on extremely well.

Overall, the evidence demonstrated instances of strong emphasis on the good interpersonal relationships between individuals regardless of confession. Early on, in rural areas, this was usually evidenced by a mutual tacit agreement over continuation of the custom of help on the land between neighbours, but without the element of social mixing, whether at formal or informal events. During the same period in urban areas there was more mingling due to simple proximity, but most social contact was still ring-fenced within confessionalised parish activity. However, the changes wrought in both inter-church and socio-economic arenas which started in the 1960s had worked through into most levels of society in the 1970s, and Bowen recorded that younger members of the Protestant community at that stage made far more contact with 'the other side' than their parents would ever have done, motivated by no longer believing that there was either the necessity or the justification for segregation. They no longer saw their fellow citizens' Catholicism or their church's power as a threat. It was also due, he argued, to the 'diminishing religious commitment of the older generation and to its growing uncertainty as to the propriety of excluding Catholics from . . . secular activities'. Indeed, Protestant youth had gained in confidence and become sceptical about the degree to which the Catholic Church could continue to dictate the form and nature of inter-church marriage. They neither comprehended, let alone shared, the plaintive views of

one strong churchman whose daughter had just married a Catholic . . . 'They think I'm too narrow. It is our church that is going to the wall. They don't see the importance of this.'[31]

Of course, it has to be remembered that rejection of segregation in general terms does not automatically mean the end of unconscious confessionalised mindsets or behaviours.

There was evidence in the interviews of a continuing Catholic perception of the Protestant tendency to exclusivity. One interviewee, a 49-year-old Catholic from an east coast town whose personal history encapsulated the social changes of the late twentieth century, related that his father was republican and abhorred everything British 'bar the coal'. However, his parents ran a bed and breakfast in the town which catered to English summer visitors and this, the interviewee inferred, broke down ethnic and cultural misunderstandings sufficiently to ensure there was no family trouble on the confessional front when both he and his brother married English Anglicans in the 1980s. However, in the late 1980s, his children went to a Church of Ireland primary school in an area of the county with a long-established and somewhat entrenched Protestant community. The enrolment policy of the school was described by another interviewee as follows:

> It's a Church of Ireland school . . . and the . . . vague enrolment policy would be, first of all, all Church of Ireland people within the parish boundaries, which are very strictly laid out. Then . . . it's all other Church of Ireland, regardless of where they're from. . . . [A]nd then it's 'other', as far as I know. . . . [A]ll schools have to have an absolutely transparent enrolment policy. . . . [B]ut obviously, because the school is run by the Church of Ireland . . . first preference is given to [Church of Ireland].

The interviewee's children were therefore admitted to the school on the basis of his wife's Anglicanism. He said of the Protestant parents:

> I thought they were a little bit clannish. Maybe because they're such a small minority. . . . [T]hey seemed to do everything together. Plus, an awful lot of what they did was based around the church. . . . I loved their Christmas carols, mind you! They know how to sing! They're great. They're not afraid to sing on, like the Catholics. They sing out . . . I thought they were a little bit clannish. . . . Kept themselves to themselves. They had their own little community, and that was it.

It has to be remembered that another factor in the distance existing between the two communities from independence up to the last quarter of the twentieth century was simply a consequence of their relative sizes: there were, in some rural areas, very few Protestants to be found. A 47-year-old Catholic primary teacher from the west highlighted this phenomenon from her point of view:

> There wouldn't have been [any contact then], because when we got married first we'd be kind-of quiet in ourselves. . . . And we would have gone to work and come home in the evening. . . . [W]e would know the immediate neighbours here . . . [my husband] might have contact with [the Protestant down the road] through the farm. . . .. I suppose, the number of Protestants in

this area isn't that great. . . . [And] where I was when I was growing up . . . I would have known Pat Nalty, who was the postman . . . but I didn't know he was a Protestant, and it didn't mean anything to me.

A 69-year-old Catholic remembered how, in his childhood in a remote western coastal area, 'there were no Protestants that I can remember. They were very remote'.

A 72-year-old rural western Catholic went to live with her elder sister, a primary teacher, when she was eight years old so she could attend the sister's school. She was then introduced to a Protestant girl of her own age, as her sister and the girl's mother were friends. Not only was this her first contact with, or awareness of, Protestants, but also from it, although it was a 'lovely, lovely contact', she gleaned the impression that

to be Protestant was to be wealthy and to have a nice home and nice clothes, and I think I remember them having an accent. Or at least I thought they had an accent, like, so that they were that bit uppity.

Later in life, she was to question the absolutism of this perception in the face of the realities she encountered. Through their travelling shop, her family had contact with two Protestants she could remember, and one of them lived in

a gate house, for what was once local landlords . . . and [he] had beehives. [My] brother . . . might have obliged him by bringing out . . . sugar . . . big quantities for his beehives, and when . . . Jimmy . . . [left] that place and [went] to Dublin, he gave over his hive of bees to our family. . . . Protestants were always held in high esteem. . . . He was actually a poor man. His family were actually poor. But he had that same kind of openness and the family towards him, too, our family towards him. . . . [W]hen I went to [college] . . . my mother wrote to me and said: Jimmy . . . is living [in] . . . near where you are, and you've . . . to go visit. And they were very poor when I went to visit them. So they didn't have that kind of, well, well-heeled background that I met in the other Protestants.

It goes without saying that remoteness and lack of personal contact was not a feature of urban living, but this did not negate the distance between the communities: instead, it led to modifications in the modes of expression of difference. A 58-year-old Catholic from a middle-class background was brought up in the city of Dublin and moved to the suburbs later in life. Her family lived in a predominantly Catholic part of the city – although there were also Jewish families living nearby – but, despite their scarcity, she stated that, in the 1950s, Protestants 'were quite normal . . . to us'. However, a distinct awareness of difference manifests itself in her description of one Protestant family, especially in her childhood ideas on Protestants, their level of prosperity and the average number of children in their families, each of which discloses forms of prevalent social stereotypes of Protestants:

> We had one family of Protestants who moved into the street, and it became obvious that they were poor Protestants. And how we knew . . . was that they used margarine. Because nobody would use margarine on their bread in those days. And admit to it. . . . But this family moved in, and they were . . . quite a numerous family. They had a couple of babies while we were there. I think in all they might have had about ten children. And this was a revelation, I realise, because in my mind. . . . I really did think Protestants usually only had two or three. . . . [I]t became evident that they were very, very hardworking . . . [so] I'm at a loss to understand . . . how they were poor.

The view that all Protestants were rich drew an apparently exasperated response – an exception to the rule of never saying publicly anything controversial – from the Bishop of Cork, the Right Revd R. G. Perdue, on the occasion of the opening of a new comprehensive school in Cork in 1975. It was reported in some detail in the *Church of Ireland Gazette.* Dr Perdue said that because the Protestant community was a small minority,

> our fellow citizens know surprisingly little about us, about our difficulties, and frustrations, economic, social and religious. There is, for example, one very widespread fantasy that we are wealthy people. If we were free to disclose the figures of income as revealed to the Grants Committee,[32] people would be amazed at the high proportion of our people who live on very low incomes indeed.

It is interesting also to note the frankness with which Dr Perdue went on to say that the minority

> gets so accustomed to its handicaps and weaknesses that it ceases to expect, or struggle for, justice and equality of opportunity with others. We have seen examples of this in the field of education and of marriage.[33]

Further on the topic of Protestant silence, even apparent pusillanimity, in the face of controversial issues, the views of Catherine McGuinness, a high-profile Protestant and eminent member of the legal profession, are interesting. In 1985, she stated that Protestant difficulties were often compounded by the fact that however bitterly controversial they might feel at a distance, they were reluctant to say, face to face, anything contentious. She continued: 'In this way, we hurt each other, and in addition, we seem hypocritical to each other. On the surface, we are totally integrated, yet underneath the distrust grumbles on.'[34] Thus, in the mid-1980s, she is confirming the continuing existence of the undercurrents of feeling that indicate continued reliance on the emotional legacy. In her view, there was no 'overt and obvious oppression' in the state, but a general feeling that it was best to leave well alone did exist. However, when members of the community *did* speak up, she said, there was a common experience of other, silent members of the community privately expressing appreciation of their public stands. Most notable is her view that:

> Generally, however, it has been left to what I might describe as unorthodox or progressive Roman Catholics, and to those who do not profess to have any religious allegiance to carry on the public fight on conscience issues. Dr Noel Browne, Owen Sheehy-Skeffington and Mary Robinson spring to mind in the political field, and there have been a considerable number of Roman Catholic priests who have expressed views on issues of conscience, not noticeably typical of the body of mainstream Roman Catholic thinking. They have not made themselves exceptionally popular thereby.

On the matter of inter-church marriages, she also had an interesting view:

> The question of mixed marriages is one which comes up in almost every discussion, and one which has probably created more bitterness than any other. Personally, I am inclined to feel that the Protestant churches take too negative an attitude in this field and tend to put the blame for all their troubles on the Roman Catholic church.[35]

For older urban interviewees there was one factor which seems to have overcome the confessional boundary strictures so firmly in place during their younger lives, and that is sport. And, it has to be said, generally middle-class sport. Rugby, tennis and even cricket featured as annihilators of confessional difference in the lives of elderly Protestants, whereas soccer did not: it was mentioned by only one interviewee in connection, as we shall see, with the issue of 'Irishness' – and then only to say that he did not play it. And that these sports helped breach barriers indicates that Catholics were indeed playing them.

A plethora of myths and resultant codes surround sport in the nationalist lexicon, not the least of which include tales of the feats of Cú Chulainn on the hurling field.[36] A significant part of the Gaelic revival of the late nineteenth century, the Gaelic Athletic Association, an amateur sporting association, was founded in 1884. 'Anti-British in outlook' it imposed a ban on members playing or attending non-Gaelic games.[37] The association was, together with the Gaelic League, 'important in drawing young people into the national movement',[38] and considerable importance accrued to it in the construction of Gaelic nationalism.

At independence, rugby, which had arrived in Ireland from England in the mid-nineteenth century, soccer and cricket were already established in the country, They were brought in originally by the military in the late eighteenth century and also by young men returning from school or university in England.[39] Soon, demonstrating the active participation of both confessions on the actual field if not the metaphysical plane, there were more clubs for all three sports throughout the country than could possibly have been for Protestants only, and some middle-class Catholic schools played rugby rather than, or as well as, Gaelic games. So, what is significant is not what actually happened, but the important symbolism inherent in the linking of the Gaelic Athletic Association with nationalism generally and with hurling and Gaelic football as exclusively the province of Catholic nationalism. Further, by its ban on members partaking in 'foreign' games like soccer and rugby, it automatically acted as an agent of exclusion by banning 'others' – both players and games – from their particular construction of Irishness. Diarmaid Ferriter maintains that, in spite of how it appeared to many, 'the evolution of the GAA was not a narrow pursuit in sporting Anglophobia but Irish sport embracing the British model of sport codification' and mirroring the global trend of the social significance of ball games.[40] Be that as it may, for a century or so, unexamined nationalist codes had it that there *was* a division: Catholics played Gaelic games, Protestants 'foreign' ones, so, by virtue of subliminal assumptions, to play Gaelic games was proof positive that one was a true nationalist and, if one did not do so, one was, by default, unpatriotic.

Ostensibly, it was the playing of matches on a Sunday that prohibited Protestant participation in hurling or Gaelic football, but there can be little doubt that the nationalist connotations surrounding it were also a factor. It was not until the late 1970s that there was a public addressing of the issue, when Dean Charles Gray-Stack, in an article reprinted in the *Church of Ireland Gazette* with the permission of the *Irish Independent*, questioned the 'Cromwellian injunctions against playing games on Sundays':

> I was delighted to see the Dean of St Patrick's attending the All-Ireland Football Final. For too long it has looked as if the GAA was restricted to representatives of one Church. . . . [S]ince Dean Griffin's more publicised appearance, the suitability of such an attendance as his or mine has been raised in the correspondence columns of this newspaper. For once we had the spectacle of members of a minority Church arguing the toss in the *Irish Independent*. I think this was very healthy for it showed us as actually involved in a real issue.[41]

Whether this was more than tokenistic, however, is another matter, as, for one thing, the playing of Gaelic games did not become a feature in Protestant schools. Eventually, reality triumphed over ideology, and by the late twentieth century the Irish soccer team for the World Cup in 1990 and 1994 eventually became 'the single most potent focus of national feeling for the Irish at home and abroad, particularly for those who had emigrated in the 1980s'.[42]

The experience of an 85-year-old middle-class Dublin-born Protestant bears further attention here, as it underlines the realities of the sporting situation. He was quite secure in his sense of his Irishness and, as an athlete as well as a player of rugby and cricket all his active life, he was also certain about the place of those 'foreign' sports in his life:

> Q. Did the difference between the two confessions ever feature at all for you?
> A. No, never.
> Q. What reason do you give for that, in Irish society, because it did feature for so many?
> A. Well, I think mainly because of sport.

A 79-year-old urban Protestant further emphasised the importance of sport in breaching confessional boundaries when she said that:

> [M]y eldest son, being a referee, he meets everyone, and he is so friendly and so popular with everyone, and really religion is the last thing that comes into sport. It's not talked about in sport. Once they're good at the rugby . . . they don't talk about religion.

The evidence of another 81-year-old Protestant brought up in a north Dublin suburb, who played hockey, tennis, badminton and table tennis in Catholic as well as Protestant clubs all her life, underlined the importance of sport as a social and confessional equaliser. Her experience was exceptional to the segregated norms possibly not only because of sport but also because of class difference. Because the middle-class suburbs around Dublin were class-constant though confessionally mixed,[43] educational confessionalisation leading to social segregation remained the norm. However, she indicated that she thought other middle-class Protestants could be insular, keeping to themselves and their kind, and she seemed also to think sport was the element that differentiated her experience. She emphasised the unusual degree to which she mixed with Catholics:

> I have to say, I never experienced or felt any difficulty with being a Protestant surrounded by Roman Catholics. Any Catholic neighbours we had, we all mixed round together and everybody was very pleasant.
> Q. Did you have any special pals who were Catholics?
> A. Yes – our local doctor, who lived in the corner house at the top of the road, he had about eight children, and they were Roman Catholics and we always went to their birthday parties and they came to ours.
> Q. Do you think your family was relatively unusual for that day in associating closely?
> A. Well, I'd say yes, probably. I knew a lot of Protestant families who never went beyond their church groups and they socialised with their own people and in table tennis clubs belonging to the church, and tennis clubs, maybe, and the Guild of Youth.

She added:

> Well, the only thing I would add is that I'm very grateful to my parents for having allowed me to mix all my life with Roman Catholics, because I think I would have missed out terribly on some of the marvellous characters that I've met and I think, I know all the reasons behind keeping you in your own church because of the falling numbers, etc, etc, but I think it, it curtails your outlook and I think you miss out on not mixing around.

Her insight is borne out by the evidence of the younger east-coast Methodist whose parents' obedience to the 'rules' of segregation caused her to lose the possibility of Catholic friends, which resulted in her continuing social isolation.

A vital factor in the opening-up of Irish society on secular as well as confessional fronts was 'the advent of a national television service'.[44] In 1957, the government, heeding public demand evidenced by the 'forest of television masts in the Dublin area' capturing signals from Britain and conscious of the need to promote economic expansion, 'indicated that it envisaged a service run by commercial interests and when a television commission was established in 1958, this proposed arrangement was modified only to the extent that a public authority was promised to control the service'. Telefís Éireann was launched on 31 December 1961. It rode in on the wave of the 1958 programme for economic expansion, breaking on Irish shores as 'the barriers, restrictions, and compulsions that were so much a part of Irish society were to be steadily eroded or removed'. According to Cathcart and Muldoon, 'There is no doubt that television stimulated the whole process of change by promoting the free movement of ideas'.[45] Indeed, no small contribution to the process of social change was played by individual broadcasters on both TV and radio, amongst them Gay Byrne and Marian Finucane, who facilitated the airing of controversial social issues hitherto unmentionable in Irish society on radio phone-in programmes on the national network.[46]

Turning to present-day inter-communal perceptions, two young Wicklow Catholics who saw confessional difference as no longer significant were in a minority. However, evidence from two other members of the younger generation from the same county demonstrated how a very different situation can exist between the two confessions in the county. A 20-year-old east-coast Protestant had thought a great deal about confessional difference, and articulated her views with exceptional clarity. She had not been aware of confessional difference in primary school, as there was only one Catholic family in the otherwise Church of Ireland environment, but when it came to

> extra-curricular activities which would mix with other children in the town or whatever, there was like a lot of questions from them. As in we didn't know there was difference [but they did.]

She went on

> I think it might be more of a thing for the Catholics in the town than the Protestants, because you just get on with it, it's sort of a background thing, you don't really talk about [it], but . . . it just seems that they want to shout about it a bit more. . . .To make sure that you know that they are [Catholic] and will never be Protestant, or whatever!

Building on her previous answers, when she was asked what she thought the Catholic attitude to Protestants was, her reply was based on her experience of interschool rivalries: 'From my observation, wariness!' She also said that she thought that, to Catholics, Protestants are still alien and

a bit of a minority. That . . . they'd see Protestants as the plantation people who came and took their land . . . or [that it] dates back to the famine and so on. I dunno, I think it can be quite alienating sometimes, just when you find out that . . . people see you differently just because of where you went to church.

She thought that this led to the realisation

that there's still, after all the progress that people have made . . . there's still an underlying . . . hatred or . . . I dunno if it's hatred, but just . . . they're at loggerheads still. . . . No one is completely accepted. Like you'd have friends, but you'd know that they'd be different . . . because it's different upbringings as well . . . religious education as well I think is a big factor in it.

Her use of the phrase 'a bit of a minority' is notable: firstly, given that she meant 'elite' rather than minority, the tone of her words, taken with the entirety of her evidence, carried within it connotations of an alienated awareness of automatic marginalisation and exclusion. This, not surprisingly, affects the way she relates with Catholics, especially those who seize on differences and bring up the issues in social settings:

[C]enturies of fighting and wars went on about this, why bother talking about this? It's not going to make us better or less friends. So, just drop the subject. . . . sometimes I think people can get into it too much. . . . sometimes . . . jokingly. . . . over a few drinks . . . someone would mess. . . . Oh ho, Jaffa cake,[47] ha ha, and sometimes . . . it would be jokey but you get irritated because . . . Why is this even an issue? . . . It's . . . ridiculous . . . it doesn't mean anything to me, so why should it mean anything to you.

Although she said later that teasing could be a two-way process, with 'Jaffa cake', or orange-centred, being countered with 'Fenian', the fact that she referred to the absurd descriptor twice, indicating each time that its use was an irritant, was another factor demonstrating that confessional difference is a live and alienating issue in her interpersonal relationships. The presence of the emotional legacy in the interaction she has with her contemporaries is also clear.

A 30-year-old Catholic from a small town on the east coast was, at the time of interview, engaged to a Protestant from the same locality. Since she met him, she had been socialising mainly with his group of friends: 'I would know a lot of [Protestants] because of [my fiancé]'. . . . [A] good, say, eight or ten people, fellow-wise, that'd be pals of his that went to school with him, and they're all Protestants'. Indicating that she, too, has been the butt of teasing based on content of the emotional legacy not only from her social circle but also within her family because of her relationship, she went on:

> And one person in particular [would say] 'Oh, you'd go with a Protestant?. . .
> Not in a nasty way, he would have a bit of fun . . . with my fiancé, and he
> wouldn't like it, but we just don't pass any comment. Doesn't mean it's
> harmful, but I know he would be very . . . patriotic. Is that the word I'm
> looking for? You know, as in he was robbed . . . years ago . . . in the famine. . . .
> I don't think it's nice, I don't like it, but there [are] some people . . . carry those
> [stereotypes]. . . . Very much so. And my brother, now, he'd be very patriotic,
> but not to that extent. . . . He would never make [my fiancé] feel any different
> in our house at all . . . he slagged[48] me when we first started going out: Oh, me
> father would turn in his grave! We were codding, and I got upset, thought he
> was serious, and he said: God, I'm only joking with you, I think the world of
> him! I'm only messing! But stuff like that now, I think you have to, I think
> people have a problem when they go on like that. I think it's sad if they have to
> worry about seeing things in life like that.

Going on to define further what she meant by 'patriotic', she said:

> They'd wear all . . . the Celtic stuff. . . . Just trying to be pure! . . . Some people
> get so wrapped up in it. . . . I think it can get kind-of messy. . . . A lot of people
> in pubs . . . when Ireland and England are playing, it gets [messy]. . . . And
> that's down to Catholic/Protestant, I think, anyway. And the same up the
> North. . . . It's just very sad in this day and age. All the years on, and still a
> bitter taste.

Furthermore, in confirmation of the persistence of outcroppings based on ethnic myth-making, she said: 'I've heard often Protestants being . . . thought upon as English'.

Moving from an east-coast county to one on the border, a 22-year-old Catholic, already quoted above on orangeism and its relative acceptance in that area, was also very conscious indeed of confessional difference. From the beginning and due to segregation at primary level, she said that 'we hadn't any close contact with, with any Protestants. I think we always thought . . . they had different lives. . . . I mean, from the age of four you've been told these children are different from you for some reason', and she and her contemporaries had 'these definite ideas that these people were very different'. Then, in secondary school, she became 'best friends' with a Protestant when they were seated next to each. This girl

> has relations in Bangor, who'd be very . . . they're Orangemen and everything else, and . . . she said . . . she was going there for a week or two, and she said: Oh, I'd love to bring you up, but . . .! And I said: 'But what?' And she said: 'Oh, if they knew that my best friend was a Catholic . . . they wouldn't be impressed.' . . . That was the only time it ever became . . . [difficult]. Like, her parents always welcomed me into their home.

Apart from confirming the extant workings of bigotry, it is interesting to note the 'shorthand' she employed to convey her meaning: it was clear that 'they're Orangemen and everything else' did not, in the context of her narrative, require further elaboration for her. It was understood, both in the context of the interview and within the narrative itself that both her friend and she, working on internalised perceptions, knew without further explanation that the people concerned would not want to have anything to do with a Catholic, and nor would they tolerate the girls' friendship. Moreover, she, a Catholic, assumed that the interviewer, whom she knew was Protestant, would also understand the implications. She had another example of exclusionary sectarian behaviour and Protestant cliquishness, this time experienced by her mother:

> [T]his little job my Mum had . . . it was this country market. . . . And she used to bake and sell her stuff on a Friday. . . . But . . . she . . . was being pushed out . . . four or five other women used to do it, and she spoke to her godmother about it one day. She was really worried, she said: God, you know, I don't feel like I should be in there! And I remember her godmother said to her: You're the wrong colour to be in there, honey! And it was, it was this kind-of notion that there were a certain clique of . . . Protestant ladies that were running the thing, and they didn't want this other woman coming in.

Not surprisingly, therefore, when she was asked whether she saw any changes in confessional perceptions in the generations, she said:

> I honestly don't know if it's changed that much. . . . maybe in the cities it has, because I know people who went to school in Dublin or whatever and the schools were . . . what's the word? Ecumenical. But . . . in rural areas . . . I don't think there's been much change.

A 22-year-old Catholic, born in the United Kingdom to an Irish father and a British mother, brought back to live in the state at primary school stage and who has been quoted already on the exclusion she experienced in primary school, was asked – given that the fact that she was born and started her education out of the state which gave her added perspective – what assumptions she had about Protestants. She replied:

> That they were 'different' . . . when I was over [there] anyone who wasn't a Catholic didn't really have a religion, as far as my grandparents were concerned . . . they don't mix with a lot of people who aren't Catholic . . . it's still very much that there was the community that they grew up in, they didn't move too much beyond that, and they still mix in the same circles . . . and you can't move anywhere without anybody knowing . . . who you are. . . . [Here] most of my friends were Catholic. . . . [But] there was a [Methodist] summer school . . . and I went from the time I was fourteen 'til I was about seventeen. . . . And I loved it down there. Had a great time. But I was very much . . . they started about the Bible and this, that and the other, and, like: No! Back off! . . . Over the line: No. Sorry, not going to convert me today!

That, although so young, she had such a strong reaction to a perceived threat of proselytism was notable, but, as we have seen, fear of it fed strongly into the emotional legacy, maintaining an exaggerated apprehension of the possibility of cross-confessional contamination.

The effects of the confessional divide quite clearly are still experienced in social contact. 'Outcroppings' demonstrating the reliance of the content of the category of 'Irishness' on the emotional legacy irrupt into everyday relationships, based on misperceptions held firmly in place by that legacy which the manner of delivery, if not the content, of the education system did little to mitigate. This leads to a situation in which, despite more mixing of the confessions both formally and informally as the twentieth century progressed, confessional difference can still be used in a divisive manner in daily communication, thereby reinforcing the Protestant perception that Catholics, despite changes in the social climate, do not recognise that they, too, belong in the imagined community of Irishness.

CHAPTER FIVE

Inter-Church Marriage

Just as it is now recognised that there are combinations of identities available to individuals in the struggle for self-definition, there are also different group definers – religious, ethnic, social and cultural – for communal identities, with a consequent multiplicity of intersecting boundaries that require monitoring. One of the most problematic areas is exogamy: as Richard O'Leary puts it, 'intermarriage has long been recognised as one of the most robust boundaries between groups'.[1] In the Irish context, he goes on, this 'continues to be the case . . . for intermarriage between Catholics and Protestants'.[2] This, he contends, is because the 'divide between the Catholic and Protestant populations in Ireland overshadowed any intra-Protestant differences'.[3] On this point, one middle-aged Protestant interviewee did, however, say:

> My aunt in Monaghan would say that in Monaghan a mixed marriage is a Church of Ireland and a Presbyterian. Have more difficulties in getting a service than a Church of Ireland and a Catholic.

This is perhaps no more than further confirmation that attitudes are more polarised in the border counties, than a contradiction of O'Leary's argument.

We have already noted how the Catholic ethos came to dominate, how the Catholic Church controlled education and how the Catholic Church's moral teaching was adopted by the state,[4] which carried it into the civil code.[5] Whether, as J. H. Whyte contends, this was indeed only to a limited extent, however, is open to dispute: Inglis's point that 'it is necessary to understand how being a Catholic occupied the minds and hearts of Irish people' is well made. In addition, the Catholic Church demanded obedience and did not tolerate criticism.[6] In the devout Catholic society that developed in the new state, the prevailing climate was one in which opposition to state policy might, even if felt, seldom be articulated by the majority community, let alone the minority. Because of this, as Bryan Fanning argued, the Catholic hierarchy did not need to involve itself in legislative processes: 'there was little need to do so . . . [because] . . . as good Catholics, legislators and voters were deeply committed to expressing their faith in the laws and institutions of the country'.[7] So, though legislation may not have been directed specifically against Protestants, the osmotic results of state policy inextricably allied with clerical power were *not* limited in extent, and could only result, ultimately, in keeping the Protestant minority as an 'outgroup'.[8]

In the early days, an example of the incorporation of a Catholic ethos into that of the state was the 1929 censorship of publications legislation, which represented the enshrinement of a narrow moral code, 'then held to be Catholic, in the laws that governed Irish society'. Granted, the Protestant community in the Free State was politically conservative in nature, and this same conservatism was also a part of their social and moral ethos. However, where the conduct of the individual in relation to debates surrounding these controversial topics was concerned, 'Protestants were generally ranged on the "liberal" side . . . between Catholics *en bloc* and Protestants *en bloc* there existed . . . a difference', resulting from the Catholic view that the code of manners and morals is immutable and the Protestant stance that change is constant, so that standards may change.[9]

Despite social change, Catholic influence remained strong until the end of the twentieth century. In the 1980s and 1990s bitter referendum campaigns were waged on whether to permit divorce and abortion in certain limited circumstances in the state. The Catholic right and pro-life organisations formulated successful policies aimed at conflating the two issues in order to divide support for constitutional amendment. In the end, 'economic issues',[10] rather than any radical changes in fundamental belief, forced change, but divorce remained unavailable in the state until 1995, when, despite the strongest of lobbying from the Catholic right, a tiny majority voted in favour of constitutional amendment to allow it.[11] A 42-year-old interviewee who was a mature student and an activist in the 1990s recalled, in an extract that reflects the contradictions pertaining at the time, campaigning for the second referendum:

[W]e were trying to get the eighteen year olds at that stage to vote . . . for the divorce referendum. . . . we were dealing with people who were studying sociology. We were dealing with . . . social policy students, we were dealing with up-coming social workers, of upcoming community workers, and when we would put this argument across, because obviously it was discussed in class . . . none of them saw the relevance of voting for a divorce referendum at the time, because it wasn't relevant to them. So you're kind of saying to yourself. . . . Give it ten years. Late twenties, twenty-eight, twenty-nine, and all working in positions probably within the State, within the Civil Service . . . because a lot of them would have ended up social workers, and you wonder . . . how much their attitude has changed to social issues? . . . When faced with the practical realities.

That it took so long for divorce to be allowed demonstrates 'the tendency in Ireland towards denial, and a hypocrisy',[12] which, by polarising opinion and decimating support for reform, permitted conservative Catholicism to prevail in the face of what was actually happening in society, for Catholics as well as for Protestants, and of the need for legal remedy for those people whose relationships had broken down.

Despite the dominance of Catholic influence in the state, however, the ecumenical movement gained momentum alongside the social and economic changes of the 1960s. The hitherto polarised stances of the two principal confessional strands in Ireland, described by Daithí Ó Corráin as a 'silent *Konfessionskrieg*',[13] gradually began to admit unprecedented ecumenical activity. Two influential Catholic journals, *The Furrow* and *Doctrine and Life* 'translated and communicated the ideas of European theologians and Catholic intellectual thought to Irish readers',[14] which helped prepare the way for Catholics for the Second Vatican Council which convened for the first time in 1962.

On the Protestant side, following early twentieth-century intra-congregational approaches between the various arms of Protestantism,[15] the Church of Ireland 'watched the Council with curiosity and hope'.[16] In 1968, in an act laden with symbolism, the wife of Archbishop Simms was the first non-Roman Catholic to address the Milltown Park public lectures at a meeting attended by President de Valera.[17] And, as ecumenism crept into inter-church relationships, it prompted optimism, a part at least of which related to the hope that the Catholic Church would find a way to modify its intransigent stance on inter-church marriages and the promises relating to the baptising and raising of children of such unions as Catholics.

However, unguarded optimism on ecumenical fronts was to be disappointed by obduracy on both sides. The conservative attitudes of the Catholic hierarchy resulted in the *Irish Directory on Ecumenism*, finalised in January 1969, underlining that Catholics and other Christians were divided on many issues, some of major doctrinal importance, a stance that emphasised the persistence of reactionary and polarising attitudes. This was despite the contradiction that key provisions of the *Directory* did indicate some advances: baptism conferred in other Christian communities was to be recognised, prayer could be offered in common, and admission of clergy other than Catholic to assist in all aspects of Catholic ceremonies but the mass itself was permitted.[18] However, while 'other Christians' were allowed to assist at mass, they were not admitted to communion 'since this requires belief in Christ's real presence in the Eucharist and is the sign that unity in faith and worship is already realised'.[19]

The Anglican-Roman Catholic Joint Preparatory Commission, 1966–8, agreed, after various consultations, that full unity lay in the future and would be attained in stages. The Church of Ireland then took part in another permanent commission which met between 1969 and 1981 to examine historically divisive issues between the two churches. However, its final report, when issued in 1982, 'was coldly received by the General Synod with . . . a grudging and graceless assent'. Ultimately, many Protestants were 'suspicious of even intra-Protestant *rapprochement*', let alone of cross-confessional treating.[20]

Two lay interviewees, one Catholic and one Protestant, were involved in the ecumenical movement in the same east-coastal community. A 68-year-old Catholic said he had long been interested in and involved in the ecumenical movement, and

> I have helped [my Protestant friend] on a few occasions to organise ecumenical activities. . . . We haven't done anything in the last few years . . . we organised . . . some very successful occasions and these were annual dinners, basically, but we had a problem, one of the churches raised some difficulties . . . on one occasion, and we couldn't get over it, so we had to cancel the dinner for that year and . . . we never started again. But then the need for these things doesn't seem to be, to me anyway, to be so great, because ecumenism . . . as far as I can see, has arrived in [Ireland]. . . . I take communion in the Church of Ireland church, and I would go along with Mary McAleese absolutely. When you take communion . . . in another church you take it with the understanding in which it is given.

The 85-year-old Protestant who worked with him outlined his long involvement with ecumenism, then said, on the topic of the annual dinners:

> [W]e ran a dinner . . . we ran it again the following year . . . but I don't know what happened after that, because we weren't able to do it any more. I mean, somebody decided not to have it and I've never found out who it was!

Despite the reluctance of the churches to grapple with the issues, the confessional communities did begin at this stage to mix more, perhaps despite, rather than because of, church leadership. A 57-year-old rural Catholic spoke about her reaction to one particular instance of confessionally ground-breaking behaviour:

> I came from Ballina [and] Mary Robinson came from a very devout Catholic family. . . . And Mary married a Protestant. . . . I remember hearing that Mary . . . married a Protestant, and it was, Ooooh! You know? It was . . . a topic of conversation. . . . I'll always remember hearing where . . . she came back, and there was such crowds going to mass in Ballina at that time . . . for a quarter past twelve mass, that if the church was very crowded, then the people were brought up onto the Altar, there would be such big crowds going, and Mary Robinson went up with her Protestant husband, up on the Altar after her getting married. . . . And he was there, yes. And I thought, God, you know! . . . I, I don't know how I felt, but thought to myself, Oh, my goodness, gracious me! This is . . . I was surprised. Mmm. . . . Yes, I was pleasantly surprised! . . . And I suppose I was surprised in the fact that here she was, and she'd done this, it's OK for her to do it – but if it's OK for her to do it, sure, it's OK for any one of us to do it. . . . So that's the memory I have. . . . Because you'd be expecting Mary to go, or you'd be expecting anybody who had married somebody of another religion, to go into the church nice and quietly inside the door, but no! But then again, if you, if you kind-of see her life today and what she's done . . . she's never gone with the flow.

There is little doubt that the most divisive confessional issue in independent Ireland on many levels was the *Ne temere* decree. The Catholic Church's stance on the conduct of inter-church marriages and the extraction of promises concerning the upbringing of the children from those unions as Catholics was resented deeply in every sector of Protestant society. However, although this was commonly perceived as only having been an issue from the early twentieth century, such is not, in fact, the case. Nor did the decree itself contain the provisions it was commonly thought to set out, as a short review will make clear.

An outline of its significance starts with the decree *Tametsi*, approved by the Council of Trent on 11 November 1563, which laid down that those who did not contract marriage in the presence of an appropriate priest and two or three witnesses lacked contractual capacity. All such marriages were null and void and the failure to observe canonical form was made an impediment. Intervening events and occasional legislation brought about a resultant unevenness in law and practice throughout Christendom lasting until the twentieth century. In 1906, in the midst of the political struggle over home rule, 'the Vatican promulgated the *Ne temere* decree in a determined effort to stop mixed marriages'.[21]

The decree, effective in Ireland in 1908, was, in fact, 'in essence a housekeeping measure, providing, for the first time, one uniform set of marriage regulations for all Catholics'. It was aimed at ending the anomolies in law and practice concerning the legalities of civil and religious marriages and, in particular, inter-church marriages. In fact, it did not directly concern itself with anything other than validity. It set out the rules for the marriage of Catholics to non-Catholics, either unbaptised or baptised. In the case of the former, a dispensation *disparitus cultus* was needed, and for the latter a dispensation *mixtis religionis*. The issue of the promises regarding the upbringing of the children was significant, then, not because of anything explicitly set out in the decree, but because of the need for the granting of a dispensation: the vital factor was the possibility of the refusal of a dispensation unless promises were forthcoming.[22]

Importantly, then, the decree was not an innovation compelling inter-church couples to promise to baptise and educate any children of the marriage as Roman Catholics.[23] It was perceived as such, however: there was a general belief that its provisions required binding promises in writing from the non-Catholic prospective spouse, and promises were, in fact, exacted on foot of that belief. Moreover, the perception was given even more weight when the promises were later given contractual status by the Tilson case, which will be reviewed shortly. In any event, the issue of inter-church marriage continued and continues inaccurately to be referred to under the blanket term of 'the problem of *Ne temere*', an example of the inaccuracy inherent in the consignment of a contentious issue to the 'mythology' of the emotional legacy.

The promulgation of the decree was followed shortly after by the notorious McCann case, which became a *cause célèbre* when it came to public notice in 1910 and public opinion rapidly polarised.[24] The inter-church marriage of a Presbyterian woman and a Catholic man broke down, amidst allegations that the husband's priest exerted undue influence on him to get his wife to convert. She refused, and the husband deserted, taking the children and leaving her destitute. Raymond Lee argues that, *inter alia*, the case generated a 'moral panic' which mobilised public opinion against home rule. As politicians in Britain and Ireland became involved in the controversy, 'Protestants became convinced that *Ne temere* was a foretaste of what might be expected if home rule were to be granted to an Ireland in which control would be in the hands of a Catholic nationalist party'. It is also possible, in the aftermath of the case, that social control of inter-church marriage was intensified: Protestant parents now had a powerful cautionary tale with which to warn their offspring, whilst Catholic priests were alerted to the necessity for ensuring that ceremonies were conducted according to Catholic rite. Inter-church couples faced decisions, at religious, familial and community levels 'with the prospect . . . of displeasing one side or the other'.[25]

Another important issue from Protestant point of view was the perception that the imperative for the imposition of promises stemmed from the Catholic belief that theirs is the one true church. Vital to understanding Protestant attitudes is the fact that the Catholic Church saw fit, in line with that vision of itself, to exercise jurisdiction over members of another faith strand, which was bitterly resented. Moreover, the terms of the procedural *Codex*, which laid down that an inter-church marriage had to be conducted by a Catholic priest in an unconsecrated building without religious celebration, were perceived as demeaning: 'the *Codex* disapproved of mixed marriages and tried to prevent them, but ensured they would be strictly controlled should they occur'.[26] It is interesting to note that Charles Flynn records the perception of a Catholic from Dundalk, who said: 'The rule was you didn't marry a Protestant and that was it'.[27]

Lee contends that the obligation – for so it was seen – to bring the children up Catholic 'dates from the eighteenth century . . . though there are reasons to believe that the promises were not always sought in Ireland'. On this point, evidence given to a select committee on the state of Ireland in 1825 by one Catholic bishop stated that 'no censure was incurred by the Catholic party if the children of a mixed marriage were brought up as Protestants'. However, this was immediately contradicted by the Catholic Archbishop of Dublin, who indicated that not only did the Catholic Church not like mixed marriages, but that they were allowed only on condition that the children be educated in the Catholic religion. This version of the situation was confirmed by evidence from an Anglican clergyman,

> who testified that he had known cases where the rites of the Catholic church had been withheld from a Catholic involved in a mixed marriage who had allowed the children of the marriage to be brought up as Protestants.[28]

Lee also considers the proposition that it was customary in the nineteenth century for male children of a mixed marriage to be brought up in the father's religion while girls were brought up in the mother's, which was common European practice, though disapproved of by the Catholic Church. This practice would have been 'consistent with the division of labour in peasant families and would have the advantage of ensuring the continuity of land inheritance within the religious group'. It appears, from anecdotal evidence at least and from comments made in passing by some interviewees, that the custom was sometimes followed in Ireland, but in the main by the middle and upper classes.

Furthermore, of great interest in respect of the effects of the Catholic Church's stance on inter-church marriages – and of Protestant perceptions of it – is research carried out by Patrick Deignan in 2008 for a study of the Protestant community in Sligo town during the period 1914–49:

> An analysis of the manuscript census returns for Sligo town in 1911 reveals that within the Protestant community. . . . of the sixteen couples in mixed marriages, where one of the partners was Catholic, there were eleven married couples that had children living with them. Of the thirty-five children recorded as the offspring of mixed religion marriages in Sligo town in 1911, all were listed as Catholics. All but one of the couples were married before 1908 . . . so it appears that the offspring of Protestant–Catholic mixed marriages were being reared as Catholics in Sligo town before the *Ne temere* decree.[29]

Although, of course, one western seaboard swallow does not make a national summer, these findings, if replicated elsewhere in the 26 counties, would indicate clearly that, far from Protestants being overly concerned about the effects of the decree, their fears concerning the loss of the children to the community were well-grounded in actual circumstance in at least one urban area. In any case, the overwhelming impression is that the path of least resistance was, and continued to be, taken by Protestants over the upbringing of children of inter-church marriages as Catholics until the last decades of the twentieth century, when changes in attitude of the laity on both sides of the confessional divide began to be seen.

In the 1950s, two notorious events highlighted the bitterness existing between the two communities, the facts of both of which are well known and often cited. At the centre of both was the issue of the promises. One of these was the Tilson case, 1950: upon the break-up of an inter-church marriage, the Protestant father placed his children in a Protestant children's home. The Catholic mother petitioned the court for the return of her children, and Mr Justice Gavan Duffy, who had, by judicial innovation, already introduced some specifically Catholic values and rules into the law of the state,[30] found in her favour on the basis of the written promises which Mr Tilson had given because of the perceived requirements of *Ne temere*. This ruling overturned the common law premise that a father had an absolute right to choose the religious upbringing of his children irrespective of prenuptial promises, and the decision was doubly disturbing because, as Bowen noted, 'Gavan Duffy justified his new interpretation of the law by referring to the constitution of 1937 which accorded a "special position" to the Catholic Church'. His decision was upheld in the Supreme Court, which, however, changed its emphasis by holding that the pre-marriage promise of a parent could not be broken because of the constitutional provisions regarding the right of parents in respect of decisions on their children's education. The only dissenting judgement was that of Judge Black, a Protestant, who wondered whether the judgement would have been thus had the inter-church promises favoured the Protestant party.[31] In short, the Tilson case confirmed for Protestants just how pervasive was the influence of the Catholic ethos.

The other polarising event was the Fethard-on-Sea boycott of 1957, in which the Protestant community was boycotted when a Protestant mother resisted pressure to have her children enrolled in the local Catholic school and took them to Belfast. Although disapproval of the tactics of the local Catholic community was widespread at all levels of society and in both communities, the Catholic church remained silent at an official level and the public pronouncements of an inflammatory nature by, amongst others, Bishop Browne of Galway, who 'publicly defended the boycott as "a peaceful and moderate protest"',[32] served to underline and validate intransigent attitudes.

The situation remained at an impasse until after the Second Vatican Council which brought about a certain degree of unofficial relaxation over the issues surrounding inter-church marriages. In November 1964 a special *Votum on mixed marriages* replaced the terms of the *Codex* and was implemented in two stages: an *instructio* in 1966 and a *motu proprio* in 1970 entitled *Matrimonia mixta* – measures promulgated by Rome for implementation by national episcopal councils in accordance with their interpretation of the national situation. Not surprisingly, the situation remained unsatisfactory from the point of view of the bishops of the Church of Ireland, because of the insuperable problem of the promises: it remained possible to impose them as a condition for dispensation. Although they might now be made verbally rather than in writing, they still formed, as had been laid down in the Tilson case, 'an enforceable contract'. So, 'the House of Bishops instructed clergy not to attend such a wedding, either as an officiant or as a guest in the body of the church'.[33]

There was also the matter of what was being taught in the schools. In the early 1950s, primary school religion classes stressed full Church opposition to marriage with non-Catholics:

A Catholic cannot validly contract marriage with an unbaptised person, e.g. a Jew or a Mohammedan. . . . The Church most severely forbids the marriage of Catholics to baptised non-Catholics, e.g. Protestants. Generally, such [marriages] bring loss of faith, great unhappiness, conflicts in the home, and grave danger to the faith of the children.[34]

The 1970 *motu proprio* was a mixture of retrogression and progress, and overall the issue of the Catholic Church's attitude to inter-church marriages remained unsatisfactory for Protestants. However, it did counsel parish priests to liaise with their Protestant counterparts so that joint support could be given to inter-church couples, and it allowed full religious rites to be celebrated before the altar. At the same time, however, the Catholic partner had to undertake to do all in their power to raise children as Catholics.

When contrasted with other countries, the stance of the Catholic Church in Ireland was uncompromising: Swiss bishops emphasised that

the religious upbringing of the children was explicitly . . . a matter of conscience for both partners. Catholic bishops in Switzerland, France, Germany and the Benelux countries accepted in principle that they could no longer insist on all children being Catholic. The French bishops made explicit allowances for not asking for the promise in difficult cases. The Dutch never asked for the promise. By contrast the Irish Episcopal Conference was coldly juridical. . . . The Irish bishops resolved that 'the Catholic party be normally asked to make the necessary promise and declaration in writing in the presence of the non-Catholic party and the parish priest', the non-Catholic party being asked 'not to impede'.[35]

Another matter for serious Protestant concern was the different degrees of stringency of interpretation and implementation of the requirements at diocesan level: at that stage, for instance, Bishop Lucey in Cork continued to demand promises from Protestant parties,[36] while Cardinal Conway persisted in maintaining that a Catholic could not be released from his duty to preserve the faith and hand it on to his children. Whilst Alasdair Heron proposed that the change in form of the promise from 'making absolutely sure' to doing 'all in their power' to raise their children as Catholics was 'an advance', the House of Bishops 'regarded the changes to the promise as little more than a modified insistence that children be brought up as Catholics'.[37]

In 1974, the *Church of Ireland Gazette* reported that an international theological consultation was to be held, at which theologians and church sociologists would review the issues arising from inter-church marriages with the aim of seeking *rapprochement.* Speaking at a press conference announcing the event, the Revd Michael Hurley, Director of the School of Ecumenics, said that the spirit of *Ne temere* was 'very much alive', and 'that Protestants will talk and treat seriously of nothing else except mixed marriages and that Roman Catholics will talk and treat seriously of everything else except this. . . . Ecumenism has not yet become a reality in the approach of the churches to the problem of mixed marriages.'[38] The requirements that the Catholic partner 'promise to do all in his power to have all children baptised and brought up in the Catholic Church', were found objectionable on two grounds, firstly, the conflation of Christian with exclusive Roman Catholicism, and, secondly, the imposition of a unilateral commitment on one partner which should be the province of both partners to the marriage.

At the end of the 1974 consultation, a public statement was issued, in which it was noted that

> the participants . . . felt all the more the scandal of disunity as revealed especially in the problems of mixed marriage. They were moved by a spirit of repentance and conversion and a desire to express this in a reform of attitudes and practices with regard to mixed marriages.[39]

After a lapse of four months, a joint 'Mixed Marriage Instruction' from the House of Bishops of the Church of Ireland was issued to all clergy, in which elaborate rules were set out for dealing with inter-church marriage and joint ministry to the resulting families. These, in retrospect, do not appear to manifest repentance, seeming little more than an attempt to retain the *status quo* with tokenistic forward momentum.[40] In any event, although the oral evidence indicates that the laity on both sides of the confessional divide have decided to follow their own consciences in the matters of inter-church marriages and the upbringing of children, with many clergy tacitly agreeing to this course of action, technically the provisions of the 1970 *motu proprio* governing inter-church marriages and the religious upbringing of children remain in force[41] and can still be subject to different degrees of interpretation: there is anecdotal evidence of people being 'upset' by things said to them in this context.

It is not surprising, then, that inter-church marriages were viewed with strong disfavour by both sides of the confessional divide.[42] John Fulton demonstrated how they were viewed as 'highly dangerous, morally suspicious, and frequently sinful', and how they came 'to have major significance in group reinforcement'.[43] Nor is it surprising that a 58-year-old Protestant, whose first wife died when their family was still young and who married again, summed up what must have been both the articulated and the unconscious attitudes of most southern Irish Protestants when he said:

> I was very . . . fortunate from the standpoint of just bringing up children . . . that I married . . . Protestants both times. . . . just looking back, I feel I was fortunate . . . finding a mate . . . both times that happened to be of the same background. From a religious standpoint. . . . I suppose I would have regret-ted . . . not have being able to send the child to a Protestant school. I just feel it would have been . . . a potential for discord, and I like the fact that my children have been brought up in the same milieu that I have been brought up in.

As a result of conforming to community precepts on endogamy, he was acknowledging – with some relief – that he had not needed to contend with the difficulties that those in inter-church marriages had or still need to face.

The fall in the number of Protestants in the state following the events surrounding independence has already been catalogued, and Bowen argued at the end of the 1970s that extinction by assimilation was an apprehension held by 'older Irish Anglicans'. Indeed, as Diarmaid Ferriter documents, 'From 1946 to 1961 the Protestant population fell almost five times faster than the overall population, and by the end of the 1960s the entire Protestant population stood at only 130,000',[44] with the result that many parishes amalgamated and churches and schools had to be closed. However, when attributing the diminution of Protestant population primarily to the operations of *Ne temere*, Daithí Ó Corráin cautions against overemphasising the connection of population decline to the decree. It certainly contributed in no small way, but so did emigration and the phenomena of a low marriage rate, late marriage and consequent low marriage fertility.[45]

Attempts by the older generation to maintain boundaries were only partially successful. Ferriter declares, 'Protestant social events deliberately did little to encourage younger Protestants to mix with their Catholic counter-parts'.[46] Early on, the social events *were* deliberately designed to perpetuate segregation, but Bowen found that, from the late 1960s and early 1970s onwards, Protestant youth itself saw little reason to accept direction from the older generation on the subject of mixing with Catholics. As a result, group barriers were regularly being breached during and after this era, even at those selfsame social events.[47] But as Desmond Carroll, a youth officer in the 1970s, noted, there were indeed ambiguities in the situation: the Church of Ireland had tended to preach a philosophy of tolerance, so that, apart from coming to see that segregation was no longer desirable, it was difficult for the younger gene-ration to maintain the hard line favoured by their parents.[48] Anyway, as Carole Holohan points out, during the 1960s, 'Irish youth, in comparison to American, British and some European counterparts was conservative'.[49] Certainly, despite the increasing breaching of barriers and *rapprochements* of this period, conser-vatism remained very much a feature of the middle-class Protestant self-image.

It is interesting to note that the 76-year-old rural Protestant who was sad to see her Catholic friends excluded from table tennis in the local primary school qualified her position on segregation – which she saw as a pity when she was a child – when, speaking as a parent and grandparent, she said somewhat ruefully:

> I think [segregation's] sad in one way, but then, on the other hand, there's so much mixed marriages today. But it wasn't in the schools they met, no. The school dances was blamed for it, but it wasn't. I have a son, he's married to a Catholic girl, she have three boys and they're going to mass. I have a daughter that's married to a Catholic . . . they have three sons and they're going to church. They've got them baptised in the [Church of Ireland]. . . . You can't stop it.

Looking back through the oral evidence, the experience of two rural Protestant women is notable for its demonstration of the strength of the internalised proscription surrounding their contact with Catholics when they were young adults. The first, aged 65 and brought up in the midlands, said that as a young adult she knew that

> there was a taboo, though, when you went to dances or anywhere, never to fall in love with somebody of the other persuasion. . . . You could be friends with them, as I say I still am, but you mustn't fall in love, and they knew it, and one knew it.

The second, aged 59 and brought up in a rural part of the southwest, said:

> [T]he people living straight across the road [were] Roman Catholics, and . . . we got on famously with them. . . . [B]ut [we were] always sort-of conscious that they were Roman Catholics and we would not be ever thinking of getting married to them, but still they would be friends of ours.

It is interesting to contrast this evidence with that of the Dublin suburban Catholic, not much older than they are, whose second girlfriend was Church of Ireland, and with that of the elderly urban Protestant who was introduced to her husband by a Catholic chemist, as it confirms the more stringent group boundary reinforcement in existence in rural communities.

So, the two of them were, like a north-western Protestant of the same era whose evidence is considered later in this chapter, compliant with the 'rules' laid down by the dynamics of Protestant group preservation. That they internalised the taboos to the extent they did and that they acted upon them without apparent questioning points up both the more conservative nature of rural Protestantism and the degree to which those who *did* contract relationships with Catholics were acting transgressively. Indeed, taking everything into consideration, it also indicates the courage that must have been required from both parties in such instances. Another western Protestant in her sixties recalled both how such relationships were viewed and the effects of such perspectives:

> You avoided it because it would just lead to too much hassle . . . with your parents. . . . And it was how they talked about others who might be involved. . . . And you would know from that . . . all the Protestants had to sign and they had to change and a lot of it was carried on in secrecy and even today you will find a certain hesitancy in Protestants who are involved with Roman Catholics, in speaking to Protestants afterwards, they anticipate some feeling. . . . I'm thinking of somebody, a girl . . . we knew. . . . I know her parents were evangelical, and they were terribly . . . anti Roman Catholic . . . she did become involved with a Roman Catholic, and did marry him, and . . . the whole thing was fraught. . . . But she could not acknowledge her former Protestant neighbours and friends for quite some years. She will now.

Thus guilt associated with transgression of group boundaries continued to exert its influence.

To return to the point on the 'unpredictability and inconsistency'[50] of church rulings on *Ne temere* and the conducting of inter-church marriages, a Church of Ireland cleric remembered that

> I grew up in the shadow of the Fethard-on-Sea boycott. It was spoken of in hushed tones throughout the south-east. When I got engaged in Wexford in 1974, it was suggested that because Barbara was a practising Catholic, we should get married in Dublin: the rules on inter-church marriages were still being interpreted in the strictest and most unkind manner by Bishop Donal Herlihy in the Diocese of Ferns.[51]

A 67-year-old Protestant gave a *résumé* of her experiences which refers to the apparent lottery of finding a Catholic venue for the marriage as well as demonstrating some of the problems that could arise upon the failure of an inter-church marriage. In 1965, she

> married a . . . Roman Catholic, and [there were] lots of coming and goings, I refused to sign papers [re the promise required by *Ne temere*] . . . and we got an altar in Dunboyne, but so did about eight others ahead of me! . . . [and the priest] quickly came home from Canada to marry us [but] my marriage was never registered. So, when I went looking for a divorce, which [my husband] said he wouldn't give me, but he would take an annulment, and I offered him an annulment straight away, and then he couldn't get an annulment either because our papers hadn't been registered. And that is the [Catholic] church being very strong.

Another Protestant, talking about an inter-church marriage in her family, said

> And at that time . . . it would have been probably the mid-'30s, and they were married in Dunboyne. . . . Because they couldn't marry anywhere else.

It would appear that either there was a particularly accommodating parish priest in office in Dunboyne on both occasions, or its location in the Meath diocese, just outside the jurisdiction of the Dublin diocese where the rules were strictly applied, or a combination of both facts, which made it the nearest available possibility for inter-church couples from the capital.[52]

A Methodist, born in 1933 in the midlands, underlined Protestant antipathy to *Ne temere*: 'My parents feared the impact of the Church's implementation of the *Ne temere* decree concerning mixed marriages from 1907 and felt hurt by its unfairness to the Protestant spouse in the marriage.'[53] Phyllis Browne, the Protestant widow of Dr Noel Browne, the socialist politician who tried to bring in the Mother and Child scheme in 1951, was quite sure that there was deliberate intent in the Catholic Church's tactics on inter-church marriages. She said:

> One of the cleverest ideas of the Roman Catholic hierarchy was to introduce the *Ne temere* decree . . . [which demanded] a promise in a mixed marriage that all the children would be brought up in the Roman Catholic faith. Some couples of course did not keep their promise, but this could bring trouble from the local priest, who would call to the house and argue with the children's parents.[54]

One Catholic who appreciated the implications of the Catholic Church's stance on marriage for Protestants was Patsy McGarry, *Irish Times* religious affairs correspondent. He came from a family 'deeply suspicious of clericalism, by which I mean the manner in which authority was exercised by our priests and bishops'. Then, as he grew older, and showing an acute awareness of the actual situation – which was also expressed in only one of the Catholic testimonies collected for this study – he said:

> I became more aware of the minority position of people of the Reformed faith in this State and what this had meant for them. In particular, I became angered at the effects of the 1907 *Ne temere* decree on that community, and the manner in which the then Article 44 of the Constitution – recognising the special position of the Catholic Church in this State – was used to bolster that decree in the civil law of the land.[55]

The evidence of one inter-church couple in respect of the upbringing of their children in the 1970s is of interest in connection with the perceptions of an English Anglican wife about the required promise. The Catholic husband said:

> When we were married . . . in London . . . [my wife] said she would bring the children up in the Catholic faith. She was asked to do so. And I suppose. . . . I would have been a more enthusiastic . . . person about my religion than [she] was about hers. And I think her concern was that [any children] . . . were Christian. . . . And so she went along with that. And the children went to Catholic schools and were brought up Catholics.

Those children, he added, were now non-practising. However, the interviewee's wife indicated that the circumstances surrounding the preliminaries to their marriage – which, it will have been noted, did not take place in Ireland – were not quite, from her perspective, those which he depicted, although she did concur to a degree by acknowledging that it was important to her that Catholicism was 'still a Christian religion'. She agreed to any children being brought up as Catholics because

> I had no choice really at that time. . . . before I was married, I'm sure I had to sign a piece of paper to say that I would bring my children up as Catholics. . . . OK, really, because I didn't know all the ramifications of it, really. I mean, you don't until you have the children and they go to school . . . it was still a Christian religion, so it wasn't as if I was asked to become . . . something else.

It was notable that, whether younger interviewees came from Protestant or Catholic backgrounds, most said they were non-practising. Exceptionally, however, a Catholic aged 22 from west Dublin, said:

> Catholicism is still a very big part of life, and now I might not go to mass every Sunday, I go the majority of the time, but if I miss one and [my grandparents] hear about it, oh God! It's, like, it's just not done!

Three interviewees, two Catholic and one Methodist, whose ages span three generations, confirmed the disfavour in which both confessions held interchurch marriages. The first extract is from a 72-year-old Catholic from the northwest, whose cousin married an English Protestant:

> [I]t would have been seen as just that, as a pity. And this is what she did, but she was only young, she was a teenager. . . . And her parents were very, very disappointed.

The second case concerned the cousin of a 47-year-old Methodist from an eastern coastal county:

> My cousin married a Catholic girl, and it was very much a no-no at the time. . . . No he wasn't [ostracised.] She was taken into the family, but there was always . . . [the feeling that it was] not really the thing to do. . . . The children were baptised Roman Catholic, but they were brought up as Protestant. They went to the

Protestant school. . . . [A]nd they would have gone to church to the Protestant church, even though they were baptised Catholic.

The third concerned the cousin of the 22-year-old Catholic from Donegal:

When I see the way my parents and the other members of my family reacted to my cousin and his girlfriend, for example. I mean, I don't think it was even the fact that she became pregnant . . . I think it was the fact that she was a Protestant and he was a Catholic that was the overriding issue. . . . I don't see much difference to the way that maybe it was approached in the 1970s and the way it's approached now. . . . I do think that the school segregation thing is a lot to blame for it.

The following evidence of intolerance in another area of the state is quoted in detail to confirm the lengths that could be gone to in trying to preserve communal integrity, as well as further to illustrate other ramifications of inter-church marriage within the families concerned. A 46-year-old rural Catholic from an eastern coastal county told of what happened with their families:

[W]hen I met [my husband in 1976] my family accepted [him]. On [his] side . . . It's only because [his father] knew my granny and grandfather that he accepted me, that's the only reason I think he accepted me. He didn't come to our wedding . . . but I didn't blame him, because he was an older generation . . . his [other] son . . . has a farm just up above where we live and he wanted to marry a Catholic girl, but his father wouldn't allow it. He said, 'if you marry that girl, I will never set foot on the place again.' So I was lucky in that [my husband] only had a half-acre site, but if he'd have had the farm maybe it was different! . . . And when we got married we had to write to the Pope for permission to get married, because I was a Catholic and [my fiancé] was a Protestant, and I had to promise and [he] had to promise that to bring the children up as Catholics. . . . [W]e invited the vicar . . . to our wedding, and he came, and everybody had a lovely time, priests and [his] side and my side intermingled, and it was lovely. [Then, as the couple and other members of her family had children] . . . as children grow up . . . they have their little tiffs . . . and . . . one day my husband did get involved, in a little tiff between two children, and he was actually called 'an English pig' and 'a Protestant B' by some of the younger crowd in the family, but it was an attitude . . . that they were learning somewhere in school or at the time they probably would have been learning about the history of Ireland, the 1916 Rising, things like that that would have affected them.

Those children, she added, now adult, 'think the world of' her husband. As well as demonstrating the gamut of reaction and degrees of intolerance, this is also, incidentally, further confirmation of the way in which pernicious messages could be relayed under the guise of history, and of their contribution to the emotional legacy.

In the main it seems, not only from Bowen's findings[56] but also from the testimony, that Protestants coming to adulthood as the twentieth century drew into its last quarter did believe they would not be affected by the Catholic Church's stance on inter-church marriage. This indicates that fear of assimilation had apparently receded by the 1970s. However, that apprehension did still appear as an undercurrent in testimony for this project in the way in which some of those adults – now parents themselves and watching, or preparing to watch, their offspring choose partners – spoke about their children's inter-church marriages. It occurred expressly in the testimony of one rural Protestant with two young children, who had his doubts about inter-church marriage:

> Just maybe that I'd like to see Protestants continue . . . [the] tradition not dying out. . . . Just continuing on.
> Q. What do you think is the best way for that to happen?
> A. Well, I suppose, the obvious way is if Protestants marry Protestants! That's the obvious way.
> Q. . . . would it ever have occurred to you to marry a Catholic?
> A. No . . . but I suppose I was always pointed in the direction of maybe trying to find . . . a Protestant girl. . . . I have gone out with Catholics. Maybe not for long, but I did.
> Q. . . . was anything express said to you by your parents or was just guidance, that you knew what they meant?
> A. Well, I'd seen it happen with my sisters. My sisters were all older than me, and I had seen it happen with my sisters . . . I could see how they were advised.

A second fear, one which also appears extant in the oral testimony, is that inter-church marriage might also mean the loss of land or a vital interest in a family business to the 'other side'. As a Church of Ireland rector from a south-western rural parish said:

> Now, there is considerably more intermarriage, and considerably less fuss about it, unless we're talking about land. Then there's fuss, you know, it's as if the land is going from one group to the other, or something, and there's quite a

lot of resentment then. . . . [S]ome just get on and live with the fact. Others then are terribly resentful, and they try as much as they can to stop the marriage and sometimes they just wouldn't turn up to weddings.

Bowen argued, as did Acheson and O'Connor later,[57] that the demarcation lines drawn between the two confessions had begun to blur if not to break down after the Second World War, with Bowen attributing this change in outlook to the growing rate of inter-church marriages after 1946. Up to that time, anyone overcoming all the obstacles to contracting an inter-church marriage was quite likely to be disowned and treated as an outcast from family and community. A 65-year-old Protestant from the west recalled how she and her sisters would overhear adults discussing such marriages and the people involved:

[I]t wouldn't have been referred as a mixed marriage, but . . . he married, or she married, somebody that kicked with the other foot! . . . Whispers. . . . Always whispers.

Through an interest in family history, she and her husband found out that some members of the family from the grandparental generation did contract inter-church marriages

and the people concerned [were] . . . lost. I'm finding them now, if you know what I mean.
Q. They were so kicked out of the family?
A. Yeah, they were, they were really, they just didn't exist any more.

Another Protestant in her mid-60s from the same area remembered how, after contracting an inter-church marriage,

my uncle was sort-of banished and he was killed in an accident . . . some years later, and . . . the family did relent and wanted him brought back to be buried locally in the local churchyard, but his wife wouldn't allow that.

This extract demonstrates how the bitterness engendered could linger, as does the following one, which also refers to the harsh treatment that could be meted out to all involved:

> In my father's generation . . . my uncle was made . . . the black sheep of my
> grandfather's [family]. . . . His mother was thrown out, which was far worse.

However, despite such treatment and the strength of the internalised messages
transmitted by the older generation, by 1961 'as many as three out of every
ten Protestant grooms and two out of every ten Protestant brides married
Catholics'.[58] Nor could the strength of the taboos and of the Protestant parish
infrastructure halt the rising rate of inter-church marriages in the relative
anonymity of urban areas, particularly amongst the members of the working
class, which rose from almost none at independence to 44 per cent in the
1970s,[59] thereby hastening the decimation of the Protestant working class
noted by Maguire.

Bowen contended that rural Protestants' 'great strength . . . lay in their
continued efforts to provide segregated opportunities for unmarried adults to
meet one another',[60] with this state of affairs lasting up to the mid-1970s in
some regions, but petering out earlier in others. Bowen went on to speculate
that, with some 60 to 70 per cent of the minority still marrying fellow
Protestants, neither full assimilation nor total integration was likely to occur
for some time. Furthermore, he thought that the growth of secular tendencies
among some Catholics apparent at that time called into question the
assumption that mixed marriages would inevitably lead to assimilation.[61] He
went on to suggest that the emergence of a broader secular movement might
enable Protestants to experience a substantial mixed marriage rate and still see
'their numbers stabilise and possibly grow'.[62] So, he saw the survival or
otherwise of the Protestant community taking place in the confessional arena
around the institution of marriage, as decreasing religiosity led to more social
permeability and increased rates of intermarriage.

Over the years, personal advertisements seeking marriage partners and
references to the Church of Ireland marriage bureau operated out of the
diocese of Tuam, in parish magazines and the *Church of Ireland Gazette*.[63] Also,
in the never-ceasing efforts to create conditions favouring endogamy, another
force was at work:

> Time was when almost every diocese in the Church of Ireland had its clerical
> matchmaker. Somehow, or other there always seemed to be a clergyman who,
> rightly or wrongly, considered that he had a special vocation for bringing
> together eligible persons with, as they say, a view to matrimony. Many are the
> tales told, when 'any other business' has been disposed of and the vestry stands

at ease, of these one-man marriage bureaux. Not all of their operations had the blessing of their fellow-clergy inside whose borders they happened to stray. But, on the whole, they fulfilled a need in dioceses where church people were thin on the ground and few and far between. And I have no doubt that many successful marriages resulted from their efforts. We may laugh at the matchmaker, as we do at the mother-in-law, but in places where opportunities to meet suitable partners are practically non-existent for some Protestants, the one is almost as necessary as the other is, barring prior decease, inevitable.[64]

That the community was and continued to be extremely concerned at the heavy loss of members perceived to be due to the problems surrounding inter-church marriage is undeniable, but it was also able to enjoy a wry joke on the subject, as witnessed by a cartoon published in 1971 in the *Church of Ireland Gazette* (see frontispiece).

The evidence of a 65-year-old rural Protestant, married in 1963, confirms the existence of the 'great strength' mentioned by Bowen of the rural Protestant community, but only in so far as it applied to herself. She gave an overview of attitudes and of the changes in them that happened over the decades. She told of how she met her husband at a Protestant social, and how, when she was a teenager in the 1950s, 'the socialising was all geared round the church, and . . . the Protestant population that was around at the time'. Inter-church marriage was never spoken about openly, but there was still no doubt that it was taboo and that segregation was to prevent it. So strong was the taboo that even friendship with Catholics was frowned upon:

> We knew instinctively that if we . . . got too friendly – I can remember . . . my mother frowned on me . . . becoming friendly with a Roman Catholic girl. . . . And going to her house.

She conformed with community rules by marrying a fellow-Protestant, but, when it came to her own children and their marriages, three of them have married Catholics.

> [Y]ou tried to . . . say to them . . . without saying it, but in your own way, tried to keep them on the Protestant line, that they would meet Protestants. I can remember a group of us, we had socials . . . I tried to tell them when they started going out, I put it in plain English to them that . . . there was a big strain on a marriage without having to put the strain of . . . different religions and that

their children would have to be. . . . And I was told . . . in no uncertain language, that they would marry who they wanted to marry.

She appeared disillusioned over what she perceived as a lack of support from the Church of Ireland in her efforts to keep them within the Protestant fold. By the time they were young adults at the beginning of the 1990s, she said,

> there was nothing for young people, even though you tried to run things for young people and bring young people together. The clergy weren't doing anything to help you – in fact, they were doing the opposite. They were encouraging us to mix more with our Roman Catholic neighbours and friends and all that sort of thing.

Ultimately, however, she appeared to see endogamy more as a necessity for the protection of Protestant ownership of land than a doctrinal matter, for, she said, on the break-up of a mixed marriage '[N]owadays . . . with farming . . . you can lose half your farm'.

Of course, this is now more due to the provisions of the Family Home Protection Act, 1976,[65] than to the operations of the confessional divide. The act 'regulates competing demands made on the family home. . . . [T]he background to this act lay in the lack of legal protection for homemakers, specifically wives in relation to their homes.' It makes it impossible for 'the owning spouse [to] dispose of, or sell, the family home without the prior written consent of his non-owning spouse'.[66] Thus, on separation or divorce, a non-owning spouse can ensure that their contribution to the marriage is taken into account when it comes to the division of property held or acquired during the marriage. So, her point that if one of the spouses concerned in a marriage split were Catholic, that would potentially be a Protestant loss indicates that she was seeing things entirely from a Protestant point of view, and not acknowledging the fact that the 'other side' could also experience similar circumstances. Part of the Protestant emotional legacy lexicon, noted by Bowen, was that 'there can be little doubt that Catholics derived considerable satisfaction at hearing of a Catholic purchase of or marriage into a Protestant farm or business',[67] in the late 1970s. Her evidence shows it remains a current Protestant concern, as does that of another rural Protestant who cited the following occurrence which took place in 2004, although she did not think such an attitude would be general now:

A niece of mine, her sister-in-law was, is Catholic and she was marrying a Church of Ireland chap and she had to turn, or he wouldn't have got the farm. That's just this month.

Interestingly, the Catholic daughter-in-law of Protestants saw their motivation in trying to steer their family towards endogamy as confessional as well as practical when, astutely, she said:

I think they were getting to the stage . . . how else were they going to get rid of their sons! But ideally, they would have preferred a Protestant girl. . . . But it was just because they . . . naturally would . . . prefer a Protestant and to bring children up Protestant and have a pure Protestant family.

In 1998, Richard O'Leary, who does not appear to have seen any amelioration of the effects of the Catholic church's stance on inter-church marriages or perceptions of *Ne temere* in the last quarter of the twentieth century, set out to estimate the rate and establish the patterns of religious intermarriage in the Republic of Ireland. He devised a method by which he was able to show an increase in the rate of inter-church marriage in the Protestant population in 1991 by birth cohort of the female partner. It showed a steady progressively higher rate for couples in the younger birth cohorts, rising to 32 per cent in that of the 1957–1961 birth cohort. He then concluded that 'the rate is still surprisingly low and is indicative of the continued relevance of religious barriers and a degree of denominational segregation in Irish society'. He also commented that the issues involved assumed 'much greater importance than would be expected' because of perceptions about the demographic effects of intermarriage through the children being raised as Catholics.[68] Given the findings so far, this is not surprising: despite the changes in outlook and emphasis over time, inter-church marriage is still a cause for concerns of one type or another.

What, then, is happening in inter-church families about the raising and educating of children? It appears from younger adult interviewees and from anecdotal evidence that children of inter-church marriages are now as likely to be brought up and educated in the Protestant partner's faith as in the Catholic's. In the case of a 76-year-old Methodist from the west, three of his five children married Catholics, but all five grandchildren were being raised as Protestants. However, both children of a 79-year-old Protestant from the southwest are in inter-church marriages, and her grandchildren were baptised in the Church of Ireland and go to Catholic schools. In another example from the same area, a Methodist mother told of how her son and daughter-in-law had followed the nineteenth-century custom, with girls following the mother's confession and boys that of the father:

> My youngest son married a Catholic girl. . . . my husband wouldn't have been that keen. . . . she's been going to the Methodist church with him since . . . the first year, but her two girls were confirmed Catholic. And then the boy is not, he's Methodist.

An inter-church couple from an eastern county have two daughters who are of different confessions, for specific reasons that had nothing to do with following precedent:

> [O]ne of them is Catholic, the older one my decision because . . . both of us were very ill . . . so I felt . . . if I die, it would be very difficult for my husband to raise her as a Protestant. And if she's going to die, she needs to be baptised very quickly. . .. [B]oth of us recovered, thankfully. . . . But then when my second daughter was born, [my husband] said . . . she'll be Church of Ireland. . . . I suppose it was in the interest of fairness. . . . it has worked out really well because I never met two children who are more interested in religion.

A 37-year-old Catholic from the northwest in an inter-church marriage said that she and her husband had chosen to have their six-year-old daughter baptised in the Church of Ireland, but to

> send her to the local school, which is a Catholic school. Now, there is a Church of Ireland school . . . a couple of miles up the road, but we go to the local school. You walk there, you walk back, you meet your neighbours, whatever. . . . the local Church of Ireland . . . I would feel it quite clique-ish, and . . . to a degree I would feel a bit of an outsider going to certain services, and stuff. Because there's . . . just a difference in confidence or attitude, or way of life. . . . But, I mean, that's not necessarily religious, that could be rural as well . . . class, whatever.

She is another Catholic to comment on the cliquishness of Protestants – especially *en masse* in the parish and school communities.

A Catholic who contracted an inter-church marriage in 1980 spoke of her experiences as the couple approached their wedding and the question of the promises concerning children came up:

[M]y mother was quite keen that I sign . . . not to create waves . . . I found the
whole thing very awkward and . . . embarrassing. . . . I think both of us had to
have an interview. . . . I think the interview probably was very minimalist . . . I
certainly would have . . . felt . . . a bit uncomfortable . . . the children were
baptised as Christians in the Church of Ireland . . . I think the reason for that
was [my husband] was probably more comfortable with that. . . . I also had big
difficulties with . . . the Catholic Church stance on various matters, and I . . .
found some of the Catholic dogma very oppressive. . . . Sin, guilt, there seemed
to be quite a heavy emphasis on that when I was growing up, on . . . punishment, and . . . it seemed to me quite harsh.

Of the Catholic interviewees, she was alone in expressing understanding of what
was at stake for Protestants in this respect. She was also aware of her father-in-
law's reservations over the marriage in case she would want the children raised as
Catholics. Further, she was later on the receiving end of Protestant strategies
used for finding out where a person stood on the confessional front:

I just remember an odd occasion, very rare, where people would . . . say: Well,
what school did you go to?. . . [W]here was I coming from?. . . because of the
diminution in the number of Protestants and because of . . . the caste and the . . .
closed group that . . . was getting very much diluted by marriage, and their own
identity . . . that's understandable, that they would be aware of that. . . . [I]f you
are part of a group and if there was a sort-of slightly siege mentality with the
Protestants because of the prevailing history over the last forty years, and
probably because if they were now starting to intermarry, and each time they
intermarried, their numbers got diluted . . . the whole caste was getting diluted.

Naturally, whilst understanding their motivations, she experienced the tactics
as exclusionary: 'there would have been odd little remarks . . . from people who
themselves might have fallen into the bigoted category'.

Three young unmarried Catholic interviewees had given serious thought to
the matter of inter-church relationships and the bringing-up of children in that
context. A 30-year-old Catholic from an eastern seaboard county contem-
plating marriage to a Protestant said that, when it came to the confessional
orientation of any children they might have:

[W]e've spoke about that. Because of course it is a bridge we'll have to cross,
please God, some day. . . . And I've decided, because of the condition of the

Catholic Church at present, I would prefer my children to be brought up Church of Ireland. . . . And I've decided this because, being in school with nuns . . . what has the church got to offer young people? Any of my friends in the thirty age group, all of us that grew up together, we don't go to mass any more. . . . Now, [my fiancé] wouldn't practise his own religion very often, either, but I think it's approached in a better way, whereas, when we were younger it was kind-of shoved down your throat. . . . [H]e said: I would like, because he only has a brother, and his father's an only child, he would like, if we had children, could we bring them up as Protestants, to carry on his family name in his church, so I've agreed to do so. And my mother and them don't have a problem with it.

A 22-year-old Catholic from a border county has also thought deeply, though not specifically, about the marriage question:

I suppose religion wouldn't be an issue for me. If I were to marry someone, I'd marry them. . . . It wouldn't be a problem, because I'm not a particularly religious person myself. . . . but when it came to the kids, I think I would just bring them up, when they were small, just bring them up as Christians. None of this first communion at the age of seven, which is ridiculous. And just let them make their own choices when they got older. . . . As for baptisms, I don't even know if I would baptise them. I think I would leave it to them when they got older. . . . Because . . . it's too contentious within families. . . . I'd just say: Look, let's forget it, we're not going to do it at all! You know, if it was going to raise issues. If one side felt really strong and the other side, or the other side didn't, I might say: OK, fine, we'll baptise them as whichever, and then . . . if they feel like changing in the future, that's fine.

The 22-year-old practising Catholic from near Dublin had also given a great deal of thought to the question, and had a different approach, based on her observations of an inter-church marriage in her immediate family. She demonstrated some wariness in response to a question about whether she might consider marriage with a non-Catholic:

I'd have to seriously, seriously think about it. Watching my aunt and her [inter-church] marriage and the difficulties that it's thrown up. . . . Especially with her two children. And now that the children are getting a bit older and starting to ask questions. . . . Watching them and their relationship, yes, I'd be willing to do it, but I'd really have to think about it.

Q. Because you would want to . . . maintain your Catholic . . . essence and your practising part of you within a marriage relationship?
A. Yes, definitely.
Q. And that would require you to want to bring up your children as Catholics?
A. Yes. Very much so.

Furthermore, despite the fact that some inter-church couples managed the complications involved without apparent stress, her perception that inter-church marriages created significant difficulties is interesting, especially in view of the fact that she had

> Protestant friends. It's not a big deal, it's not something that divides any of us at all. . . . [But] with my parents' friends, I know it does make a difference with them. . . . [M]y Mum's friends, I know two of them are Protestant, and it's very much a big thing in their lives, and they will have arguments and debates about it.

Given the disfavour with which such unions were viewed from both sides of the confessional divide and the resulting wariness, it was nevertheless obvious from the evidence that, when an inter-church marriage occurs, many couples and their families take a pragmatic attitude. One such couple conducted a ten-year courtship, though not only because of their confessional differences. However, it certainly gave them time to work out the details of how they would deal with them and with the raising of children in the future. Another Protestant in her seventies spoke of what had happened in her family:

> [T]he two boys . . . are both married to Roman Catholics and . . . they are like daughters. They are daughters. . . . They're lovely. . . . [A]nd they're so nice to me and [my husband]. Yeah. And they sort-of said, why don't you do this, that and the other, and I said: Oh, no [my husband's] keeping his money for when, if one of us go, we'll have to go into a nursing home. 'Don't you worry about that, we'll take you!' . . . That's the sort they are! They're lovely. . . . [But my daughter married a Catholic and] that was a little more difficult. . . . [I]t was a wash-out.

There can still be considerable problems for those involved. A young Protestant told how, taking on board the community's attitude to exogamy and although she had always intended to marry another Protestant, she had ended up in an inter-church marriage:

> [I]t had always been my intention . . . to marry somebody who was Church of
> Ireland as well! So as not to have had any of that conflicting rubbish that one
> can have. . . . It's both conflicting and rubbish.

For cultural as well as confessional reasons, her fiancé's family found it very
difficult to countenance the idea of their son contracting an inter-church
marriage, and opposed it from all points of view. Aspersions were cast on
Protestants in general and on her in particular, with an emphasis on the
inferiority of the Protestant faith, and it was forcefully stated that all inter-
church marriages were bound to fail. The couple persevered, however, and his
family attended the wedding, though very much on sufferance. On the
question of which confession any children should be raised in, she said 'I have
always intermittently . . . been church-going', whereas her husband went
'through the motions', 'for me, there was no contest. . . . We were married in a
Church of Ireland church and . . . the children have been baptised [Church of
Ireland]'. It was, then, less a doctrinal issue for her and more that she had a
stronger identification with belonging to Protestantism in its cultural as well as
its religious guise, as it were, than her husband had with belonging to
Catholicism.

An arresting point on the nature of southern Irish Protestantism was made
by a 40-year-old Protestant which goes both to the root of the last interviewee's
attitude on the practice of her religion and its place in her Protestant cultural
identity and to questions of identity under examination in this book:

> I really do think that the Church of Ireland is a culturally Protestant church
> rather than a theologically Protestant church. . . . [W]e're very culturally
> Protestant, and proud of it.

Thus even a person who takes the path of atheism can still identify strongly
with being a southern Irish Protestant. Of course, the same strength of
identification can be said to occur for those born into Irish Catholic families,
but the minority status of Protestants in the state is the factor that brings the
issues into sharper focus for them.

On the point of the perception of Protestantism as inferior to Catholicism,
another Protestant born elsewhere but brought up in the rural south-west
spoke with some emotion of how she had been perceived to be a 'souper' by
Catholics drawing on the tenets of the emotional legacy. As we have seen, to
call someone a souper still resonates today with multiple implications of

apostasy, betrayal of national and group identity, even of personal weakness, and, as such, is firmly anchored in the emotional legacy. She said:

> There's nothing about me that's originally from [where I live] . . . but the whole tradition of . . . the soupers . . . I would be branded to be part of that whole forcing people to turn their back on their religion so as to be fed . . . even though I just happen to be Church of Ireland and from [where I was born] . . . . So, I find it interesting when a few people have said to me, oh, you're just a souper [and] I just happen to [live] in [this part of the country].

Finally, the evidence of a 90-year-old Protestant who retired back to the south-west in 1980 after a nursing career and marriage in England is examined. She gave a fascinating lifetime's perspective, when she spoke of the changes she has witnessed in confessional dynamics, of what happens in families and of the creation of fresh barriers:

> The biggest change, were all the mixed marriages. I mean, there wasn't a family that I knew that didn't have a mixed marriage in it. . . . A mixed marriage, say, forty years before, was hardly spoken about, except to say something that wasn't very nice, maybe. . . . [In 1980] it was all mixed marriages. . . . You can't have a proper conversation . . . because . . . you'd be frightened you'd upset one if you said something to the other. . . . While closing one barrier, it created another. . . . I notice that, particularly, in our own family. . . . Several of my nephews and nieces, who were brought up . . . strict Protestants . . . had married Catholics, and that has created a barrier. Not on the outside, because . . . we meet and we invite each other to our christenings and our weddings and parties and 90th birthday parties, and all the rest of it, but . . . there's always a limit to what you say. . . . A constraint. . . . that is sad, too. Because it's another division. . . . [M]aybe one or other doesn't go to their own church. . . . we believe you should if possible keep that up. . . . [T]hen you have the problem of the children. They don't have to be Catholic but there's always the undercurrent: if they're brought up Protestants, the Catholics, they don't care for it, and vice versa. . . . one of my nieces married a Catholic and when their son was born . . . the father, went to the priest . . . to arrange the baptism, and the priest said all right, . . . [the father] said the godmother would be . . . a Protestant. And the priest would not accept her. . . . And never, since that day, has that young man been to his own church to worship.

To sum up, then, the essence of confessional difference coalesces around inter-church marriage. Although now there is much more individual freedom being exercised about choice of partner and about which faith strand the children will follow, the topic remains highly charged on the emotional front and can still cause conflict ranging from overt rows to constraints upon freedom of speech. Terence Brown noted an apparent diminution of anti-Protestant feeling shown when, in 1977, 'Mícheál MacGréil reported on his research findings on prejudice and tolerance in Ireland which showed that in Dublin 73.4 per cent of the sample group surveyed were ready to admit a Protestant to the family by marriage'.[69] Whatever about conditions in the city three decades ago, we have seen that such attitudes did not prevail in provincial Ireland.

CHAPTER SIX

'There's No Such Thing as a Poor Protestant'

Religious differences aside, examination of resentments based on economic imbalances between rival communities is an obvious route to take when seeking out the roots of inter-communal tension. Niceties are soon forgotten in the morass of antipathies engendered by unequal distribution of wealth, and no-where has this been truer than in the Irish context.

The perception that *all* Protestants belonged to a wealthy and privileged elite is captured in Brendan Behan's descriptions of an Anglo-Irishman as 'a Protestant on a horse', someone who 'only works at riding horses, drinking whisky and reading double-meaning books in Irish at Trinity College'.[1] They encapsulate more than one myth securely located in the emotional legacy, tapping neatly into historical, class and economic resentments, and relegating Protestants to a monolithic category of the rich and feckless. However, this did and does not represent reality: it hardly needs to be pointed out that the Protestant community in the Republic has always resembled the surrounding majority community in its internal diversity.

Another example of the use of the association of 'mini-mythical' confessional attributes occurs in the work of John Banville's *alter ego*, Benjamin Black. In *Christine Falls*, a novel set in Dublin during the 1950s, the protagonist, Quirke, a consultant pathologist, takes his niece – a young Catholic girl romantically involved, to the horror of her family, with a Protestant – to the Shelbourne Hotel:

> The Friday evening horsy crowd was up from the country, all tweeds and sensible shoes and braying, overbearing voices. . . . From an opposite corner of the room an elderly fellow of military bearing, with polished bald pate and a

The chapter title is a quotation from Jack White, *Minority Report: The Protestant Community in the Irish Republic* (Dublin, 1975), p. 158

137

monocle, appeared to be regarding [Quirke] with a fixed, affronted glare. . . .
The monocle . . . marched past the table, displaying an equine grin and
extending a hand to someone behind Quirke's back.[2]

The words 'horsy', 'braying' and 'equine' conjure brilliantly the cluster of
stereotypes – although there is some doubt in this instance as to whether the
quadruped in question is equine or asinine.

The reductive and unflattering portrait of a feckless class lurks in prevailing
myths of Protestant economic superiority and consequent oppression of
Catholics disclosed in the oral evidence. However, these images do not exist
only within that set of unconscious assumptions triggered by the word
'Protestant' for Catholics. They have also pervaded the sense Protestants have
of themselves, internalised as a result of the dynamics of their 'established and
outsider' status, identified in Mennell et al.'s study. As their elitist position in
Irish society was eroded and Gaelic Ireland took over, and as their numbers
continued to decline, Protestants found themselves not only numerically over-
whelmed but also in an invidious psychological position. Elements deriving
both from their former established status as well as from their new outsider
status began to contribute to their new construction of identity, and they internalised some of the negative feelings associated with Catholic views of Protestants.[3]
Their right to belong to the imagined nation and to claim Irishness was
accordingly challenged, not only from without but also from within. Amongst
other things, this has resulted in the adoption of a defensive posture in respect
of their claim to Irishness.

A 20-year-old Protestant from a rural background in Wicklow showed both
a degree of resentment and an awareness of the operation of the stereotypes
when she said:

> I suppose most people think Protestants are generally rich, upper-class or . . . at
> least middle-class, but . . . I'd be a working-class Protestant . . . Mum would be
> as well, and Dad, but people just generally I think they expect you just to be
> snobby if you're Protestant . . . and just generally to have a better start in life,
> but you don't necessarily . . . not at all. . . . I mean, no one's going to hire you
> because you're Protestant, or . . . no one's going to give you a college place.

From the tone as well as the content of her evidence, it was obvious that she
perceived herself as unfairly relegated to a fictive category in which she felt
stranded. She was also unaware of the ways in which Protestants formerly

helped 'their own' – as, of course, did and do all groups: it is one of the charac-teristics of group cohesion – through parish and social networks.

Bowen related how Protestant employers with vacant positions would inform the rector, who then announced this information from the pulpit. Employers also kept in touch with the leaders of the major youth organisation in the poorer parishes, the Boys' Brigade, so that 'the Captain always looked after his boys when they left'. He outlined other forms of support the Protestant protectionist network took: the secondary school, with headmasters ensuring a flow of suitably educated candidates for jobs in Protestant firms; the contact provided through sporting clubs and, not least, the good offices of the Freemasons.[4] The last, as might be deduced when Catholic resentment of the masons is recalled, was an aspect of communal protectionist behaviour which could produce particular resentment.

Historically, it was not only the fact of Protestant wealth compared with Catholic poverty that fed antipathies but also the fact that their riches came from occupation of land that Catholics perceived rightfully belonged to them that added substance to their multiple grievances. The fierce attachment to land also gained substance because of the reliance of the people on agricul-ture to make a living. Hence, as little industry was established in the state, the majority of people remained directly connected with and dependent upon the land. Also, and significantly from a psychological point of view, during the nineteenth century land ownership became conflated within the ideological concepts of national identity and independence,[5] and, by the 1880s, the Irish nation had been reimagined as excluding the settlers and their descendants, leaving them eternally marooned in the category of usurper.[6]

Indisputably, Protestants held the economic high ground in Ireland for a long time. That this led to abuses on multiple fronts is also true. There were landlords who were unjust to Catholic tenantry and who mismanaged their estates badly. The Dáil debate on the 1923 Land Act encapsulated the popular consensus on this aspect. It epitomised the polarised situation by tapping into the *zeitgeist* which saw the necessity for the erosion of Irish landlordism as 'an integral stage in the move towards independence', and drew on rich seams of mythologised elements of the emotional legacy in support of the cause of depriving proprietors of any remaining vestige of their former glory – or infamy:

> There were those who would gladly have expropriated landlords' lands and who venomously denounced them as 'bloodsuckers' and the 'descendants of Cromwellian planters'. Some TDs harped upon Cromwell's edict of 'To hell or

to Connaught' and reminded their parliamentary colleagues of the 'emigrant ship'. And 'the blood spilled by our forefathers' during the Land War.[7]

This set of attitudes took no heed of the fact that that there had been some landlords who ran their estates in a manner which, given contemporary economic circumstances and in the prevailing mode of more-or-less-benevolent despotism common to all of Europe, did not, or did not intend to, treat the tenantry badly. These were the so-called 'improving' landlords, like Lord Farnham in Co. Cavan or John Foster in Co. Louth, who were 'active advocates of farm improvement'.[8]

Undeniably, the landlord's role was all powerful and central to the community; he held the destiny of his tenants in his hands.[9] A relentless war of attrition was waged over rent: all too often a rent that would have made reinvestment in agriculture possible was far in excess of the tenant's ability to pay, which meant not only desperate hardship for the tenantry but also, with an inevitable circularity, meant that estates became unviable. All in all, it is not difficult to comprehend how the emotional legacy mustered around myths of universal oppression which, by their nature, could not accommodate any allowance for actual conditions. It also ignored the fact that, by 1870 'there were a number of Catholic landlords . . . including the Earl of Granard who owned around 15,000 acres in Longford and Leitrim'.[10] Fr Thomas Conefry, local leader of the Land League in 1881, described him in words that spoke volumes as 'a good-hearted man who would not oppress you if he could avoid it'.[11]

The 'land war' that started in 1879, a campaign of agrarian unrest that ranged from the withholding of rents to the physical prevention of evictions and other acts inescapably accompanied by violence, saw the irruption of traditional tenant grievances linked with a serious economic downturn in agricultural incomes. It rapidly became 'a campaign against landlordism *per se*' orchestrated by the Land League under the leadership of Parnell. Concessions to tenants made by Gladstone's government, which came to power in 1880, led to a partial mitigation of the anti-landlord campaign. However, 1882 saw the ending of only one phase of ongoing agrarian unrest: it was to last until independence and pervade the Troubles, when Protestants were targeted both at the landlord and the tenant level.[12]

Though Catholics had been first deprived of their land and then forbidden by the penal laws to repossess it by purchase, not all the side-effects militated against them: whilst some did very well out of land as tenants, others were forced into diversifying into the areas of trade and commerce, where they attained an increasing degree of success in the nineteenth century which was augmented in the twentieth. Furthermore, as their legal disabilities were eroded, Catholics also began to enter the professions.[13] After the Great Famine, many landlords were financially ruined,[14] and, with the subsequent redistribution of land to the tenantry, which not only took away the source of much of Protestant prosperity but also symbolised the end of the ascendancy,[15] Catholic advancement continued on all fronts.

Bowen maintained that 'the economic dominance of Protestants in the South had been broken by 1922, since they had lost control of the country's major productive base – namely the land'.[16] However, it is important to remember that centuries of elitist economic and educational advantage still accrued to the benefit of Protestants, and this advantage continued, giving them a head start, as it were. Thus, even as their political power drained away, the manner in which the community withdrew into itself, put its energies into private enterprise and fostered the protectionism that saw them looking after 'their own' with undiminished diligence well on into the opening decades of the new state, fortified the remnants of their economic dominance. So, although at the same time Catholic advancement proceeded, Protestant economic advantage was slower to dissipate than other areas of influence.

Following independence, the Irish economy had serious problems to surmount. Firstly, in the mid-1920s only 14 per cent of the working population was engaged in industry, and, by December 1923, 80,000 people were out of work. Even more dismaying was the fact that between 1926 and 1930 no more than 5,000 new jobs were created. This state of affairs reflected the fact that the newly formed state was heavily, if not entirely, financially dependent on the agricultural sector. Nationalist politicians believed that 'national development was synonymous with agricultural development [and] that the interests of the farmer and the nation were identical'.[17] Cumann na nGaedheal's Minister for Agriculture in the Free State government, Patrick Hogan, was to develop agriculture further by encouraging greater production and improving quality and efficiency. He saw agriculture as the only realistic source of economic growth, and his policies were aimed at maximising its export potential.[18]

In accordance with this philosophy, completion of the transfer of large land holdings from Protestants to mostly Catholic tenant farmers, which had begun before 1922, was given priority by the Free State government. Its 1923 land bill, designed to complete the process of the transfer of land and to relieve congestion in areas of particular poverty, was an immensely complex piece of parliamentary drafting. The situation was even more complicated because landlords were unrepresented in the Dáil, and the republicans had refused to take their seats because of the oath of allegiance issue.[19] The confusion created a situation wherein the overall consequences of the legislation, particularly the financial ones, remained obscure and ambiguous. Whilst the bill's apparent intentions appeased the owners of uneconomic holdings and landless persons with promises of compulsory acquisition, in fact the terms offered protection to the class of large farmers from whose ranks the government drew its support.[20]

The post-independence demand for land was ferocious. Hogan wrote to the Taoiseach in 1924, saying that there were 'one and a half million landless men and only about 30,000 holdings for them, and these landless men are at present prepared to exercise their claims with gun and torch'.[21] Indeed, what Terence Dooley calls the 'primordial impulse to own land' was no less important an issue in independent Ireland than it had always been, with land ownership being essential to social standing in rural communities right up to the 1970s.[22] The passing of the land from the hands of landlords into those of the people was, then, a factor of great psychological and symbolic importance in the imagination of the new Irish nation, and, after 1923, Dáil Éireann legislated for the redistribution of land to those 'for whom and by whom the Irish state was created and consolidated'.[23]

The ambiguities inherent in the land legislation led to great difficulties in its implementation. As a consequence, practices for transferring land were developed *a posteriori* which were eventually given statutory recognition in Fianna Fáil's first land act in 1933.[24] In all, it took 13 subsequent land acts, a process that lasted up to the mid-1980s, to complete the work of the Land Commission, which had been set up in 1881 and had undergone several procedural modifications in the interim leading to its 'in effect [becoming] the landlord for untenanted land that it subsequently divided for the benefit of small farmers'.[25]

In the decades after independence, the mindset that saw agriculture as the anchor of the Irish economy was challenged and displaced slowly after Fianna Fáil's successes in the 1932 and 1933 elections. The disastrous economic 'war' with Britain over the period 1932–8 began with the withholding of land annuities payable under early land reform legislation to the British government. Britain retaliated by imposing heavy duties on imports of cattle and other agricultural produce, to which Ireland's answer was to impose duties on the import of British goods. In October 1932, the *Church of Ireland Gazette* reported that, having almost killed off the cattle trade, the government then tried to stimulate it by giving a bounty to farmers which was taken from other citizens by taxation: this, it considered, was topsy-turvy.[26]

A leading article in the *Gazette* in July 1932 had been full of foreboding about the effects of the economic war on the Protestant population, for, if Fianna Fáil were to continue with its anti-British policies, it feared it might lead to another exodus of southern Protestants and to a further decrease in numbers of the community.[27] In any event, the immediate effect was that, in common with the rest of the population, Protestants generally suffered hardship during this period. Indeed, later in the year, letters were published from clergy looking for used clothing for impoverished parishioners,[28] which also tends towards the view that that Protestants were aware of their own poor and did seek to aid them.

Fianna Fáil's ultimate intention was to achieve national self-sufficiency insofar as this was possible in an under-industrialised state, and the standoff between government and its policies' opposers did eventually lead to fundamental changes in Irish agriculture. These included a veering away from beef towards tillage, the widening of the search for alternative markets, infrastructural development and more industrialisation. These changes were, broadly, the result of the innovative economic policies of Sean Lemass, described by Brian Girvin as a 'developmental nationalist', in that he was involved, after Fianna Fáil's success in the elections of 1932 and 1933, in undertaking that party's republicanisation of the nation whilst at the same time seeking to develop the economy to be more competitive in world markets and, vitally, less dependent upon Britain. However, as a party, 'Fianna Fáil was never fully united behind the radical economic and social policies' later identified with Lemass. The multi-faceted reasons for Ireland's lack of economic success at that time are still in contention, but the relevant point here is that Lemass's policies, conceived as early as the early 1930s, did not begin to show results until the 1950s.[29]

In Bowen's view, 'Irish Anglicans were much more successful in preserving their influence in farming than they were in the rapidly expanding urban environment'.[30] On the other hand, he also noted that, after independence, in the expanding urban economy Protestant 'influence had fallen to below half its 1926 level by 1971'.[31] As a result of the policy of land redistribution, however, the 1961 census showed that 58 per cent of Protestant farmers had holdings of 50 acres or more within the Republic compared with 33 per cent of Catholics, thus sustaining an actual, though diminished, advantage.[32] The origins of their advantage in rural areas are exemplified in what occurred in Monaghan, one of the border counties, where, as a direct outcome of plantation policies, Protestants generally owned larger farms on better land.[33]

However, Protestant advantage in the agricultural sector was no protection against economic forces, whether national or international. In the 1930s, the Irish economy was still in thrall to 'economic nationalism' and, during the economic crises of that decade and the following one, large farmers 'were affected not just by worldwide economic depression but the shift towards agricultural protectionism in the UK, Fianna Fáil's emphasis on tillage at the expense of dairy farming, the economic war and the emergency, which pushed them off the pedestal of comparative advantage'.[34] One of the older Protestant interviewees, a Presbyterian aged 80 at the time of interview, one of a family of seven, came from a hundred-acre farm in Co. Monaghan, an area where more than 40 per cent of the population was Protestant.[35] Despite the fact that the family farm was 'big in that day and age,' she described hard times and poverty, 'and just no money' in the locality in the 1930s.

Perceptions of residual economic imbalances did not appear to hamper neighbourly interactions in the countryside and the giving of assistance at labour-intensive seasons such as harvest. Bowen commented that this 'tradition of neighbourliness [had], if anything, grown stronger' in the 1970s, although mechanisation diminished the need for manpower.[36] However, the hostility that could arise over the passing of the ownership of land or business interests to the 'other side' in the context of inter-church marriage has already been alluded to, and it also figured in the context of one western Protestant farming couple's desire to expand and improve their holding. In response to a question about whether she had ever experienced sectarianism in their area, the wife said that it had 'showed itself' against them as a couple, in the guise of claims under the land redistribution legislation. In the late 1960s, they decided to bid for a farm that adjoined their land with the aid of a bank loan. She described how 'once it was known that [we] had bought the land, then [local Catholics] began to agitate for it'. Her husband said:

> I was considered a lunatic. Having taken . . . on such a size of a loan at that time, to do so. . . . I suppose I took an innovative step in my time and I was probably lucky that the bank loaned me the money. . . . [A]nd there was the carrot at that time that . . . Ireland would join the EU and that things could be much better in the future. . . . But then all the people round about were congratulating me on doing it . . . then we ran into trouble . . . the people started a campaign to . . . take the land that I had bought. . . . I think it was a religion matter. . . . I feel to a degree it was a religion matter. Because before I bought the property, it was presumed that some of the business people in [the nearby county town] were

the ones who would buy that place. They had bought several places round about . . . and . . . they seemed to do it with impunity. And I was quite taken aback when I did encounter difficulty. And I think the people that helped me ultimately realised that it was partly a religious thing. But if it was a religious thing . . . it could be shown that . . . they were all Roman Catholics that lived round about and . . . whether they were Roman Catholic or Protestant, that they were entitled, if they'd small holdings . . . to enlarge their holdings . . . but then why didn't they do it to the other people who bought the other pieces of land . . . in the locality? So, maybe it was sectarian to a degree. . . . The Land Commission inspector that came here, he says: . . . I'm not doing this because I think you're a nice fellow, he says, I'm doing this because I want to see fair play. . . . Now . . . there was one Protestant family who were . . . supposed to have put their names in, as it were. I think there might have been ten or fifteen people, but there'd probably be only . . . land for five people in it. . . . Everyone was having a go . . . our Rector at the time, who was a keen fisherman and who had a friend who was also a keen fisherman and who worked in the Land Commission . . . at a fairly high level, and he put my case in front of him. Which of them succeeded, I don't know. . . . But then, the same thing happened a few years later with another [Protestant] farmer . . . just a little bit nearer [the county town], and they . . . wanted to expand, and they went through the same sort of hassles as well.

In his even-handed analysis of what happened, the interviewee saw all sides of the situation, and did not even appear to be surprised that fellow-Protestants tried to climb on to the land redistribution bandwagon.

It also highlights an instance of an Irish form of old boys' network, and is reminiscent of Jimmy O'Dea's joke, related by R. V. Comerford, about 'the harp being the appropriate symbol of Ireland because of its being an instrument operated by pulling strings'.[37] It is tempting to add that it might also qualify because harping on about old grievances is a regrettable national pastime. In any event, it would be very interesting to know whether influence or inspector prevailed in obtaining the outcome.

There is no doubt that the task of the Land Commission Inspector was not an easy one. He had to enquire exhaustively into the circumstances of every claimant within a mile radius of the land in question, and 'it was not unknown for inspectors to receive death threats from disgruntled applicants for land'.[38] It would appear, however, that the obsession with ownership of land had mutated somewhat. The target was no longer the Protestant landlord – who had virtually disappeared in fact, if not in myth – but simply anyone who stood in the way of a claim on land, whether or not it was rightly conceived, with a dash of sectarianism added for good measure.

Turning to the worlds of the professions, private sector business and commerce before independence, Jack White maintained that Protestants held a commanding position in the professions and business up to the Great War:

> In 1914 they held 70 per cent of all positions in the bank service and 66 per cent of the jobs in insurance, and they accounted for 60 per cent of the practising lawyers. As late as 1926 they still counted more than one-half of the bank employees, not much less than one-half of the chartered accountants, over one-third of the auctioneers and one-third of the insurance officials. In the professions they numbered over one-third of the lawyers, one-third of the dentists and about one-fifth of the doctors.[39]

Bowen stated that 'by 1922 Catholics had . . . made considerable headway in overcoming their subordinate position within the economy',[40] and he estimated Protestant influence in the professions had fallen by the last quarter of the twentieth century due to 'an immense increase of 177 per cent in the number of Catholic professionals and a virtually static rate of change among the minority'.[41] The change in the balance did not, however, diminish resentment at perceived Protestant dominance and affluence which, allied with other attributed characteristics, served to preserve the gap between the communities. The myths of universal Protestant economic exploitation of Catholics and perpetration of exclusionary tactics were too deeply entrenched within the emotional legacy to be shifted easily.

In the professions, White stated that 'the 1961 census return shows some 56,000 men and women in "professional and technical occupations", and of these just about one-tenth are Protestants'. He also argued that the 'long-established custom' which saw one Protestant judicial appointment to the High Court was probably what would now be called positive discrimination, but went on to say that this was defensible as a guarantee of equal treatment under the law for the minority.[42] However, the incorporation of Catholic moral precepts into state law bears another mention here, and the appointment of one Protestant judge did nothing to stop that.

The Catholic ethos that came to predominate in the state also had an important effect on Irish society when it comes to the medical profession and the health and social services. At independence the new state inherited a health system that was partly public and partly private, but always confessionalised – something that was not, of course, peculiar to Ireland. Historically, in the early eighteenth century, charitable support for the sick began to be channelled through hospitals and dispensaries administered by Protestant medical charities. There were four types of institution, of which voluntary hospitals and county infirmaries were two. They 'were imbued with a strong Anglican ethos and bias. Nepotism, sectarianism and divisive politics were part of their very fabric'. The other types of institution were fever hospitals and dispensaries, and, in the 1830s, a network of workhouses was set up across the country for the poor with some government support.[43]

By mid-nineteenth century, the number of Protestant charities were 'notable . . . for their number and range . . . while the Quaker community contributed out of all proportion to its small population'. The penal laws had prevented the open endowment of Catholic charities, and neither had they permitted charitable endowment of lands by Catholics. Some relief of these measures was granted in 1832, but it was not until 1860 that Catholics could effectively grant land for charitable purposes, at which time there was an upsurge in Catholic charities.[44] From mid-century, the existing system had ceased to cope with the demands placed upon it, and the Catholic religious orders responded to what was identified as a major social need. Following emancipation, major Catholic hospitals under the patronage of the bishop or archbishop of the diocese had been established nationwide.[45] The overall result was a form of apartheid: 'by a happy accident it turned out that the best-qualified candidate in a Catholic hospital was always a Catholic',[46] and *vice versa*. And, from that time on, as Ruth Barrington observed, 'Ireland [was and] is probably unique in the extent to which the Catholic Church has influenced the development of health policy'.[47]

From the beginning of the nineteenth century Catholic and Protestant doctors alike attended the destitute and poverty-stricken lower classes, in the growing network of hospitals without charge, so that they could learn to practise their professions and then make their living from treating the rich privately with the skills learned in those hospitals. In the second half of the century, efforts of the Catholic nursing orders to become involved in treating inmates in the workhouses were opposed by some Boards of Guardians, who did not want to see publicly funded institutions developing a Catholic ethos. However, some institutions permitted their involvement because their services were free and their help was needed – and appreciated – by patients.

In 1911, when the Liberal government tried to bring in legislation implementing unemployment insurance and medical benefit throughout the United Kingdom, the Catholic hierarchy, taking its cue from the propertied classes, opposed the introduction of such measures in Ireland. Members of the medical profession allied themselves with the bishops, and they succeeded in partially blocking the reforms, so that medical benefit was withheld and the Irish health system was left in their combined hands, creating a hegemony that was hardly to change over the next century.

The situation at independence was challenging. The voluntary hospitals under the control of both confessions had to contend not only with financial burdens but also with the immense changes that had occurred in medicine since the mid-nineteenth century. They relied increasingly on income from paying patients and their commitment to treating the poor declined. The new government, determined to keep taxation low by running public affairs as economically as possible, was not sympathetic and refused to increase the value of parliamentary grants to the hospitals.[48] Eventually, a solution was found through the legalisation of a sweepstake on horse racing from which funding was to be provided, on condition that public patients were treated. In 1932 a letter published in the *Church of Ireland Gazette* noted the fact that the Protestant-run Adelaide Hospital and allied institutions would not take money from the Sweep because of disapproval of its provenance.[49]

John Charles McQuaid, Archbishop of Dublin from 1940 to 1972, was strongly opposed to state involvement in the provision of health and social services, and wanted to establish services that would be largely under the control of the Catholic Church.[50] Indeed, health care came to be the source of much political controversy by the mid-twentieth century, and, in Tom Garvin's view, not least of the problems encountered was that 'health was an ecclesiastical obsession because of its close connection to matters of sex, reproduction and marriage'. Overall, a situation existed wherein public health was a major concern, with tuberculosis, polio, diphtheria and venereal disease common. 'In the case of VD in particular, ideological and psychological barriers militated against the disease being tackled scientifically'.[51]

In 1944, there was a confrontation between the Catholic Church and the then Minister for Local Government and Public Health, Sean McEntee, over reorganisation and, more importantly, control of the health services. The state prevailed, and a 'regular' Department of Health was formed. This was the first 'Catholic Church versus state' clash since 1922. The next one came in 1951, when Dr Noel Browne, who had spearheaded a successful TB eradication scheme drawn up and initiated by the previous Fianna Fáil government, tried to tackle infant mortality and maternal health with his 'Mother and Child' scheme. This resulted in a head-on clash with the hierarchy, backed by the Irish Medical Association, and Browne was destroyed politically.[52]

Another notorious episode occurred in 1949, this time 'essentially a clash between the Knights of St Columbanus and the Freemasons who competed to gain positions of influence for their members'.[53] The Knights, an order of Catholic laymen dedicated to the service of Christ in all aspects of daily life including the workplace,[54] gained a majority of votes at the Protestant-run Meath Hospital AGM, unseated the old management and took control. A High Court action by the unseated board was unsuccessful, but the government intervened by way of a private bill, creating a new mode of representation on the management committee that was acceptable to both sides.[55]

Fianna Fáil returned to power in 1951, and, despite opposition from the Catholic hierarchy, eventually managed to bring in considerable reforms to the provision of health care in the state. In Barrington's view, the Catholic bishops' opposition was 'only understandable as a defence of the interests of the powerful Catholic voluntary hospitals, their consultant staff and associated medical schools from further state encroachment'.[56]

In view of all this, Barrington's argument that 'the triangular conflict of state, church and medical profession of the 1940s and 1950s left its mark . . . on the health services to this day', is no surprise. The first effect she noted was the enshrinement of the means test as a mode of access to health services. The second was the defence by the medical profession of their private practices, which led to an extraordinary degree of such practice, making it difficult to distinguish between public and private. The third was a way of controlling the appointment of medical consultants, which needed the co-operation of the independent hospitals and was effected through Comhairle na nOspideal. On the positive side, this organisation brought about a major rationalisation of medical specialties in the country. On the negative, the nature of the approval system has resulted in the small number of consultant posts in the state, particularly when compared with other countries.

Fourthly, a source of continuing disquiet not only for Protestants but for others in the increasingly pluralistic society that is developing in Ireland, the alliance between the Catholic Church and the medical profession has ensured the predomination of the Catholic system of ethics, which consequently affected access to family planning in all its aspects and to abortion, particularly on therapeutic grounds. It has also proved politically impossible to define the circumstances in which legal abortions may take place in Irish hospitals, and, because of the relatively easy availability of abortion services in Britain, to which many Irish women resort each year, politicians have evaded the need to address this issue.

A particularly interesting piece of evidence on the political and moral controversies surrounding the respective rights of foetus and mother was given by a 47-year-old rural Catholic, who related what happened when

> they were arguing that they weren't quite sure what would happen – oh, it was the right of the mother over the unborn child, if there was a danger that she could die. . . . [T]here was a query about ectopic pregnancy and a whole load of stuff like that, and I remember that it would have been the first time that big debates had really happened round that issue, and I was curious to see what my Dad would think. Right? I kind-of thought that I knew what he was going to think. Well, I tell you, was I in for a surprise! And he said, Look at, he said, I have four daughters: any one of them, he said, could land up at the hospital in the morning, he said, with an ectopic pregnancy. And, he said, if that ruling goes through the way the church wants it to go through, he said, they'd be allowed to die. And he said, that wouldn't be a viable pregnancy in the first place. And, he said, there are loads of other positions, he said, they could find themselves in, and their lives would be in danger, and he said, so I'm voting, and he was voting the same way I was voting at the time. D'you know, my Dad's in his seventies, he's 76 now. . . . That's – wonderful! Absolutely! Absolutely! And I remember looking at him, and I saw him in a completely different light, because he would be very religious, and he'd be very good at . . . going to regular confessions and mass and doing all the right things . . . and would have dragged us along with him whether we, kicking or screaming or not.

The alliance of Catholic Church and medical profession also ensured that the voluntary Catholic hospitals, and other Catholic-run welfare services, remained outside the controls imposed on other public services, even though more than 90 per cent of their funding came from the taxpayer. Some of the results of this immunity and lack of accountability have been seen in the disclosures of abuse of all types in religious-run institutions, which ultimately accelerated the almost-entire withdrawal of the religious orders from the care of orphaned or neglected children.

The two main Catholic teaching hospitals in Dublin, the Mater Misericordiae University Hospital and St Vincent's, are run by religious orders. In view of the fall in vocations, it cannot be predicted how long these orders can continue to remain active in the hospitals, but, until for one reason or another they withdraw their services, they continue the perpetuation of the Catholic ethos in the medical arena.

Another pertinent question is what is to happen when those who wish to choose a service not available in a Catholic hospital, but to which they are legally entitled now or in the future, such as legal abortion, sterilisation and 'artificial' contraception, or who may take issue with the use of extraordinary means to prolong life. In a pluralist society, whilst it does not seem reasonable to require hospitals to carry out procedures that are incompatible with their religious ethos, government should ensure that people can avail themselves of legally permitted services in another institution.[57] The evidence of a 58-year-old Protestant health professional is pertinent to this point, pointing up as it does an unfortunate experiential outcome of absolutist ethical principles. She said:

> I worked in . . . a very Catholic hospital, and I did find . . . that it was just very Catholic and everything, you know, the priest would come in and the nurses would go down on their knees, he'd ring his little bell, but I wouldn't do that . . . this woman . . . was losing the baby and she would have had to go down . . . to theatre . . . you have to do a pregnancy test, and if the baby's still alive, then you don't take them down. But the baby's dying . . . and [the nun] made this remark. . . . I said: Is she going for a D & C? [She said] This is a Catholic hospital – we don't do abortions here. And I just thought . . . it was prolonging the woman's agony and . . . nobody wanted that.

In the 1980s, lack of economic viability saw the closure of all but one of the Protestant institutions, and the Adelaide Hospital was left on its own to provide health care for any citizen of the state who, for one reason or another, preferred not to enter a Catholic hospital. Long and protracted negotiations were conducted with the aim of its becoming part of the new hospital complex at Tallaght whilst keeping a Protestant ethos for patients who wished to exercise choice over ethical concerns implicit in their medical treatment. Eventually the hospital charter was amended by statute in 1996 and the Adelaide became part of the new institution whilst retaining its character and ethos. As Rosemary French, who was involved in the negotiations, said, with more than a degree of ironic delicacy,

I remain puzzled as to why it should have been so difficult to get agreement for one hospital in the State to have a multi-denominational and pluralist character. It was a lonely place to be but one could feel the winds of change blowing in the country and the Board of the Adelaide Hospital received incredible support from people of all denominations and of none throughout the whole country.[58]

The legacy of the 'triangular relationship' between Catholic Church, state and medical profession outlined by Barrington might explain the difficulties.

In the world of commerce, Bowen advanced arguments of particular relevance to the perpetuation of the emotional legacy where it is mustered round Protestant economic privilege. Because, until the 1970s, most businesses could be easily identified as either Protestant or Catholic, the risk of class conflict 'was increased . . . because the existence of separate Protestant firms made the material advantages of the minority all that much more visible to Catholics'.[59] When it came to hiring policies for those Protestant firms, there is no doubt that there was huge resentment at the practice outlined in White's example of three advertisements in the *Irish Times* in 1927, two of which stated that any applicant should be Protestant and the third of which required applicants to state their religion when replying to the advertisement.[60] Indeed, a 59-year-old Catholic interviewee showed detectable emotion when he said 'Now, before the [Second World] War, there was an awful lot of that, if there was a job going it'd state very clearly "No Roman Catholics need apply". That was commonplace.' As he was born just after that war and did not enter the workplace until the early 1960s, when he said he and his contemporaries 'were all too busy trying to earn a living and make . . . ends meet' to worry about sectarianism, this must have been something about which he had been told and which did not derive from his own experience. However, it was obvious from his demeanour that the story had gained in the telling and is therefore an example of the emotive hold of myths making up the emotional legacy. The evidence of another 57-year-old rural Catholic confirms how the myths were relayed:

I was told by my father, there was a big firm in [a local town], and they would have sold all kinds of drapery, shoes, you could buy a suit of clothes in it, you could buy a yard of material, they were that kind of firm. . . . [B]ut they had, at one stage . . . a little notice up in their window saying that they were looking for staff, but 'RCs need not apply'. . . . [B]ut I myself had no memory, certainly, and I worked [for a] builders providers, and there was Protestant and Catholic staff in it, and there was no discrimination. . . . There'd be no teasing certainly.

White suggests that, at least in the early decades of the state, the society inhabited by the separated communities supported the right of those from both communities involved in the private sector to 'look after their own'. Bowen also referred to this phenomenon, and pointed out that Catholic business proprietors not only practised their own form of protectionism, but were also relatively tolerant of it when practised by Protestants because they understood and identified with the concept.[61] So it can at least be hazarded that, in this instance, such practices were less the result of sectarianism as of nepotism, but that the resentment felt by workers placed it firmly within the ambit of sectarianism and made it part of the emotional legacy.

Given the prevalence of stereotypes of Protestants as oppressors, it is no surprise that there are tales that show Protestant employers in the private sector in a bad light, as more than meriting an exploitative reputation. A 91-year-old Dublin Catholic had several examples that occurred before and around the time of independence and in the mid-1930s. First of all, she stated that her father worked for Guinness's, then, in a way that indicated that it was something quite unexceptional, she continued 'but he was never promoted'. When asked why, she said baldly: 'Because he was a Catholic'. White stated that 'firms like Guinness's were notorious for employing only Protestants in senior posts', adding the comment that, among Protestants, the firm were also notorious for their preference for Oxbridge graduates over those of Trinity, 'which suggests that their bias may have been social rather than religious'.[62] However, the working-class Protestant father of another interviewee also worked for Guinness's in the capacity of lorry driver, which tends to show that the firm did, in fact, employ Protestants at lower levels.

The 91-year-old Catholic interviewee went on to relate that she

had an aunt who was married, she was a cook for Lady Shaw, and she married a gardener. . . . [H]e was working for this man, I think it was Serpentine Avenue . . . and the man came to him one day, and he says: Eh, could you get somebody to paint my railings who is not a Sinn Féiner? And Jim looked at him, he says: Ah, sure, we're all Sinn Féiners! But he was out of a job the following week!

Another relative worked for a large Dublin hardware firm, and she told how one day some fellow there . . . passed some very derogatory remark about the nationalists, and Tommy hit him. Knocked him down! And he lost his job. So, that was two of them had it. . . . [T]hat kind of thing went on for a while. There was another, a little girl in Sandymount [who] was going to the tech in Ballsbridge, and . . . she applied for a job in [a Protestant firm] and was accepted and told, yes, you start on Monday. But on Monday she went in and the lady who had interviewed her for the job said: Oh, by the way, there was one question I forgot to ask you. What school did you go to? . . . So she said: Lakelands Convent in Sandymount and the technical school. Well, sorry, the place is filled. And that kind of thing went on for quite a while. . . . But gradually it eased off.

So, at a time when, as might be expected, the positions of the confessions were at their most polarised, tensions continued to come to a head in the relationships between employer and employee, Protestant and Catholic. That, in those days, *all* employees of the lower classes everywhere suffered similar insecurity and went in fear of dismissal without testimonial by their masters for the flimsiest of reasons must not be forgotten, but the religious and political content of discrimination in Ireland undoubtedly added elements of danger for those without power.

In a pamphlet published in 1946, W. B. Stanford addressed the topic of 'jobbery', first of all by stating, unexceptionally, that 'justice prescribes equality of opportunity for every citizen, and that work and rewards should be given on merit, not on hereditary qualities of class, creed or race', then giving details of 'an actual case':

A young skilled worker in Dublin is offered better paid work in another firm. He gives notice, and in due time goes to the new firm. Within a few days of his arrival the manager calls him for a private interview. He explains that pressure has been put on him by customers and others not to employ a Protestant worker. [63]

It would appear, then, that by mid-twentieth century the employment boot might have been on the other confessional foot – for those in the lower echelons, at least, if not for management.

Confession-based jobbery and protectionism were, to a greater or a lesser degree, both practised and tolerated by both sides in the private sector in the early days of the state. However, the exercising of privilege in the public sector was another matter altogether. After the Union, whilst Westminster legislated for Ireland, 'the actual administration of government and the judiciary still remained at Dublin Castle, which was the centre of the Irish executive',[64] and, according to Jack White, under this administration, discrimination and patronage were rife in appointments ranging from judges to rate collectors.[65] Fergus Campbell has suggested that Lawrence McBride's view, set out in *The Greening of Dublin Castle* (1981), that the Irish administration transformed itself between 1892 and 1922 so that Protestant unionist senior administrators were replaced by Catholic nationalists, was possibly overstated. Campbell argues that there was significantly less 'greening' than McBride claimed, and that the British state appears to have regarded Irish-born Catholics as potentially disloyal, with the result that it implemented a subtle system of ethnic discrimination at the upper levels of the Irish civil service. He argues further that the existence of this version of the 'glass ceiling' provided young educated Catholic professionals with a powerful motive for participation in the 1916 rising.[66]

Not unnaturally, in the new state Protestants feared that the tide of preference would flow against them, but White maintained that 'in fact, the Free State set a high standard of equity in the matter of public appointments'. However, to take the Civil Service as an example, he continued, few Protestants thought of making a career in it, probably from an expectation that they would feel out of place.[67] Returning to the 91-year-old Catholic interviewee's own work experience, after trying other jobs she ended up as a typist in the civil service and eventually was appointed to the Prices Commission, where

> most of . . . the chartered [accountants] were Protestants! . . . But then we, when the war broke out, we were under Sean Lemass at the time, and we had to get . . . four new accountants, so they advertised the job, and we got one from Liverpool, and a Cork man, and another Cork man who was working in Dublin, I think, and one from Belfast . . . the Belfast one couldn't come until he fixed up in Belfast, and he was late coming in, and one of our men said to . . . a typist, [who] was a Protestant . . .: I think . . . we've to get another . . . accountant yet, he hasn't come yet. I'm sure he's one of yours! He's coming from Belfast. And she said: What's his name? Vincent Hedley L. And she says: Well, Hedley might be ours, but not the Vincent! And she was right. So I married him!

The typist was, apparently, teased about her religion, but she reciprocated in kind: '[W]e used to joke her sometimes, and say: Oh, H, some day you'll see the light! You know, this kind of thing would go on . . . [S]he'd take the same fun with us'. So, as the interviewee pointed out, by the 1930s the polarised confessional situation had 'eased off', and, although most of her colleagues were Catholic, there were Protestants at both senior and junior levels in the civil service. Another interviewee who also worked in the civil service in the 1930s confirmed this situation:

> [T]here were a few [Protestants] . . . Yes . . . there were two.
> Q. And what were relationships like in the office?
> A. Grand. Fine. I think indeed the supervisor was Protestant. I couldn't really tell you, but I think she was. Fine. There was no such thing as any, religion was never mentioned.

So, there was apparent fairness in the process of appointments to the public service and, from the point of view of two Catholics, good relationships in the workplace in the 1930s, despite the acknowledgement of a bit of reciprocal teasing with the Protestant typist, which was something that went on in both public and private sectors – and still does, as will be seen.

However, what happened in the workplace was not always benign when seen from a Protestant perspective, as the experience of a 64-year-old Protestant woman from the west, recently retired at the time of interview from a long career in the public sector, confirmed. Referring not only to sectarian discrimination but also to Catholic assumptions about Protestants and the Irish language, she said:

> [T]here would have been discrimination. That would have been accepted. And I, I, the only way I could work it out why in recent times some have got things and others haven't. . . . I remember a colleague . . . I took over a case from him, and the woman was a Protestant, had married a Roman Catholic, become a Roman Catholic and she had a family, a largish family and there were all sorts of difficulties. And she was a bizarre woman. . . . [H]e saw the root of [her psychosis] being in the change of religion. It was so bizarre, I couldn't follow it. I've never heard anything like it. And that did tell me something. And . . . he made a statement . . . it was very anti-Protestant. . . . [At the time of] the blessed referenda. . . . the abortion and all the rest of it.. . . He was very angry that Protestants didn't come . . . on TV and argue it out with some of the Roman

Catholic bishops. . . . So that was the atmosphere. . . . [Y]ou learn to . . . watch and observe. . . . I wouldn't readily make comments or anything like that. And sometimes there were definite misunderstandings when you'd give a point of view. . . . And the silence that would follow it would mean that they probably weren't accepting what you were saying. . . . [I]t came up in, in conversation one day . . . I said something about Coláiste Moibhí, a friend going to it, or somebody I knew, and . . . they were absolutely gob-smacked that a Protestant would attend, or that there was even, under Protestant . . . ethos, an all-Irish college. . . . Or that I went to the Gaeltacht. That was unheard of.

Apart from the 'bizarre' incident based on bigotry, her experience of the assumptions held by Catholic colleagues about the relationship between Protestants and the Irish language displays not only an oblique form of discrimination but is also an example of exclusion from an Irishness constructed with a pivotal place allocated to the national language, whether or not Protestants were fluent in it.

And, notably, another civil servant, a Catholic this time, was frank about whether sectarianism existed within the service in the present day, confirming that it did:

We would have a number of people from both Catholic and Protestant backgrounds, and we would have one or two people who were Jewish, as well. And I certainly have heard what I would regard as sectarian comments made about people, eh, behind their back, by certain individuals . . . which, I think . . . would not really be regarded as politically correct or acceptable. Now, among ourselves, people that I would be friendly with, who are from different backgrounds, it would certainly be a matter of some kind-of humour, at more or less, at times. . . . [B]ut . . . certainly, it would be known that there are . . . particular people in positions who would have issues around religion. . . . [I]t's not widespread. . . . I would hasten to add that there . . . are just a small number, but certainly I have become aware of it. . . . [T]he incorrigible small per cent, but some of those people are in very important positions, unfortunately! . . . I would have seen it as an abuse of power, at times, yes.

An 81-year-old Protestant pursued her career in the banking sector. She spoke of what, in her experience, happened in the 1940s as Protestant dominance of one of its bastions was, in fact, eroding. She stated that 'in the south, the Catholic church liked to make sure . . . that Catholics got . . . more than a fair share, because they liked them to get the jobs', and cited an instance where a Catholic clergyman – before the recording of the interview, she had said he was a bishop acting at the behest of the parish priest concerned – interfered with the appointment of a Protestant, who

> was moved because the bank he was in was a country branch and the priest there thought there weren't enough Catholics in the bank and he asked . . . the bank to change the position and put . . . more Catholics in it, so my friend had to leave and they sent him up north then to a bank up there. . . . He was a Protestant, he had to shift. . . . [And the] lady who was in charge of the female staff, a very capable person, they wanted her to be replaced by a member of the Catholic church, because . . . there were more Catholic women, which it was true, in the banking world, than there were Protestants, so they should have had a Catholic. . . . But . . . I don't think the staff wanted that, because they all admired and trusted the woman that was there, and they didn't want her replaced. . . . It was external, outside, you know, it was the church wanted greater representation of Catholics.

Thus it can be seen that, in her experience, a Protestant had suffered detriment in a sector in which many would have expected him to be in a secure position because of Protestant preference. It can also be inferred that, at least occasionally, employees' wishes, as distinct from any policies handed down from above or imposed from outside, were *not* governed by confessional imperatives.

Bowen found that at the end of the 1970s 'the minority was showing signs of a new willingness to take up careers within the Catholic world'.[68] He also noted that a Protestant manager might, in the climate of growth and change in management practices of the time, have argued that 'religion doesn't enter into it any more'. However, he went on, such 'sweeping statements must be viewed with some suspicion'.[69] Furthermore, the report on Irish values and attitudes, part of the European Value Systems study, carried out in March/April 1981 and published just before Bowen's study, found that, despite increasing Catholic advancement, Protestants were much more likely to be or have been in professional/managerial or other white-collar jobs, and much less likely to be in low-skilled manual work or in farming.[70] This situation possibly reflects the continuing advantage accruing to Protestants from their previous elite position and might have contributed to the perpetuation of perceptions of excessive Protestant domination.

What, then, is it like in today's workplace? There is, of course, always the possibility that to notice 'outcroppings' might betray a morbid sensitivity. But in any situation where religion and politics are concerned, a minority is bound at least to notice, if not to resent, such slips and what they indicate. The same can be said about the type of teasing where fun is made of someone because of their beliefs or the characteristics they are assumed to possess as a result of confessional or other types of orientation. Without labouring the point, in an age when it is recognised that teasing can rapidly become bullying, especially in school or work environments, the fact that it is deemed acceptable to tease co-workers on such matters at least requires examination.

Although teasing in the workplace was not a universal phenomenon, it did happen to two Protestant interviewees, the first in her late twenties and the other in her late forties, both of whom are referring to current conditions. The first said:

> Now, you get slagged off a little bit at work, you know, and maybe I draw it upon myself you know by not being afraid to say that I am different, that I don't go to Mass, and I actually am Protestant, and I don't find a problem with it. . . . And just those . . . small things in work . . . that there would be just slagging off. You know, just messing, Arragh, sure, you don't believe in Lent, do you? Those kind of little things, you know. I suppose lack of education brings that about.

The second confirmed: 'You get the odd kind-of slagging, Oh, she's a Prod'. Both had a robust attitude to the phenomenon, and did not display the 'silencing' experienced by the 65-year-old recently retired Protestant quoted earlier who, because of her awareness of sectarian undercurrents in her relationships with colleagues, had learned to watch what she said for fear of adverse reaction. However, it is clear that, whatever the reaction on the part of those being baited, Protestant stereotypes are frequently evoked in everyday co-existence in the workplace, and Protestants are deemed to be 'fair game'. A 44-year-old Protestant with 20 years' experience of working in a Catholic-dominated area was not as magnanimous about being singled out as were the two interviewees already quoted. She did have one positive experience to relate, but it was in itself also a signifier of difference because of the use of the descriptor 'your kind':

> I certainly felt conspicuous. . . . [P]eople would talk to me about being Protestant. . . . [A]nd a lot of [the bosses] would have been member of the Knights of Columbanus. . . . [F]unnily enough . . . when I was doing the

interview for Rathmines, there was a journalist on it from the *Irish Press* . . . who was on the interview panel, a wonderful man, and when we were coming towards to end of his course . . . he said:. . . tell the Protestant girl to come in to me. . . . I went into the newsroom . . . and he said: I'd hate to see you not getting through, not making it, because not enough of your kind come into this profession. And I thought this is wonderful, this is the *Irish Press*, and here's this man, sticking his head out and we wouldn't even have allowed the *Irish Press* through the door at that stage in our family! My father was staunchly *Independent*, and my mother bought the *Irish Times*!

Another Anglican woman, raised outside the state and trained as a nurse but living in Ireland and working in a different capacity, was clear about how confessional discrimination directed at singling her out was practised in her workplace. She did not disguise her exasperation with the way she had been treated:

I hate to say, the only time I really experienced [discrimination] was . . . at [work]. . . . Now they put it in the form of a joke, as you often do: Oh, she's Protestant, Protestant, Protestant . . . I got this continuously. It drove me . . . ! At first it was funny . . . but then it got irritating. . . . And then it just was. . . . Oh, I didn't respond . . . after a while. And it got so that sometimes I would even say: Oh, I'm doing this because I'm Protestant. . . . For . . . example now – I'm sure you've experienced this, too – you do teas at church, you do bake sales, you do bazaars, and there you are, from the time you are knee-high . . . with your mother, you're doing teas, you're doing tray-bakes, you're doing all of these things, and to me that's the mode. We have a coffee shop at [work], so, here am I . . . as a nurse, you clean. As . . . a Protestant woman, you . . . tray-bake! You tidy, you, you don't sit around. You bustle. Now, this is a stereotype, of course. You don't sit around, you bustle around, you're helpful, you're positive . . . you know?. . . my natural inclination anyway, is to tidy and clean and do that kind of thing. So, I was minding the coffee shop, in the best way I could. And this was not approved of. And I can't believe that, even now . . . they would not be happy that I would be happy to work and clean and polish! Almost as if there is some kind of resentment that I was doing it, and they weren't!

A 34-year-old Protestant described what happened to her when employed by an Irish concern in London:

I suppose because my name was 'as Gaelige' it was always assumed I was Catholic. And people would find it almost . . . duplicitous, if that's the right word, that I would be Protestant masquerading under an Irish surname. People would have . . . felt that I was almost trying to hide my Protestantism . . . and my boss . . . goaded me about being Protestant, and how could I be Protestant with an Irish name? And me saying: but I can be Protestant and Irish. And that that would have been . . . Protestant and . . . speaking Irish. . . . [The boss's remarks] would have been somewhat tongue-in-cheek, but utterly meant, nonetheless. . . . [W]e brag that part of the Irish sense of humour is that we like to slag people and be slagged and everything else like that. So, if you're slagged about being Protestant and don't take it as a joke, you're just proving that you're not Irish to begin with. Oh, yeah.

Later in the interview she commented again on the incident with her boss, saying that, given legal developments that recognise the unequal power relationship existing between a superior and an employee and that abuses of that relationship are rights of action, 'nowadays you'd probably sue'.

To counter this evidence, however, the experience of a 61-year-old Dublin Protestant who started work in the 1950s is notable on two fronts. Firstly, he averred that he had met with no bigotry whatsoever, and, secondly, the workforce was confessionally mixed at all levels:

[W]e didn't notice [confessional difference in the workplace]. . . . [T]he two owners . . . one . . . was a Protestant, went to Wesley College, [was] Latvian by extraction . . . his parents were Latvian, and his mother never really spoke English properly. They came over at the revolution. And his partner, was [an] absolutely fervent Roman Catholic, a daily Communicant . . . who wrote scripts for Old Mother Reilly and the pantos in the Olympia. . . . [H]e used to try out the scripts on us. . . . But . . . I overheard [him] telling another employee about when I came for the interview . . . there was something like fifty boys came for the interviews, and . . . he said that he knew that [his Protestant partner] wanted me, but didn't want to say so because I think I was the only Protestant . . . but [the Catholic] said that he wanted me, too, because he thought I was the best, or whatever, but he strung [his partner] along . . . he let him dangle. . . . [There was] absolutely no bigotry . . . none whatsoever. And the firm employed . . . about ten of us, and I'd say there were four Protestants in it. . . . A high percentage, I think.

We shall consider further evidence from this interviewee later, when addressing the issue of what does or does not constitute 'bigotry'.

An 81-year-old Protestant from a middle-class area of Dublin spoke of how the Protestant network operated, and had various points to raise on difference in the workplace. She never married, worked all her life and thus had extensive work experience over a long period. She spoke of how staff were recruited through personal contact when she was looking for her first job in the private sector at the age of seventeen:

> I don't know whether this . . . applied to all offices, but in M's, for instance, if they wanted a new bod, they would tell the staff: we need a new invoice typist, or someone. And they would ask the staff if they knew anybody. . . . I knew a lot of people in the secretarial college at the time, and I actually got about three different girls into M's because I knew they were looking for jobs. As it happened, they were all Protestants, but it was just because they were . . . in the same school as me . . . if I'd known there was a Catholic looking for a job, I would have mentioned her name just the same. But, that was largely the way, that happened a lot in those days. Because you see, there was no such thing really as CVs and things in those days, and you just went for an interview and if the person who was interviewing liked you and thought you were the right type, they took you on, and that was it.

She said that she had met with 'a few isolated cases' of confessional victimisation in the workplace, but, in relating one incident where a Catholic girl left a job because of a row with a Protestant member of management, her desire to avoid being specific led to the point of the story being somewhat obscured. In the main, however, she went on, she shared offices with Catholics and got on well with them. She was somewhat atypical for her age and her class, however, in that, up to starting work, she said she had

> no particularly strong political leanings one way or the other, because of . . . my father being English, and I was born just after we got independence here, so a lot of my older relatives, my great aunts and uncles, would have all grown up under British rule and politics really weren't discussed in the family, but . . . they were sort-of royalists. . . . I became very friendly with a girl who was a couple of years older than me, but was a rabid republican. . . . [A] Catholic. And she lent me books, I remember Dan Breen, the life of Dan Breen, and it was the first time I had ever read anything like that, connected with the republican

movement. And of course I could see then a lot of things that I didn't know and we were never taught in school, anything about the famine or the landlords throwing the people on the side of the road, etc., etc. So I lapped this up, and became, while I never became a rabid republican, but my sympathies were with the Irish and I became very friendly with this girl.

Of course it is only possible to speculate, but it could be that this explicit identification with the nationalist cause may well have protected her from teasing in the workplace experienced by other Protestants. At any rate, in a subsequent job,

> for years and years I worked very closely, like as close as you are to me, in a room with a Catholic fellow-shorthand typist. And we were like that! And she came from a republican background . . . but . . . we certainly never fought over religion, or republicanism, or politics. But . . . at one stage, we were in a big office in Mountjoy Square . . . and . . . we needed something to put on . . . the bare walls, and I had a lot of tea-towels from around the world . . . so I brought them in and pinned them up, and one of them had a picture of Churchill on it, and she objected!

A 65-year-old Protestant from Dublin's city centre described her work experience and gave an instance of the involvement of the clergy in finding suitable employment for parishioners which demonstrates the difference between her generation's experience of the Protestant network and that of the younger interviewee who did not know of its existence. In her first job,

> practically all the . . . office staff . . . was Protestant, but the packers . . . were Roman Catholic. . . . I don't know of any Protestant that worked in the packing when I was there. I was there for five-and-a-half years. . . . [Then] I didn't think I was getting on . . . [and] the accounting machine was coming in . . . and . . . I wanted to learn it. So, I was in the book-keeper's office, I was a cashier. There was four men in the book-keeping, all with big ledgers, I used to help them now and again, so . . . I looked out for another job. . . . I asked Canon Kerr . . . the rector . . . I heard that he was very good for getting jobs and I just asked him one day would he know of any jobs going, so he said he'd have a look out for me. In the meantime, I was answering ads myself. So, I got this job in . . . Baggot Street. . . . [Then] . . . Canon Kerr said . . . Oh, by the way, there's a job going in . . . [a Protestant firm]. Will you make arrangements for to go out for an

interview? . . . So I thought that that was better. . . . And I was there for nine-and-a-half years, working on machines. But it wasn't NCR, it was Burrows, and they were dreadful old machines, always, always breaking down. . . . And we were always working overtime. . . . And I got kind-of fed up with it. . . . [T]here was a mixture of Protestant and Catholic there. . . . Even in the office, there was. The whole place was, there was a good mixture. . . . [Then] I saw an ad in I think it was the Evening Herald . . . [for a job in a Protestant firm] In Dawson Street. . . . I really wanted to work in town again. . . . I got that job, and it was great. We were just facing the Mansion House and we were seeing all the activities going on. . . . I was there for about nine-and-a-half years, and I suppose I would be still there only for they went into liquidation.

The last two extracts confirm confessional integration as well as good relationships in the workplace for some, at any rate, in Dublin.

In at least one area of the provinces, similar conditions applied: a 51-year-old Protestant from a small midland village described the process by which she was 'vetted' for a job. She heard that a Protestant shopkeeper in a nearby town was looking for staff, and

I went in. I was only sixteen at the time. And [I] applied for the job. . . . And seemingly he did some checking on my background, I found out later, to know who I was and where I was from and all that. Now, I don't know whether I was Church of Ireland that I got the job . . . it turned out . . . he had half employed Church of Ireland and half employed Catholic. . . . There was two men now, they were Church of Ireland, they were in the Men's department. And I was in the Shoe department with George S, he was Church of Ireland as well, and then in . . . Ladies Wear . . . the other section, and Underwear . . . there was all Catholics, you know, he had employed there, so I mean there was no discrimination as such. But . . . I heard he did a bit of background checking to know who I was. Well, I suppose in those days they did check your kind of pedigree, or whatever. Who you were, and where you were from and . . . I suppose it was easy to find out, you were in a close community like that, anyway. And of course he said to me: where do you come from? . . . [S]o all he's to do is lift the phone. His clergyman . . . would ring, I suppose. I suppose that's the way they would find out. I don't know if that was how I got the job or not.

The evidence demonstrates not only operations of the Protestant network, but also shows that, even in the 1940s, there was a degree of mixing of confessions in the workplace, albeit with a rigid class distinction in force in respect of the division between office and shop-floor workers in the earlier years in the Dublin example. Moreover, they confirm Bowen's findings that few Protestants were employed by Catholic firms, that working-class Protestants often worked alongside Catholics and that segregation was often an internal matter of Protestant office workers, Catholic labourers and a Protestant managerial level in Protestant firms.[71] It also appears that not only the working-class but also the lower middle-class employees were likely to be integrated in the city firms. However, by the 1970s at least, there was an even-handedness at work that belies the myth that all Protestant employers *always* discriminated against Catholics. Of course, there was more than a desire to be seen to be fair involved: firstly, there were simply not enough Protestants to fill all the vacancies in Protestant firms, and, secondly, after the mid-1940s, it became a commercial tactic when it was realised that employing Catholics might be a way of attracting Catholic custom.[72]

A 59-year-old working-class Dublin Protestant, the daughter of the Guinness's lorry driver, worked in a large Protestant-owned confectionery firm. She 'never noticed' any discrimination in the workplace until she experienced the silencing effect surrounding the irruption of sectarian violence in the North in 1969:

> You'd hear people coming in and saying . . . Oh, did you see what happened yesterday? I never used to open me mouth, I never gave an opinion, because I felt it was not worth it . . . I felt it was better not to . . . cause problems!

The evidence of another working-class city-centre Protestant in her seventies, whose father was an employee of a famous O'Connell Street Protestant grocery firm, demonstrated another arm of the Protestant network, family connection:

> Mam got me a job then . . . where she used to work [in a distillery]. And I was there for 23 years. . . . I was in the factory. . . . We done everything by hand when I went in first, and, of course, then . . . worked more to machinery, but I liked it there. . . . [I]t was [confessionally] mixed, even then.. . . I got on all right [with everyone].

Another lower-middle-class Protestant, aged 77, found a good job through family connection and the Protestant network:

I got a very good job. It was in Francis Street. . . . .They were tobacconists, manufacturers.. . . . I was there for a number of years, and the salary was very good there. I got £4. 10s. 0d. with 2oz of Bendigo plug tobacco as a perk! And my father was thrilled to bits! . . . When I brought this home. And I didn't go in until ten. I came home, left there at half-twelve, I didn't have to go back until half-two, and finished at four. . . . I think my father used influence to get me this job. . . . That was important, influence.

Q. [T]hat would have been the Protestant network?

A. I reckon.

However, in a different workplace later in her career – which, atypically, continued up to retirement age although she married and had children – she found out that she had unwittingly bested the system and avoided discrimination:

One of the head men, on his leaving the company, retiring, I was at the reception with him, and he said to me, casually: we never knew you were a Protestant. And I turned and said: would it really have mattered? Did I ever do anything wrong? Oh, no, no, no! I said: did it really matter? He hesitated, now, but we'd always got on alright. But they didn't employ, I gathered, Protestants. I don't know why they didn't find out. . . . I handed in references, but obviously Howth Road School and Norwil College didn't identify me.

An 81-year-old Protestant who worked nearly all his life for Protestant firms had miserable experience of them as employers. He is quoted at length because, in one lifetime, it gives insight into the long work history of a Protestant lower middle-class Dubliner as well as demonstrating that being a Protestant emphatically did not gain him preferential treatment from Protestant employers:

I worked for Protestant firms. . . . I left school at fourteen-and-a-half, and I worked in this hardware [store] . . . [in] Aungier Street. . . . [T]he boss man . . . wasn't . . . a very nice man because . . . I used to have to cycle in to work . . . and he used to stand there with his pocket watch at the porch when you'd go in, and he'd say, say: what time is it? . . . [W]hat time am I paying you from? . . . he was a very strict man. . . . [*Interjection from his wife*: What was worse for you . . . was you were serving your time, and you'd a five year apprenticeship, and on the fourth year, he said: I won't be able to afford you on the fifth year.] . . . Because . . . you were coming on more money . . . when you finished your apprenticeship. . . . But you couldn't leave [a job if you didn't like it]. . . . Because if you left, and they rang up your employer and he said he had a job here for him but he left, you'd be stopped six weeks on the labour exchange. . . . [And] you wouldn't get a reference. Your reference was your certificate into another job. . . . I was out of work for the six months. . . . And then I went into a firm . . . a wholesale jewellers, and I went in there when I was nineteen. . . . And I worked there for thirty-one-and-a-half years. . . . when I left, I didn't get my last month's wages . . . and they went into voluntary liquidation about two years after that. And at that particular time, a firm that went into voluntary liquidation could take the pension scheme in with the liquidation. . . . So I lost my pension. [*Interjection from his wife*: Worse still . . . was that every time you went for an increase, he said: but sure I'm paying your pension!] [T]hen I went into K's of Westmoreland Street . . . I was redundant there. . . . [T]hen I had to go into [security]. I was fifty-two years of age at that time. . . . I was in [security] for two-and-a-half years. . . . And then I left there and I went in to S.F. They made all the copper fittings for pipes and everything like that, you know, and they were the best firm I ever worked for. . . . I began to see good money, like, you know. And happy times. . . . Every year, for about five years or six years, I went up to a Christmas party . . . and they gave you a full . . . dinner . . . and then they gave you a cheque for about £40, £50. . . . That was the best firm I ever worked for . . . [*Interjection from his wife*: It was a Catholic firm.]

In the main, both sides claimed that relationships in the workplace were generally harmonious, although this was likely to have been as a result of the avoidance of controversial matters, particularly by Protestants with their custom of keeping below the parapet, rather than because of the absence of potential areas of controversy. Moreover, as the polarisation that surrounded independence faded and as economic necessities became more pressing, class was seen to be a more significant factor than confession in predicating the treatment meted out to employees, in that working-class people of both confessions were, for too long, at the mercy of harsh employers – or the whim of unjust ones.

Overall, there is no difficulty in comprehending where the content of the emotional legacy on economic and employment tensions comes from. But, by the time the state came into being, Protestant domination of the economy was giving way to increased Catholic participation and growing control, and, by the middle of the twentieth century, Catholics had ceased to be dominated by Protestants in any sphere. There had been Protestant domination, and there was injustice, but this was followed, for a time, by discrimination by Catholics as radical changes in the balance between the communities did away with Protestant advantage.

The oral evidence shows that marginalisation of Protestants is an extant phenomenon in the workplace, whether public sector or private. It does not have a material effect in that they are not in danger of losing their jobs or missing out on promotion because of their confession, but their difference is seized upon and made apparent in a manner that reproduces alienation. At the least, it becomes, quite simply, tedious. Furthermore, many Protestants will identify with the tactic employed by the woman who, after a while, began to say she was doing certain things *because* she was Protestant in order to forestall teasing. Where it occurs, such baiting is symptomatic of Protestant exclusion from the majority's construction of Irishness. First of all, it marginalises them in a manner that prevents them from feeling part of the group, whether as a co-worker or, by extension, as citizens of the state and as members of the nation. Secondly, it reinforces the self-protective tactics caused by internalisation of that alienation. Protestants are singled out in the course of the daily round because of their confession and this contributes in no small way to their alienation from the rest of Irish society at a metaphysical level. Even though some did not appear to be adversely affected by it, nevertheless their marginal status in relation to the majority community is still persistently paraded and brought to consciousness, which has been shown to have a negative effect on at least some of the interviewees.

Finally, an anecdote told by a young Catholic recalled a conversation with a Protestant friend she had known from early childhood. The Protestant

> went for a job . . . with Fás, counselling long-term unemployed men on the north side of Cork city, and I remember . . . both roaring laughing and her saying . . . the one thing she was not going to say in the interview was that she was the daughter of a large Protestant farmer from just outside Cork city, because she didn't feel this would really qualify her at all for . . . the job.

She knew her place in the pecking order.

CHAPTER SEVEN

Protestants and Irishness

In the early decades of the state as it evolved after independence, Protestants and Catholics, already separated by historical confessional, ethnic and cultural differences, became even more estranged, with inescapable consequences. The longevity and subtle depth of the gulfs that separated them sustained the resultant tensions, despite the assertions of those who did not want to admit to their continuing presence. And that the problem is extant is attested to not only by the oral testimony collected for this study, but also by the findings of the recent study that found that children reflect attitudes and values from the society that surrounds them when forming their sense of identity. It demonstrated that, even as recently as 2006, 'assertions of Irish identity may revolve around being white, Catholic and part of the settled community. Minority ethnic groups, such as Travellers, Jews or black Irish are often considered outside this norm', and it also found a distinct 'anti-English bias, with . . . children who had returned from England, or who had parents who were English, . . . singled out for their difference, manifest primarily in their accents'. Indeed, one child was quoted as saying that a classmate was called an 'English bastard' because of his accent.[1] This indicates that, despite progressive lessening of the degree of segregation from the late 1960s onwards, the divisive components in Irish identity construction continue and the oral evidence has shown how they can surface in 'outcroppings'. What is also clear is that these findings do not carry a positive message for multicultural Ireland.

From early on, Protestant settlers developed a distinct Irish identity for themselves despite their allegiance to the British crown. After independence, whilst always adhering to a strict code of civil rectitude as far as loyalty to the new state was concerned, the emotional attachment to empire gradually faded. On the cultural front, their identification with their 'Anglo' cultural roots did not dissipate altogether, and this continued to pose some problems, not least for themselves. On the one hand, they were unable to rely on their 'Anglo' background in the face of ongoing general confusion over the differences between political, cultural and ethnic identity, particularly in an environment where anything Protestant was 'Anglo' and 'Anglo' was automatically perceived as anti-Irish. On the other, they obviously could not claim with any validity the alternative in the Irish context, that is to say, an alignment to Gaelic roots as defined by the majority. This ambiguous locus did not stop them, however, eventually becoming conversant with Irish history, language and culture through exposure to the state educational curriculum. Young Protestants in the new state studied the history and the language of their nation, and incorporated new aspects of 'Irishness' into their Protestant construction of national identity. And, as far as the language and government policy on its teaching were concerned, they worked out an accommodation to it to at least as much a degree as many Catholics. However, shifts in Protestant attitude and self-image seem to have remained invisible. The *force majeure* inherent in the accretion of power to Catholic religious and political interests allied to the sheer size of the community made it possible for the majority's construction of Irish national identity as Catholic/nationalist, with the addition of the foregrounding, even if at a iconic level, of the national language, to remain dominant. Vitally, it also enabled identification of this construction with the ethos of the state.

A middle-aged Catholic from the west epitomised exclusionary assumptions when, having been asked what he thought about Protestants' place in the category of Irishness, he said: 'I hadn't given it too much thought! Because there are not many Protestants around.' He went on to give a stock definition of Irishness from a Catholic point of view – as well as, incidentally, a description of himself – when, having said he would find it very difficult to sum up Irishness in one sentence, he went on:

> [W]hat makes us Irish I suppose is the religion . . . primarily, and . . . the music. . . . The language. They're the things . . . And that that you're born and reared here! . . . [So that] You look like the rest of them, somewhat.

His placing of Catholicism in a central position was automatic, and adherence to 'Gaelic', or traditional, culture in the form of music and the language as necessary components was laden with significance, because stereotypical views of Protestants see them as universally hostile to the Irish language, to Irish traditional music, and to 'Gaelic' sports. He continued, changing from the inclusive 'us' to the more distancing 'you': 'And that you're born and reared here! . . . [So that] You look like the rest of them, somewhat.' When his words were considered in the context of the interview as a whole, the apparent retreat from the dominant construction conveyed in the change of person to 'you' did not, in fact, include Protestants, even though being born in the country had been offered as an 'including' component of Irishness. Also, for him, looking 'like the rest of them' implied a belief that there are 'national' physical attributes which distinguish Irish Catholics from others. All these components were founded in an unconscious reliance on an origin myth[2] attributing common 'Gaelic' ancestry to the truly Irish person. Accordingly, Protestants – and any other minority – can only remain excluded.

However, it was also possible to think of Irish identity outside the usual confines, and an original, intriguing and non-sectarian conceptualisation of Irishness was provided by a 60-year-old Catholic brought up in the midlands:

> [I]t'd be like a green cabbage. . . . With all the layers of it!. . . I actually thought at one stage . . . of maybe doing a painting . . . whereby you would have the different typescripts . . . the Roman and the Celtic and the Ogham . . . superimposed one over the other . . . as far back as you can go in history, and the more archaeology develops . . . the more clear you can see the underlying ones.

Across the confessional board, some of the answers to the 'Irishness' question relied on stereotypes, in that interviewees had never thought about what it meant to be Irish or questioned their Irishness: they *were* Irish, and that fact did not require analysis. The following two quotations typify this approach. A Protestant from the rural south-west said:

> I suppose you just feel Irish . . . if you've been born in Ireland, and you've lived in Ireland, your family's all Irish . . . then you're Irish. . . . I'm as Irish as they come.

A 69-year-old Catholic farmer from the west echoed her views:

> [W]hat makes them Irish? . . . I don't think I think, I don't think about it, really . . . I just . . . I am. I'm part of it. I'm there, but . . . it's not something that I think about, or not something that I'd say: well, I have to be more or, or less of, it doesn't matter to me.

For others, there was an acceptance of stereotypes as definitive and a trite list of what are usually termed characteristics would follow. 'Friendly', 'welcoming', 'easy-going', were the most usual, the capacity for 'craic' another, and so on. The first three were equally likely to be chosen by either confession as being something identified with being Irish, so there was no impediment to Protestants claiming them, which was consistent with their own view that they do possess an authentic Irish identity. The 'craic', however, signifier of a 'Celtic' type of fun, was another matter – for older Protestants, anyway: they might consider that they are capable of enjoying themselves and having fun, but they were unlikely to call it 'craic'. Expressions of pride in Irishness were present in most of the contributions across confession, class and generation. It seemed to be necessary to articulate it, often in a manner that implied insecurity, as if there was an expectation that the claim might be questioned.

The problems surrounding Irishness provoked other emotions as well: an elderly Dublin Protestant became agitated when trying to assemble her thoughts. Perhaps stimulated by her distress, she then covered most of the confessional and ethnic content of the category for Protestants, certainly for those of middle age and upwards. Her reply also illustrated most aptly the marginalisation of Protestants:

> [B]eing Irish, what would I say? I don't know . . . it would be restricted, I think. . . . I'm Irish. I am Irish, but I'm not Irish to the extent where I'd have to talk about the troubled times, and all the things that went on in those olden days, while I'm Irish. I know I'm Irish. But I'm not Roman Catholic Irish. I, I can't describe that any more than that. . . . [We] never felt really Irish. Never really felt a hundred per cent Irish. We're on the outside looking in . . . at the people. At Ireland. . . . . You feel English. I don't know why you feel English, because you're Protestant. . . . I've heard people say: . . . you speak like that, and you're Irish, and you're not English? . . . [I]f you're in a bus . . . they'd say to you: Oh, you were at Mass today . . . they take it for granted that you are one of them.

Her words 'We're on the outside looking in . . . at the people. At Ireland', bear repeating for the way in which they capture the emotion surrounding feelings of marginalisation. They disclose the isolation at the heart of, in this case, Protestant exclusion, but they could indicate 'outsider' experience in other contexts. It is also interesting that, to begin with, she used the emphatic first person – 'I'm Irish. I am Irish', and then, later, having alluded to the perceived effects of not being 'Roman Catholic Irish', she changed the mode of expression and continued: 'You feel English'.

For the oldest Protestants in the cohort of interviewees, the question of nationality was, on the face of it, simple: before independence, politically and regardless of confession, all the Irish were British. One 90-year-old Protestant said that her parents' loyalties had lain

> definitely with England. My mother always kept a very large, a very large print of a huge photograph of the Royal family pinned on the wall over the fireplace in our kitchen, and it was King George V and Queen Mary and their huge family.

For her, like most Protestants at that time, it can be assumed that British allegiance did not discomfit them because of their identification with British culture[3] – even if the community was not all unionist politically speaking. The fact of Protestants' British nationality did not, however, mean they did not think of themselves as Irish. Retiring back to the south-west after a career and marriage in England, she demonstrated a strong identification with 'Irishness', despite her nationality at birth and long residence in England, when she said:

> [A]ctually, I was always considered British [but] I feel Irish . . . my birth is registered at Somerset House . . . because we were under British rule . . . my father and mother, even though their forebears came from . . . [Scotland and England] . . . were born and bred here.

None of the Catholic interviewees of her generation referred specifically to having been born British. One 88-year-old gave his nationality as Irish and ascribed his parents' loyalties as being 'on the Irish side . . . when the British ruled here', but making no specific mention of the automatic fact of British citizenship before independence.

A 90-year-old Protestant from the midlands was also quite sure of her national identity:

A. Oh, Irish.
Q. Even with your, your Scottish mother in the mix?
A. No . . . that didn't make any difference . . .
Q. And being born in 1914?
A. I was born here, and I was brought up here, and my surroundings were Irish.

A poignant exception to the generality on this point was the evidence of an 85-year-old Protestant, daughter of a Church of Ireland rector and an English mother whose early childhood was both isolated and segregated from neighbouring Catholics. Illustrating the alienation of her class and background as well as the lifelong effects of her immediate familial circumstances, she said, in response to the question about nationality:

> I'm a bad person to ask that question, because . . . I always count myself as being stateless, with my English mother and my Irish father, and he couldn't have been more Irish. She couldn't have been more English. And I'm trapped in the middle, and I don't actually know what an Irish person is. I honestly don't.

A Protestant, who said he understood and tolerated the use of the term 'West Brit', although he would not self-designate as one, recognised that the facts of his birth and upbringing – son of a rector, educated at preparatory and public schools modelled on the British template even though in the state – might put him in the category in the eyes of others. However, this did not inhibit his claim to Irishness. As a boy in the post-Second World War years, he said 'I didn't feel English, but I certainly had sympathetic feelings towards England', but he now feels 'thoroughly, thoroughly Irish', and 'I want to live in this country, I have worked in this country . . . this is my country, and I feel thoroughly Irish. I don't play hurling . . . but then I don't play soccer, either'. It is interesting that he used sport to illustrate how he envisions his claim to Irishness – and intentionally subverted a stereotype in so doing.

Another 66-year-old Protestant brought up on a midlands farm said:

> I'm Irish, with a bit of English . . . my mother [was] English. . . . We were . . . taught we were privileged in having been able to have an education and a nice house, and because of that we were expected to behave in an exemplary manner. . . . Unfortunately, because of my voice, some [people generally] perceive me . . . [as] well-to-do English . . . some Protestants will perceive me as being much more well-off than I am because of the accent. . . . [O]ne can actually have just as bad snobbery from Protestants as Catholics nowadays.

Thus she constructed her Irishness with partial reliance on her ethnic background. Also, she consciously underlined two of the main stereotypical views of southern Protestants: 'Anglo' accent and perceptions of wealth and privilege.

An elderly rural Protestant said Irishness was 'loving your country. Doing what you can . . . for your country. I suppose, having been born and bred . . . a feeling of belonging.' When asked what was her nationality – 'Irish' – she had replied in a very emphatic manner, and confirmed that she felt absolutely secure in her Irishness, despite her confession. Then she went on:

[A]t boarding school in Dublin, I was rather a bit of a rebel, I think, as Irishness went, and I can remember my history teacher looking at me aghast, that I was so Irish! . . . I was [very much a nationalist] at that stage. I've calmed down a bit since then!

A 67-year-old Protestant from Dublin was another who adverted to her 'mixed' ethnicity. Having said: 'I don't really know . . . what [Irishness] really means at all', she nevertheless went on to claim Irish nationality without equivocation before going on: 'But, of course, I'm a quarter English . . . if you think about it . . . because Granny was totally English on my father's side', then introduced an interesting instance of being perceived as 'different'. When her marriage broke down

somebody . . . said, oh, but I thought as you were a Protestant you could get a divorce! . . . [I]t was horrifying to me that people felt the law of the land did not affect me because I was of the minority religion. I couldn't believe it.

A 65-year-old Protestant from the west placed rectitude in civic matters in the centre of Irishness and he also adverted to obedience to the laws of the state:

I think your Irishness, it's something you're tied to, that you're tied to it. . . . That you were born here, and that you live here and that you do your public duty . . . live as a law-abiding citizen and that you . . . support those people who are democratically elected, although it has a contradiction in itself, that . . . you may be supporting the people that you didn't elect.

A 60-year-old man, from what is now a west Dublin suburban area but which used to be a village on the outskirts of the city, was born into the Catholic faith, but, after a period of withdrawal from, and antipathy both to Catholicism and religion in any form, eventually converted to Anglicanism. He was very clear on the issue of nationality: 'I'm Irish. I have Canadian citizenship. . . . That's not to be confused with the passport, now! . . . What I feel inside? . . . I'm Irish!' Asked what he thought made up Irishness, he said:

[I]f you're born here, you're Irish. If your parents are Irish, and even if you were not born here, you might consider yourself Irish! It's very complex!. . . I think really the essence of Irishness is to be got from growing up in this society . . . I have a niece and a nephew . . . who grew up in London . . . to me they are not really Irish, because they grew up in that culture . . . any little flavour of Irishness in them . . . they would have got it from their parents. . . . I really think you have to grow up in Ireland . . . to understand . . . the nuances . . . of Irish society . . . the good, the bad and the ugly, all of it!

A 65-year-old Protestant born and raised in the inner city of Dublin said she considered herself to be Irish, and gave as the first requisite for Irishness that 'you're an Irish citizen', and then, in response to the question: have you always lived in Ireland? said: 'Yes, except the year I've lived in Northern Ireland'. She was also one of the few who said she had never felt that she was considered not truly Irish by Catholics. Her perceptions of what constituted 'Ireland' contrasted directly with those of a 56-year-old Protestant who went to boarding school in the North and who said 'I would have said to you that I never lived out of Ireland. I didn't think that going across the border to school was out of Ireland.'

A 59-year-old Dublin Protestant demonstrated that she had thoroughly internalised her father's attitude – that of doing nothing that would disturb the peace with Catholic neighbours – and incorporated it into her concept of Irishness when she said:

[I]t's the country you were born in, and you have to kind-of just remember that you're Irish, and you do what's in the state, you know, and try and live as good a life as you can, and without antagonising other people.

Responding to an invitation to expand on whether she thought Catholics considered Protestants 'really' Irish, she related the following incident, which she said had happened in approximately 1994:

I was in a bus one day . . . talking to a friend of mine. And this woman behind said: Oh, all these Protestant people should be all up in the North. They shouldn't be down here. They've no right to be down here. . . . They've no right to be down here, that this is a Catholic state and should only be for Catholics.

She then recorded how her friend expressed a strongly felt perception that Protestants were undervalued and, by implication, excluded, in today's Ireland:

[She said: 'W]e don't count down here. We're nobody. If you go to the Pro Cathedral and there's anything on, you'll see loads of police. And if we've anything on at the [city-centre] church, you're lucky if you get one, maybe two.'

A 44-year-old Protestant thought that things were changing in respect of Irishness with the advent of a multicultural Ireland, but during the mid-1980s when working in a Catholic-dominated environment she

had people assume that I've a lot of relations in England. Or that I should go home . . . where did your people come from? . . . And none of my relations came from England. Well, maybe they did, about 1600 or something, back before we can trace.

A middle-aged Protestant who can trace his descent from a 'planter' was quoted on how he was taught by his parents that he was Irish, but that Irishness had been 'hijacked by our neighbours'. Consequently – and ambiguously, given that he was taught he was Irish – he saw his national identity as implicitly defined in opposition to that of those 'neighbours', especially after he had gone to school in England. However,

later in my life . . . Irishness became a feature of . . . who I was and what I was doing . . . I've always [carried an Irish passport.]. . . . [I'm] Irish. By virtue of the passport, if nothing else. . . . There's a citizenship element to it . . . if people want a definite answer to something, well, one has to point to a definite piece of paper or a definite record, and in my case it's the Irish passport that defines me when I travel.

A Protestant had highly developed insights into different facets of her identities. From an inter-church family, she identified strongly with the Church of Ireland part of her heritage whilst claiming aspects of Irishness more usually perceived as attaching to a Catholic/nationalist construction. She contracted an inter-church marriage, and the children were baptised into the Church of Ireland. However, they were given the Irish form of their names 'so that they can get away with hiding their Protestantism in years to come!' Citing examples of exclusionary behaviour she experienced in different contexts, she was very angry about how she thought she had been perceived:

[W]hen people say that I don't have an Irish accent, that really irritates me, because I would admit that I don't have a specifically Cork or Dublin accent, but I most emphatically have got an Irish accent. Or when it's suggested that being Protestant, or non-Catholic, makes me less Irish. . . . It gets to me, it really does. . . . I suppose [I] enjoy in some ways being a contradiction insofar as I can speak Irish and that my maiden name is Irish, but that I'm Church of Ireland. . . . I very much see that the two can go hand in hand, and it galls me, it pains me that other people most emphatically don't see it that way.

Her reactions might be construed as hypersensitivity by a confident and insensitive majority. However, they indicated areas of real distress, and the degree of feeling apparent in her interview resonates with that of other Protestants, most notably the elderly Dublin Protestant who became upset when talking about Irishness and with that of the young interviewee who spoke of her irritation at the Jaffa cake jibe.

A 29-year-old Protestant from the west coast was sure of her own national identity and has constructed a satisfactory 'Irishness' for herself, even though she appeared to hold some mutually exclusive ideas and knew she did not fulfil several of the criteria regarded as fundamental to the dominant construction:

I would class myself as being Irish. . . . But I don't know many soldier songs . . . because I suppose of the nature of my upbringing. . . . I probably know more about English history and government and . . . the royals and that kind of thing, than . . . my contemporaries. . . . And, maybe somebody would class that as being less Irish and more of a royalist, and a unionist . . . definitely a Protestant. . . . [W]hat is Irishness? I really don't know . . . the land of a thousand welcomes . . . freedom to . . . call in. . . . What is Irishness? . . . [I]t's the Irish language native to this country . . . if you're a gaeilgeóir . . . that makes you more Irish. But I don't know what makes one person more Irish than another . . . the usual things . . . would be music and language. . . . I don't think that supporting a particular political party, having leanings towards nationalism . . . makes you any more Irish than the next man. If you don't support a united Ireland, it doesn't make you a royalist. I think it makes you maybe more . . . logical.

Taking up her point on being an Irish native speaker, she exhibited a degree of confusion in allocating an added status to native speakers of Irish but then said she did not know what makes one person more Irish than another. However, she also said of herself that 'I'm not brilliant at it, but I watch TG4 [TV channel in Irish]', so she attached both a personal and a generalised significance to knowledge of the language as part of an authentic Irish identity.

For the older members of the Protestant community, the issue of the Irish language can be epitomised in the account of an 82-year-old Protestant. When asked what the creation of the new state had meant to her, she said:

> I think the biggest problem was with . . . my generation and the Irish. . . . Having to pass Irish to pass exams. And then, once you did that, unless you were in a specific job that needed Irish, you never used it again. So what was the point? And we all resented that very much. And it was a major problem.

For her, problems arising from the language policy were pragmatic rather than ideological and did not influence how she constructed her identity. When she was young and the state was new, although her father was English and her mother's family would have been what she called 'royalists', 'politics really weren't discussed in the family'. However, she claimed and had no doubt about her national identity from young adulthood:

> I am definitely a republican now . . . have been for years . . . I wouldn't go out and wave flags . . . but . . . I consider myself Irish, not English, and I have great sympathy with . . . the Irish.

In couching her views in those terms: feeling Irish, yet sympathising with 'the Irish' she appeared ambiguously to place herself both within and outside the category. Overall, however, she constructed an Irishness for herself which took account of her Protestantism as an active member of a city-centre parish, went further than the more usual 'nationalism with a small n' politically speaking, and did not include an ability to speak the Irish language as an integral component.

The following extract emphasises the extent of the problem of compulsory passes in Irish in the intermediate and leaving certificate examinations for older interviewees. An 85-year-old Protestant man from Dublin, capable of learning Latin, German and French and who went on to a successful career as an accountant, failed the leaving certificate because he did not pass Irish:

> They didn't give you a leaving certificate . . . if you failed in Irish . . . I did very well . . . I was amazed that I won so many prizes for different things . . . I did Latin, I did German, I did French.

Overall, however, there was by no means a universal rejection of Irish by Protestants, and where there was objection to the imposition of compulsory

Irish it was on practical, rather than ideological or cultural, grounds. The 60-year-old interviewee with dual Irish and Canadian nationality was quite clear on what he thought was the place of the Irish language in the construction of Irishness:

> I've come across enough people . . . who'd say: Unless you understand the Irish language, you're not Irish . . . I don't accept that at all . . . I and many, many people like me, were brought up in the English language. My parents were brought up in the English language. . . . Our introduction to the Irish language was that forced system in school, which I didn't like. It actually turned me against it . . . we are an English-speaking nation, and those who want to learn to speak Irish and use it for cultural reasons, for enjoyment . . . please, be my guests!

So far, it is clear that Protestants of all ages consider they have a claim to an Irish national identity, that they construct their Irishness with or without the Irish language as a component, and without needing to assert allegiance to anachronistic forms of nationalism – an issue clearly distinct from loyalty to the nation and the state – and without feeling that their confession disbars them. A Protestant businessman introduced an interesting concept of flexibility when he said: 'We [Protestants] as Irish . . . have the ability to slip in and out of Irishness in a way. I mean, I'm Irish, but I'm a West Brit, I'm an Anglo'. This view, and that of the younger Protestant who, although angered by exclusionary perceptions also enjoys 'being a contradiction', underlines the infinitely flexible nature of the construction of identity in general. It also goes towards refuting Philip Roth's assertion that identity labels have nothing to do with experience by demonstrating that, just as identity colours experience, experience shapes identity. People adapt.

The 47-year-old Catholic, a teacher, already quoted on the cocooning of Catholics, gave a very full list of the components she thought went into being Irish, including a sense of the connection to the physical quality of the land:

> [T]he connection that Irish people have with Irish people is different to the connection that other people, other cultures, would have. So, to my mind, being Irish has nothing to do with politics, it has to do with where your space is, what you feel about the land around you, what you feel about the culture that's part of us. . . . [C]ulture is changing all the time, and it's not culture . . . unless it's growing . . . it's a living thing. And I suppose the language would possibly, the language definitely has a part of it, because our phrases and sayings that

have transferred over to the English language are ours because they're direct translations from the Irish . . . being Irish . . . is having a good sense of humour and being able to connect with people very quickly. . . . [M]y view of Irishness would be that kind of a hospitality where you're curious about other people and you're open to them, you welcome them in, you have this grá [love] for things Irish. . . . I would love to go away for a year and see what it is I would miss.

Apart from her ideas on the uniqueness of the personal qualities attaching to the category, three things are immediately obvious: firstly, the Irish language was important in her construction of Irishness. Secondly, despite her views on 'culture', she still saw stereotyped characteristics as central to the category as a whole. Thirdly, she did not expressly link confession into identity. However, after further questioning, she took some time to work around to speaking about this aspect, and then was reluctant to accept the notion of Protestant exclusion. Eventually, she conceded that possibly 'Protestants are not [seen as] Irish' in the abstract but not in the particular, naming a neighbouring Protestant couple with whom she and her husband were very friendly. She was, in effect, either unwilling to acknowledge difference or being extremely sensitive about it, which might have been partly because of the confessional background of the interviewer, but also because her awareness of the problems involved in confessional difference had been raised as she had one Protestant in her confirmation class.

The evidence of a middle-aged suburban Dublin Catholic also identified strongly with the physical existence of Ireland, its 'presence'. In its awareness of and tolerance of difference, her testimony stands out from, and is different from, the mainstream. The first criterion, however, birth in Ireland, was cited by most of the Catholics interviewed, and would at face value appear to include Protestants in the nation, but on further examination does not do so: a clear demonstration of how tenets of the emotional legacy do not stand up to analysis. To her, Irishness is something intrinsic that she did not have to think about or to proclaim: it is, she said,

kind of an accident of birth. . . . You are . . . born into a country . . . I was born here, so I'm Irish. Now, I love being Irish . . . I love Ireland. . . . I love the landmass of Ireland. I [have] great affinity with Irish people . . . it's a difficult question to answer . . . I have a brother . . . who's very . . . 'I'm Irish', and he lives in Australia, and I said: For God's sake, you go on with so much nonsense, I'm Irish, and I live in Ireland . . . and I feel I don't have to keep saying it.

It is worth noting that she had never lived abroad, and so had not experienced the intensification of feelings, positive or negative, surrounding national identity that can result from adjusting to a different culture and finding that it throws one's own identity open for examination. To stay with this point about intensified feelings about national identity in emigrants, a negative example was given by a 38-year-old Catholic. Having said she was 'very wary' of entering into discussions to do with Irishness because it was 'such a minefield', she went on to illustrate the ambiguity and confusion that so often surrounds it. She has

> two siblings who left in the '80s and have a real chip on their shoulders about Ireland and are always giving out about Ireland. And yet they're going on about being Irish. You know, this really pisses me off. . . . That they'll always knock Ireland. . . . But when they're out of Ireland, they're Irish, and they wear the little T-shirts with shamrocks.

Returning to the evidence of the Dublin Catholic, she was quite clear that confession should have no part in Irishness:

> It shouldn't matter what religion anyone is . . . if you're living here, if you're Irish, you're Irish. It doesn't matter whether you're Catholic, Protestant, Jew, atheist, Muslim, whatever.

Her perceptions about the *inclusive* nature of Irishness appear to stem from her family background and her early surroundings, and she has carried them on into adult life. She associated freely with Protestants who lived near her family while she was growing up. And this freedom of association continued despite strictures from the nuns at her first school about 'not mixing . . . with people of . . . a different religion'.

A 75-year-old rural south-western Catholic, another of the few who used the distancing third person when speaking about this topic, said that 'Irishness' brought to mind

> Irish culture? And Irish games. And [an] Irish attitude to life. . . . They feel Irish themselves, they want to be Irish. They feel if they're not Irish, or if they're taken as not Irish, they're being deprived of something. . . . [W]hat makes an Irish person what he or she is, is their culture, the way they look at themselves and they look at their country, and they way they look at things generally, and what they feel is part of them and what they feel is not part of them.

His observation on deprivation identifies the element of alienation. He also said that he thought that Protestants who live in the state now 'want to live here and they certainly don't want to be excluded', with an implication that in the early days after independence even when Protestants elected to stay on they would have preferred not to live under the new order.

A 40-year-old Catholic from the west listed what she thought were seen as the confessional and political components of the category from a Catholic and republican point of view when she defined Irishness as

> generally . . . Catholic, for starters . . . and I suppose nationalist . . . from the old IRA style . . . way back. That, all Ireland should be Ireland . . . when I think of Ireland, I always think of the whole of Ireland . . . Irish versus English. That's a big part of our green . . . upbringing as well . . . I'd be proud to be Irish.

A 91-year-old Catholic, brought up in south Dublin city and a keen member of the Gaelic League in her youth, had an interesting perception on what did *not* comprise Irishness in the early days of the twentieth century. Naturally, given her interest in it, she thought the Irish language was an essential component, and she went on to say her mother, from Galway, spoke a little Irish, but

> my father had no Irish, he was from Dun Laoghaire and Glasthule, and his family were very . . . in Irish you'd call them 'shónins'! They weren't Irish by any means! . . . The Dun Laoghaire people are very near England, and a lot of to-ing and fro-ing there between Ireland and England and they had no Irish traditions.

So, despite his Catholicism and his political and cultural nationalism, her father could not unambiguously qualify on the Irishness front because of his proximity to the perceived taint of Englishness.

A 70-year-old Catholic retired primary principal brought up in an Irish-speaking family on the west coast said:

> Irishness . . . Well, first of all there's . . . the physical side of being born in this island. Born in Ireland . . . anyone born in Ireland has a right to call themselves Irish . . . I'm not sure that I know where to go after that. . . . The mentality, the attitudes. . . . The environment, the background.

On whether or not there had been Protestant exclusion from Irishness, he said, somewhat reluctantly, for he, too, did not want to offend:

> In one sense, I'd be a bit surprised. . . . And then in another sense I wouldn't be, because . . . I'm trying to visualise that situation. . . . Ignorance is an awful thing. And people . . . are afraid of what they don't know. . . . [It makes for] Shallow nationalism, if you like.

'Shallow nationalism' would, he was implying, automatically operate to exclude Protestants.

The evidence of a young Catholic gave an interesting glimpse of how tensions surrounding the construction of national identity, Irishness and exclusion on ethnic grounds have affected her family over the generations. She spoke of her grandmother's experience and of the perpetuation of exclusion – because of the grandmother's perceived Englishness and despite her Catholicism – that also affected her daughters, one of whom was the interviewee's mother. The grandmother was born to an Irish Catholic father from a small coastal town in West Cork, and raised in the East End of London, where he had gone because of lack of work at home. She often came to Ireland on holiday to visit relatives, and married an Irish Catholic from her father's area. She did what she could to integrate into the community, even to the extent of trying to learn Irish, but was laughed at for her London accent and so gave up. This demonstrates a proprietary attitude to the language on the part of the community in which she was living: speaking Irish was a badge of 'Irishness' to which she had no entitlement because she was not *of* the community, not truly Irish. In this case, her religion and her ethnicity were not sufficient to overcome her cultural shortcomings, and her granddaughter said:

> I think she spent her entire life in West Cork feeling that she would never be accepted there, and that she would never be regarded as Irish, no matter what she tried to do. . . . [C]ertainly both her daughters, my mother and her sister, now live in England . . . [and] would say that . . . even now, they feel more accepted in England than they felt growing up. . . . . As daughters of an 'English' mother in . . . West Cork.

On Irishness from her own point of view, and in furtherance of the point of 'birth in Ireland' as a qualification for belonging, she commented that her generation's sense of themselves is very different from that of their parents:

[W]e have millions of Irish citizens all over the world. Some of them have never set foot in Ireland. . . . Irishness – it's a . . . very important layer of your identity. It's your sense of affiliation to this island. . . . And to . . . certain ideas. . . . And awareness . . . of certain traditions. . . . [W]hat makes us different? . . . it depends on . . . who you're comparing yourself to . . . the fact that we were a colony, I think, rather than a coloniser, makes us different . . . we have a sort-of sympathy with the underdog . . . we don't have the same kind of delusions of grandeur or authority that you come across if you're working in the EU. . . . [T]here is certainly . . . a healthy scepticism . . . of authority . . . a willingness to challenge rules . . . it's not unique, but it is distinctly Irish . . . we're a very talkative people. . . . Irish people are actually quite nosy . . . if you are a country with a tradition of emigration. You need to be curious . . . to suss things out fairly quickly, it's . . . a survival mechanism.

Thus she provided another list of characteristics tending towards the stereotypical, but which at the same time allowed for generational changes. She did not comment expressly on the confessional aspect of Irishness for herself and her coevals or upon Protestant exclusion, but did speak about having a Protestant friend whom she has known since childhood:

[W]e used to play together most weekends. . . . I went to a primary school in the city . . . she went to . . . the Church of Ireland School . . . when I would stay with them for weekends. . . . I would go to church with them. And [she] would come to Mass with us. So, we would have been very aware that there were differences between the two.
Q. [A]s two girls, did you ever talk about it?
A. Oh, often! Often. And we would now, still, as adults looking back. . . . We would kind-of laugh about [it] . . . we would now talk a bit about our experiences of prejudice.

A 22-year-old Catholic from a border county provided a novel view on the flexibility, amounting almost an *à la carte* quality, of national identity from the point of view of a member of the youngest tranche of interviewees, disagreeing with the point made by so many others that birth in Ireland was necessary:

I don't think you have to be born here. . . . I think it's where you feel at home . . . that defines it . . . if I feel at home in France, and I've lived there for twenty years, I could be French, I don't have to be Irish! But I probably would stay Irish!

On confessional difference, however, she instanced multiple occurrences she had observed. She said difference under this head did not matter for her, that she would not, for instance, let it influence her choice of marriage partner, and that she would like to raise any children she might have as Christian rather than either Catholic or Protestant. She was firm on the point that, inculcated mainly through segregated schooling, the confessional divide had been a constant presence in her life.

The significance attached to emblems of Irishness and the ambivalence of some claims to Irishness based on symbols like the harp and the shamrock was referred to by one Catholic, who said:

> [T]here is a tradition that the harp and shamrock . . . are part of our Irish heritage . . . the RUC . . . used a harp and [a] shamrock, and yet the strong nationalists . . . [wanted] all that to go. And I . . . said: Why would you want that to go? Surely . . . that's some of the basic symbolism? . . . Oh, yes: but there's a crown on it.

At a personal level, a 47-year-old English Protestant, who came to Ireland on holiday 26 years ago and stayed, said, not surprisingly when she went on to define nationality, that she considered herself British. This was despite what amounts to total immersion in Irishness stemming from long residence, marriage to an Irish Catholic and raising a family in the state. She said: 'I believe that you are what you grow up . . . [what] your tradition is', and she underlined this by declaring 'I wouldn't wear green on St Patrick's Day, because I don't feel I've got the right to wear green!'

A 22-year-old practising Catholic, born in the United Kingdom and raised in a west-Dublin suburb, initially gave a broad base to her definition of Irishness but questioned the iconic status of so-called 'national' symbols:

> 'Irishness' especially for me is something that is broad. . . . I know Irishness for a lot of people is you were born here [and] you grew up here, that's it, and that's not what it is for me at all. . . . I suppose it's belonging to a place and belonging to . . . a group of people . . . I was born in England, I don't feel English at all . . . if someone described me as English, I don't get offended, but I do question it. . . . I think from a certain point of view [Irish music, GAA are] evidence of being Irish, they're national games, they're national music. . . . I don't consider them as something . . . that would deem you to be Irish. . . . I've never been to Croke Park – shocking!

We have already considered the testimony of the 72-year-old Catholic from the west, who summed up the main stereotype held by Catholics about Protestants when she told of how she thought being Protestant meant being 'uppity'. By extension, she implied, carrying such an 'uppity' label, denoted principally by how one sounded, was the antithesis of Irishness. Such notions are current and not held only by Catholics, but also by Protestants about other Protestants, an example of the infinite capacities of the process of 'othering'.

Another example of internalised negative perceptions held by Protestants occurred in the testimony of the 31-year-old Catholic from a small village on the east coast engaged to marry a Protestant. She did not find Protestant feelings of exclusion difficult to credit. Attributing them to perceptions of ethnic difference and demonstrating how they come to be internalised, she said:

> It doesn't surprise me. No, I've heard often Protestants being . . . thought upon as English . . . [my fiancé's] grandfather might have been in the English army . . . [but my fiancé] says, like, 'But I'm not English!'. . . [H]e would have that stigma himself, as in maybe they were teased at school . . . he would often say, people think you're English because you're Protestant! [He was] born and reared down the road . . . his mammy's from Kildare . . . you can't get more Irish than that . . . can you?

Her use of the word 'stigma' is telling.

As we have seen, accent has come up more than once, usually to single out Protestants. However, another aural aspect surfaced in what a 75-year-old Catholic farmer from the western seaboard had to say. He had great difficulty in articulating his ideas on what constitutes Irishness until he thought of his six adult children, who have all spent considerable periods of time out of Ireland, and the fact that they 'have not a bit of an accent. You'd think that they never left here. And I think that is great! I think that is one Irish thing that I love.' He was indicating that they had not picked up English or American accents, and so had, according to his system of values, retained their allegiance to and connection with their true Irish roots.

The 38-year-old Catholic, whose emigrant siblings have ambiguous feelings about their Irishness, also spoke of her mother talking about a neighbouring family and demonstrated confirmation by reversal of the prevailing stereotype:

> [My mother] would be quite negative about some of her [rural] roots, and . . . the attitude of people . . . because of the whole Catholic/Protestant thing . . .

their neighbours are Protestants . . . but . . . they were poorer than them. Because the perception . . . is . . . that Protestants are always better off than Catholics. But they had the large family and the poor farm, too.

'Differentiating' views on Protestants and their relative prosperity were not limited to rural areas in the provinces. We have already considered the evidence of the 59-year-old Dublin Catholic who, in describing a poor Protestant family in the neighbourhood where she grew up who used margarine instead of butter, referred to three of the most often-rehearsed perennial myths about Protestants: that all Protestants were wealthy, that they personified a particular, confessionalised form of the work ethic, and that they had small families. She went on to say that when she was a child 'It never occurred to me to wonder about anybody's religion'. This would seem to indicate that she did not see Protestants as outsiders. However, taking her youthful views on them and how, using them, she pinpointed the three stereotypes of work ethic, poverty and family size, it is possible that, at that stage, she *did* see them through a different frame of reference when compared to the majority. This indicates that there was an unconscious – as opposed, of course, to any knowingly sectarian – and differentiating set of defining criteria that she applied to them. She also described how Irishness was not something she thought about until early adulthood, perhaps because she felt she was securely within its ambit:

I suppose I never . . . felt very Irish when I was in Ireland. It was only when I went abroad that I discovered that I was Irish. . . . [Now] I do feel that I am more Irish than somebody else of Chinese ancestry born in Clondalkin . . . . By virtue of the fact that my family has lived here for generations.

She referred to this statement again later in the interview when she mused on the concept of multicultural Ireland:

[H]aving said what I said to you about the Chinese from Clondalkin, I think we are going to have a very interesting country here . . . as a result of all this . . . immigration. And I think we could probably do with new blood . . . from all kinds of points of view.

She worked in London in the 1960s and so was able to relay an outside perspective on the confessionalised religious component of Irishness, the telling of which disclosed both her relationship with her religion at that stage of her life and further intricacies of the process of 'othering', illustrating as it does how groups discriminate *ad infinitum* against sub-groups. There was, she said,

> one English Catholic on the staff [who] said: Oh, my God, an Irish Catholic . . . now she'll be looking for time off to go to mass on holy days, and she probably want to say the angelus at twelve o'clock! . . . I just found it so funny . . . but in fact she was a much more observant Catholic than I was, which I think a lot of English Catholics are because they are in the minority there.

This incident indicates one of the ways in which minorities in general tend to behave, in that they adhere strictly to regulated norms of behaviour in the interests of survival, a tactic which we have seen was employed by the Protestant community in the early decades of the state.

Returning to the topic of multiculturalism, a Protestant underlined the marginalised position of Protestants in Ireland when musing on current conditions in the state:

> I think that the advent of multiculturalism in Ireland and the influx of people from other nationalities has made Protestants feel as if they're more, not as if they're more Irish, but has allowed them to be perceived to be part of the state in a more inclusive way. . . . [W]e're now seen as more similar.

Although there is a conflation of 'nation' with 'state' in her idea, she was driving towards the theory that multiculturalism permits the imagination of a nation inclusive of Protestants on the grounds that they are less 'other' than other immigrants. Although it is easy to comprehend how she arrives at this idea, it is somewhat problematical, because it envisages a hierarchy of rights to Irishness, and because it permits Protestants to enter the imagined nation only by default. From the evidence given by Catholics, in the majority of instances they were unaware that their identity-formation processes were excluding Protestants. If they were to exclude them consciously, it would entail operating from within an acknowledgement of residual confessional, ethnic and cultural difference as applied to uniquely to Protestants, and attitudes to multiculturalism, in their application to recent immigrants to Ireland from other cultures and faith streams, would not necessarily be affected by such perceptions.

The evidence of a Catholic-born 76-year-old retired teacher combined confessional difference and an aspect of 'Britishness' so that she saw continuing Protestant exclusion from Irishness as inevitable because of Anglicanism's

former established status in Ireland: 'Anglican Protestantism . . . unfortunately . . . it's a State religion and it represents in a huge way . . . the British state
. . . I see Anglicans as part of that system'. She tried to lessen the impact of such
an absolute exclusion when, in placing the Irish language squarely at the core of
Irishness alongside religion, she expressed her amazement at the part played by
nineteenth-century Protestants in the preservation of Irish, but she was
ultimately unable to detach Protestant interest in the language from their
outsider/oppressor status because she referred to what was, indeed, one of the
motivating forces behind their promotion of the language in the early nineteenth century – the use of Irish for the purposes of proselytism by evangelists,
but which now is of no significance, save in that it forms part of the emotional
legacy.

The interviewee quoted on 'uppity' Protestants responded to the question
on nationality with an uncompromising: 'Gael! Irish'. She went on to give
interesting insights into how she construed the confessional component of
Irishness. First of all, in response to being asked what she thought made
up Irishness, she said:

> [B]eing born in Ireland, and being immersed . . . in the history, and the cul-
> ture . . . being proud of it . . . willing to pass it on. And maybe having to correct
> it where there were imbalances in the past . . . it's such a wonderful thing to
> be able to claim Irishness. . . . I would want to be always very proud of
> my Irishness.
> Q. Do you think religion plays a part in it?
> A. I would say that there was a time when I thought it did, and that it should.

She did not clarify when, or to what degree, her attitude on the confessional
aspect had changed, but later, when asked if she was surprised to learn that
some Protestants felt excluded from the category of Irishness, she repeated,
somewhat tartly, that her first definition gave birth in Ireland as an necessary
qualification, but then said: '[I]f it's defined through religion . . . it would be
inevitable that they would', and continued, ruminatively,

> one of my brothers-in-law came from Belfast, and for a long time I didn't
> regard him as an Irishman. Until . . . he corrected my thinking. And I said, Oh,
> I didn't even know I thought that way! . . . I could see . . . how Protestants could
> have felt . . . that they were outside the glow of being Irish.

Thus, whilst reflecting on the issue, although missing the point that the problem is a Catholic perception and not the way Protestants see themselves, she provided a perfect example of the unconscious workings of the exclusionary mindset.

A 68-year-old Catholic gave a thoughtful response on the issue of Irishness and confession. Having given a summary of the historical relationship of Protestants and Catholics in relation to nationalism in some detail, he continued:

> I think today there's little doubt in my mind that it doesn't matter what religion you are, we are all Irish . . . in the twenty-six counties. . . . [T]oday this feeling that Protestant means British, West Brit, Catholic means nationalist, that is weaker than it ever has been before in history [but] . . . It hasn't disappeared. No. Not entirely.

It was difficult to gauge whether his not being really sure about the remaining extent of the confessionalisation of national identity was due to doubts he held himself, or to the fact that he was considering what he said very carefully.

Returning to the issues of the language and of culture in the sense of shared beliefs and practices, a 55-year-old Catholic from the west emphasised knowledge of the Irish language as central to Irishness:

> I still feel, that . . . it's nice to think that you . . . can speak a bit of Irish. It sets the Irish people apart . . . you do feel Irish if they're kind-of looking at you as Irish, if you can talk about Irish culture, if you can demonstrate a bit of Irish music or sing an Irish song.

On the other hand, the 57-year-old Catholic from the west, who had been terrified by her teachers to the extent that she could not learn Irish, whilst listing interest in cultural and sporting components as necessary components, did not think the language was essential – for the very practical reason that, in her case, as she had not had good experiences of learning Irish at school, she could not speak Irish now. She said:

> Irishness . . . would be folklore, learning about our past and learning all about our heritage . . . I don't think the Irish language . . . because . . . I was never any good at Irish. . . . [I]t is lovely to be able to, to speak a couple of words in Irish. . . . Particularly if you're abroad . . . and nobody will know what you're saying! . . . [T]o me, that's Irishness . . . céilidh dancing. . . . I do think that . . . Protestants

haven't the same interest in . . . céilidh dancing, Irish singing . . . as we would have. . . . Because you would never see Protestant children doing Irish dancing . . . Protestants don't play . . . Gaelic football, either. . . . Maybe a bit of soccer . . . they do play rugby. But you wouldn't get any local Protestants playing football.

She undoubtedly thought that Protestants marginalised themselves, and her use of 'we' opposed to 'Protestants' is interesting. Another 70-year-old Catholic produced some surprising views on the language issue:

I've very mixed feelings about [the language.] Because I would have started . . . more at home with Irish than with English as a child. . . . I loved Irish. But . . . there was such pressure on learning Irish, that I'm afraid I lost whatever Irish I had. And it is only in recent times . . . I've got back to it, and I'm often sorry that I haven't worked harder on, on it. Because I love, I love the Irish language . . . schools are like a damper.

It is worth underlining that wherever it was mentioned throughout the testimony, there was universal condemnation of the state language policy.

On the issue of the claim to the uniqueness, and place, of Irish history in identity formation, a 42-year-old non-practising Catholic from the eastern seaboard claimed 'special case' status for Ireland and thought that this was the essence of Irishness:

Ireland has a very specific history that a lot of other countries don't have. . . . I think to me Irishness is very based in the roots of where we come from. . . . We could go obviously all the way back to the potato famine and come all the way forward, but I think there's a sense of history there that I don't think other countries have . . . that history . . . makes us that little bit [different]. . . . And to me that's . . . Irishness.

A 52-year-old psychologist raised in a Catholic family in the midlands, also thought Ireland's history had an influence that, for her, surfaced in unexpected ways: 'I think Irish people are bright . . . and they're questioning. They're interested. . . . Maybe it's because of their history, and so on'. We have seen how a 40-year-old Catholic had an arresting view of Irish history as a series of rebellions 'where somebody betrayed everybody else', which she blames for the melancholia she sees as part of national identity. On the language issue, she said:

I think it's time we dropped the Irish language as essential to being Irish . . . it's . . . a millstone round our necks in the schools . . . we're doing it a disservice . . . it's dying out in the Gaeltacht areas, unfortunately, but it's a beautiful language, and . . . we should treasure it for it's cultural . . . knowledge, and for itself.

Further, she said: 'I always hated Irish music as a child and as a teenager, but I actually like it now', showing an attitudinal shift mounting to a conscious desire in adulthood to identify more with Irish culture.

Specifically on the issue of Catholic views of Protestant exclusion, a western Catholic in his fifties said, with more than a degree of irony:

[I]t's probably true to say that Protestants are not as Irish because they've only been here a short while. And they've only associated with the country for a short while. You want to give yourself time, don't you? . . . Couple of hundred years!

A blunt piece of testimony was given by the 75-year-old man whose children have retained their Irish regional accent. When asked about Protestants' perceptions of exclusion, he said:

I honestly think that . . . if the average person was asked . . . if they said, all the Protestants in the area are going, the people would say, well, good luck to them . . . for no particular reason [other] than they're not one of us.

To him, it appears that Protestants are not 'average' persons, nor are they of 'the people', and they are firmly located in that no-man's-land of not being 'one of us'. Given his age, his confession, where he lives, and despite the fact that he numbers neighbouring Protestants amongst his friends, it is not surprising that he made such a statement. However, in coming to that conclusion, it has to be acknowledged that certain assumptions about how one of 'them', an elderly Catholic from the west, might think, have been employed. However, taking the words at face value, it seems a hard-line position to express.

Catholics seemed to find it easier to express ideas of Irishness than Protestants. They were less likely to fall back on the concepts of nationality and citizenship in their answers. For one thing, the need to articulate the category of confession was hardly ever seen as relating to them: being Catholic was an automatic qualifier. For another, the question of the language was central in importance but ability to speak it was not vital: if not fluent, most expressed the view that it would be good to be able to speak it. Those who spoke of birth in Ireland as a necessary component of the category did so without realising the ambiguities inherent in that view, but only one referred to the citizenship rights of the 'diaspora', many of whom had not even visited, let alone been born in, Ireland. However, it bears emphasising that citizenship is not the same as membership of the nation.

Arising from Catholic perceptions that most Protestants are superior and condescending, there is another factor that needs to be addressed: that the occurrence of 'outcroppings' was seen to stem only from negative Catholic perceptions of Protestants, and no examples of a reversal of this situation were given. There are, of course, numerous characterisations of the Catholic Irish in Protestant consciousness typified by nineteenth-century 'disobliging character-isations . . . in *Punch* by Richard Doyle'.[4] Another example of the objectifying of the Catholic Irish in fiction occurs in the works of Somerville and Ross, who relied on a host of politically incorrect stereotypes of the Irish in their *Memoirs of an Irish RM*, portraying them as anything from clownish to sly. Other derogatory and reductive portraits might include the 'thick Mick', who, whilst acting the part of the fool, is laughing up his sleeve or the 'cute hoor', running rings around everyone. However, Protestants only employ negative stereotypes of their fellow-citizens in very safe company: they may think certain things, but they will not admit to holding such ideas, let alone express them. It is possible to speculate that this is not only because of the relentless pursuit of middle class respectability but also for reasons of discretion – it being the better part of valour in more than one sense of the word. The important overall point here is that more irruptions of the emotional legacy focusing on the past mythologised history of conflict between the confessions appear to have attached themselves to Catholocentric modes of expression and to refer to the minority. Overall, Protestant modes of expression in the interviews exhibit a greater awareness of the possibilities for misinterpretation and of ambiguity and, hence, the presence of care. That is not to say, once again, that Catholics were overtly anti-Protestant in what they said: it was more a case of not realising that their words could be capable of bearing inimical connotations.

We have already seen some examples of how the Catholic/nationalist construction of Irishness affects Protestants, and there are more. The views of an 82-year-old Protestant from a farming background in the south-west were typical of other elderly and middle-aged interviewees. Although a gentle and softly spoken person, she appeared angry when she spoke of having been considered less than truly Irish:

I've got that feeling years ago from some people, that I wasn't really Irish, which made me very indignant because I consider that I'm as Irish as . . . Certainly I'm not, I'm not any other country!

She continued, noting the improvements in inter-communal relations, but confirming the continuation of the phenomenon as well: '[Religion] used to matter far too much, but I don't think it is as much today. . . . I suppose there is a tiny bit there, but it wouldn't be anything like it was'.

A 77-year-old Protestant brought up in a north Dublin suburb was quite clear on the conflation of Protestant and English by Catholics:

I've never thought anything other than I'm Irish . . . and I'm very proud to be Irish. And if I go on my holidays, even up North, or to England, I let it be known that I'm Irish and proud. So it means a lot to me . . . [But] I'm quite sure [Catholics don't think I'm Irish]. . . . They always thought I had an affinity to . . . England.

Some, though by no means all, from the youngest age groups also felt that confession no longer mattered so much. For instance, it is quite clear that, although the 20-year-old student from an east-coast town has been made feel an outsider on the basis of her confessional identity, she does have Catholic friends. This is the main difference between her and her mother's generation: her 47-year-old mother's wistful evidence describing her regret and feeling of loss arising from the enforced segregation of her childhood has already been noted. The 81-year-old Protestant who developed republican sympathies in young adulthood was one of the exceptions to the generality in that she did not think she had been regarded as *not* Irish by Catholics, but qualified that by adding she could not really say, because they had not discussed the point specifically.

Returning to the phenomenon of denial, as well as those Catholics who do not wish to admit the possibility of Protestant marginalisation, there are southern Protestants who want to deny that being Protestant in the Republic of Ireland has been anything but a positive experience. Out of the 64 Protestants interviewed for this project, 60 recounted or implied feelings of exclusion. Three felt that sport had helped towards their integration into society to the extent that sectarianism did not matter to them – although they acknowledged it existed for others. And only one stood out strongly from the rest in his resistance to the idea of discrimination. In his early sixties, from middle-class Dublin origins, his childhood was strictly segregated:

> [I]f I give an impression that I never suffered from discrimination, that's true. I never have, never have. But then, at school, I went to Protestant schools, so it wouldn't have, it wouldn't have impinged anyway, and certainly in work and maybe, maybe the printing business is different to other businesses, but nobody ever, ever once, never have I, I have never suffered for my religion, in other words, unlike Cranmer and others!

All the same, he said, at work there was a 'bit of badinage at times, you know. Ah, you ol' Prod, you, you know, you would say that, or something, you know. But no, nothing.' However, having spoken of his lack of contact with Catholics in his early life, he moved on to touch on many of the heads of discrimination acknowledged to have been problematical for the minority community. Amongst them, he cited the all-pervasive *éminence grise* influence of John Charles McQuaid, Roman Catholic Archbishop of Dublin from 1944 to 1972: he had the ear of the political establishment, was 'profoundly suspicious' of state involvement in the provision of health and social care, and wanted 'to establish a Catholic health and social service that would be largely independent of the state and under the control of the diocese'.[5] The interviewee noted 'the disparaging way . . . [McQuaid] spoke about Protestants', and said 'it was a time when Prods kept their heads down', . . . '[y]ou didn't rock the boat'. He continued:

> I think it was shameful the way the Republic was ruled. I mean, I remember Costello's remark about being a Catholic first and . . . an Irishman second. . . . I mean, I think that's appalling, absolutely appalling. And they all went along with it.

From this, it can be seen that he was construing 'discrimination' in a specific and narrow sense: he was not prepared to say that he had in any sense been martyred for his faith, but, whilst he could provide a digest of the issues of unequal treatment which affected the minority community, his mindset did not admit subtler manifestations of 'othering'. And, in spite of his views on how the state had operated, his conception of Irishness not only shows his absolute identification with the Irish nation, but also illustrates the ambiguities of identity issues for so many Protestants of his generation. When asked whether he had ever been made to feel that he did not have the right to call himself Irish, he said:

No. No, I never have. . . . I mean, there would have been times when I was very young . . . in the late '40s [on] Remembrance Sunday, in St Patrick's . . . the congregation . . . would sing 'God Save the . . . King'. . . . And the Coronation film wasn't shown in any of the cinemas here, but every parish hall in . . . Dublin, had it and we went to them all. So I suppose there possibly was a certain ambivalence there. . . . No, I've . . . absolutely no doubt I was always Irish, Irish, Irish. . . . we wouldn't have looked to England, or Britain, but there was that residue, I suppose, of Unionism left.

From this, it is perhaps easy to see how certain perceptions of Protestants as 'Anglo' persisted in the nationalist canon, but three things are pertinent: firstly, he is referring to the situation over 50 years ago, and things have changed; secondly, Protestants who remained in the country after independence consciously opted to row in behind the new state, although their cultural allegiances perhaps lagged behind their civic ones until subsequent generations internalised the effects of the new directions taken by the reformed curriculum and intermingled more; thirdly, despite retaining apparent residues of British allegiance, this was the period during which Protestants were simultaneously emerging from the isolation of the first three decades of the state, communal barriers were crumbling and social integration with Catholics was starting the process of normalisation.[6]

All in all, we have seen examples of Protestant reactions ranging from bewilderment to hurt and anger at perceived Catholic attitudes to them. Naturally enough, the persisting manifestations of the emotional legacy which result in unexamined perceptions of them as oppressors and land-grabbing 'planters' wound, and being called 'English pig', 'Protestant bastard' or 'black bastard' give both offence and hurt. But the sense that, quite apart from abuse, the subtle but nonetheless obvious attitude of some Catholics to the effect that they do not see Protestants as fellow-members of the imagined community of the Irish nation is the most difficult of all to swallow. Indeed, it also appears that southern Catholics simply do not notice southern Protestants at all except when they appear 'over the parapet' to say something unacceptable to Catholic/nationalist sensibilities.

Interestingly, greater polarisation of attitudes came from areas which suffered notably traumatic historic events, which testifies to the strength of the hold of the emotional legacy. West Cork still showed evidence of Protestant 'muting', which arose from fear of reprisal during the Troubles surrounding independence. Wicklow and Wexford, where the 1798 rebellion was particularly bloody, produced examples of a startling degree of antipathy to Protestants, particularly over inter-church marriage. The West of Ireland, where effects of the famine were so harsh, demonstrated a lingering distrust of Protestants in general. Unsurprisingly, another area where bitterness has coalesced is in the border counties.

One issue remains to be addressed: did Protestants collude in the process and perpetuation of marginalisation? It is obvious that, in the early days of the state, segregation was seen as vital by both Catholics and Protestants: the churches wanted their doctrinal sway over their congregations to remain undiluted and unchallenged. For Protestants, it was also fundamentally important to maintain their ethos, their culture and their social practices intact in the face of the multiple threat they perceived in the face of Catholic numerical superiority and increasing political power. The fear, whether articulated or not, that they would have to pay for the sins of their ancestors, must also have been present, and, as Stephen Mennell says in his 'Introduction' to *Untold Stories*: 'It is scarcely surprising that two centuries of Protestant triumphalism were succeeded by several decades of Catholic triumphalism in the south after independence.'[7] Public Irishness in the early years of the state was clearly Catholic as well as culturally and politically nationalist and took no note of plurality. Therefore it was not something a Protestant, despite the conscious ethical compulsion to exercise civic rectitude – reinforced by directives from the Church of Ireland and prominent Protestants – could accept wholeheartedly, especially on an unconscious level. Consequently, that the community would collude in its own confessional and social exclusion from an Irishness so inimical in its components to its sensibilities and its own understanding of the category is not surprising: it was a defence mechanism that, for historical as well as emotional reasons, was irresistible to a group many of whom, at that stage, could not see how they might reach an accommodation with the new order. Decades of living at close, if segregated, quarters with the 'other' had to pass before sufficient confidence was aggregated to the group to facilitate any degree of rapprochement. The Protestants' segregationist drive did not, however, extend to the realms of the metaphysical category of Irishness when applied to themselves. They considered themselves Irish and as entitled to claim Irishness as any Catholic.

Another aspect for consideration concerns the different types of Protestantism within the community itself not only based on sub-sect, social and class differences, but also on the urban/rural divide, proximity to the border, degree of isolation, and so on. A 65-year-old Catholic from a border county, where emotions ran stronger and harder lines were drawn, saw Protestants in her area as deliberately isolating themselves. Looking back to her childhood, she said:

> [C]oming up to the 12 July . . . the Protestants would gather . . . with their sashes and they would be marching up and down banging their drums and singing . . . all the Catholics in the town would have been aware that this was going on. And it would . . . have been enough 'in your face' to get up people's noses. . . . And you always had the view that the Protestants . . . in our area would much rather have been in Northern Ireland. Under British rule. Than been in the south, under supposedly Catholic . . . and I would be very aware that all the . . . Protestant people in the town who were wealthier than the Catholics, and who had the businesses, all those would have been involved in . . . this marching season thing. . . . So . . . I think certainly at that stage they very much isolated themselves.

This is an instance of aggressive Protestantism used deliberately to delineate and affirm group boundaries. Such anachronistic attitudes are still to be found, somewhat muted and with the 'honours' more evenly distributed, but nevertheless present. In the course of her work, the young Catholic who attended an orange lodge picnic in Co. Monaghan and witnessed both the strong community feeling amongst the Protestants and the rivalry between the confessions epitomised by the dual between marching and pipe bands in the locality during that event. She said: 'I accept that Protestants can feel that there is a perception that they're not . . . proper Irish people, but . . . they possibly could integrate a bit more'.

Indeed, northern Protestantism, with its hard-line behaviour and attitudes, is regarded with more than a degree of dismay by many southern Protestants. A 72-year-old Protestant from the southwest said:

> [T]he Protestants in the North: they're so negative. 'No' is their favourite word, I think! . . . and Paisley!

She then told how a cousin had counselled her not to consent to being interviewed for this project:

> [T]here are a lot of Protestants and they're very insular, too. . . . That could be associated with this fear on the telephone that I got this morning, you know: don't say anything! . . . [J]ust to keep yourself to yourself.

The fear referred to was that of reprisal for speaking out, a remnant of the sectarian violence in her area of West Cork at the time of independence.

Urban working-class Protestant interviewees from Dublin, most of whom were aged from their late fifties to their eighties, had been frequently at the receiving end of street hostility from Catholics, and had always done their best to avoid doing anything that might be construed as giving offence by minimising contact. The middle classes of both confessions tended to think that the confessional situation had changed for the better, and that they mixed more now. There were, however, qualifications, as well as a degree of self-consciousness. The 47-year-old English Protestant who did not feel entitled to wear green on St Patrick's day did not agree with the proposition that confessional relationships were always better now. She and her Catholic husband were two of the several who thought the Protestants encountered at the Church of Ireland schools where their children went were cliquey.

What, then, can be concluded about the nature of Protestant Irishness and exclusion? In assessing the oral testimony in this study, it cannot be forgotten that only 100 people were interviewed in total, and therefore the sample is far too small to be quantitatively significant. However, the voice of personal experience is a powerful one and one worth heeding, for how people feel about things, as opposed to how they think about them, so often governs how they actually behave. Thus if Protestants – or other minority groups – feel excluded, they will tend to behave as a marginalised group, thereby both justifying exclusion in the eyes of the excluders and suffering continuing detriment to themselves.

Protestants in independent Ireland behaved in a predictable manner given that they felt excluded from membership of the imagined nation. It has been demonstrated how segregation, with the consent of both sides, operated to keep the two communities apart and Protestants colluded in this and with their marginalisation in the early years because it was, they felt, the only way they could maintain their collective identity. This has had still-discernible results: as a 40-year-old Protestant said, 'I think Protestants want to be different, but we don't want to be that different'. This might translate as the desire to be seen as distinctively Protestant *and* Irish.

We have seen how southern Irish Protestants have their own views on their relationship with Irishness: from the oral evidence, it appears that their personal identity still melds with their communal, cultural and confessional identity, in that their sense of themselves as individuals is still connected to the commonality of being Protestant. In this they are not dissimilar from Catholics, who are just as bound together in their confessional identity. For Protestants this element is emphasised because of their minority status: they seem to have more need of, and investment in, what defines them as a cohesive group. They, too, have a sense of belonging to Ireland, by long association and through long chains of predecessors – in the sure knowledge that this concept remains strongly contested – and any identification with Britain or with Englishness is long past from their point of view. However, the important point is that their view of themselves *vis à vis* Irishness is not – at least at 'emotional legacy' level – allowed for by the majority, and that the latter does not appear to want to address the issues involved. There is some evidence that people in the early middle-aged group and young people on both sides of the divide are starting to discuss the issues with each other, but that there are tensions involved that import a degree of risk into the process.

The view that a Protestant construction of the category of Irishness, as they perceive it, is still not allowed for by Catholics arises from the facts that the latter's right to claim centrality in the category on confessional grounds, let alone ethnic or political ones, was unquestioned by so many of the inter-viewees and that the assumptions of class and economic privilege adhering to Protestants still exist – and rankle. This was shown by the testimony of all age groups, but its effects surfaced most significantly, and perhaps disturbingly, in that of young Protestants, who, strongly in some cases, perceived themselves to be confessionally marginalised. In particular, the qualified contention by both Protestants and Catholics that things had changed for the better was rebutted by several interviewees, in particular the 20-year-old Protestant from the east-coast town: at best, it could be said that, though difference is something which is beginning to be discussed – which may or may not be a development for the better, depending upon whether the issue is approached with flexibility – but that it has not disappeared. Even in the face of evolving multicultural Ireland, Protestants – on the specific foundation of the history of the long-drawn-out situation of conflict of varying degrees of severity between the confessions – can still blatantly be constructed as 'outsiders'. It has also been shown that, to many of the Catholics interviewed, the idea that Protestants might feel excluded from the category of Irishness, might perceive that they were not permitted to belong, was novel. Some, having thought about it, acknowledged that it might indeed be the case, but others were loath to concede the point.

We have already seen evidence disclosing a self-conscious Protestantism and, arising from that, conscious decisions to act in particular ways, a cognisant 'performing' of being a Protestant. Performativity is a process by which an identity 'constitute[s] the identity it is purported to be',[8] with the result that individuals act in certain ways because they are perceived in a particular manner. One example was the young Irish-speaking Protestant, who challenged Protestant stereotypes and said she enjoyed 'in some ways being a contradiction insofar as I can speak Irish and that my maiden name is Irish, but that I'm Church of Ireland'. Another was the Canadian-born Anglican who consciously adapted her behaviour in the face of confessional baiting in the workplace deliberately to draw attention to the aspects of that conduct indicating underlying assumptions of inherent Protestant traits. The third was the Protestant businessman who referred to Protestants slipping in and out of Irishness at will.

Joseph Ruane, after alluding to the uneasy relationship still extant between the Protestant and Catholic communities in the Republic of Ireland, argued that two things prevent the reconciliation of the Protestant communal narrative with the narrative of the state and the nation. One is the ambiguity, arising from the dominant construction of Irishness, leading to questions about whether the state is a republic in the generic sense or simply the state of the Gaelic-Catholic tradition on the island. The other is the reluctance of the minority community to articulate its attachment to its own historic communal identity and traditions, so that southern Irish Protestants are not 'demanding' a version of the nation that includes them, and 'each advocates a pluralism that allows it to conserve its traditional difference'.[9]

Two points arise from this. The first concerns the attachment of Protestants to the past, and *their* past in particular as a central tenet of their identity construction. The emotional legacy stems from the record engraved on the national consciousness of the history of the nation, and not only do Protestants rely on this for identity formation but *both* communities have a stake in its maintenance in the furtherance of their self-definition. Also, it has been noted that attachment to the historical past materialising through 'outcroppings' of the emotional legacy appears to feature more for Catholics than for Protestants. In 'Memory and forgetting' Paul Ricoeur considers two short essays by Freud, the first of which deals with resistance and repression in psychoanalysis. In it, Freud posits that in order to reconstruct an 'acceptable and understandable past' it is necessary to get beyond a stage of mere repetition of incidents to attain a state of reconciliation through the use of 'memory as work'. The second essay concerns mourning and melancholia, and Freud uses the concept of the 'work' of mourning. Ricoeur maintains that

> it is quite possible that the work of memory is a kind or mourning, and also that mourning is a painful exercise in memory. . . . Hence, mourning and 'working

through' are to be brought together in the fight for the acceptability of memories: memories have not only to be understandable, they have to be acceptable, and it is this acceptability which is at stake in the work of memory and mourning.[10]

There are two aspects here that concern the southern Irish context: the first, to 'work through' memories of old hurts in order to get past the element of mere repetition which underpins the emotional legacy, and the second to acknowledge a need to mourn the alienation.

The second point arising from Ruane's article is that Protestants have not, and do not, articulate, let alone demand, changes in the narrative to accommodate their self-conception. This is not only an outcome of the content of their own narrative, but also because theirs is a very small voice indeed in the national choir which is not heard over the main theme of the majority construction of Irishness. In the past, fear prevented them from speaking out; now, it is the feeling – indeed, perhaps even the knowledge – that they will not be heard, or heeded. In this respect, their situation is analogous to the locus occupied by women in phallogocentric discourse, that of an impotent entity with neither voice nor right to make meanings with which freely to negotiate their lived reality.[11] In this light, and taking the evidence disclosed by this study, is it really so difficult to discern the continuing causes of residual Catholic/Protestant problems?[12] It was indeed fortunate for the Protestant community that the new state did at least seek to treat them scrupulously on the legal front. Otherwise, it would have had no hope of keeping the distinctiveness which it retains.

It is recognised that, in the face of the denial surrounding the issues, there are those from both sides of the confessional divide who will not wish to accept that southern Irish society still operates within the ambit of denominationalised perceptions and assumptions anchored to a troubled historical past. However, it is hoped that this exploration may give substance to the concerns of those southern Protestants who feel they have been silenced and erased from the nation to which they are as attached as are those who fall within the dominant construction of Irishness.

Those concerns were admirably summarised by a southern Irish Protestant who grew up in West Cork. In 2005, in a letter to the *Irish Times*, he cogently synopsised all the findings of this study. In particular, the last three sentences underline the sense of futility and the fear surrounding the notion of 'speaking out' for those who share his views. It also permits access to the depth of alienation experienced by some Irish citizens as a result of simply being southern Protestants:

> We have been unable to fully celebrate and maintain our diverse heritage.
>
> The formation, definition and national identity of this state was based on a Roman Catholic and Gaelic tradition.
>
> In this exclusive nationalist identity the vast majority of the Protestant community felt alienated. Our cultural differences were suppressed in a hostile environment.
>
> This repression has caused and maintained silence over our cultural demise.
>
> The combination of the political, media, sporting and educational system has selectively displayed a cultural and historical amnesia towards us. . . .
>
> Today, few Protestants would want to be quoted by name, in public, if they are saying something even slightly contentious. . . .
>
> When they do have the confidence to speak, they are met with either suspicion, ridicule or contempt and are fearful of a more subtle, isolated persecution.
>
> For a quiet life, we have said nothing.[13]

Are Catholics open to changing the ways they see Protestants? We saw how an elderly Catholic, reflecting on the issue of Protestant exclusion for the first time and recalling how she had perceived that her brother-in-law was not Irish because he came from Belfast, provided a perfect example of the unconscious workings of the exclusionary mindset. The fact that, when challenged, she changed the way she thought about the issue showed willingness to revisit automatic assumptions. A point to note, however, is that, given that other personal testimony disclosed deliberate use of, as well as unconscious reliance on, the content of the emotional legacy as overt abuse amongst young people,[14] the problem needs to be addressed early on, in the state's schools as well as in its homes. Again, this is not only in the interests of improving relationships between Catholics and Protestants, but also, by extension, of facilitating the integration of immigrants who have settled in the Republic.[15]

Are Protestants prepared to examine their construction of Irishness and articulate it, rather than staying silent – and resentful? Silence can, after all, be a powerful weapon. In the past, as a community, Protestants in the Republic avoided confrontation whenever possible: in the violence of the period surrounding independence, they were muted by the threat of physical danger; this danger gradually receded but Protestants stayed muted, for the most part because they did not want to provoke latent sectarianism. Many felt, in any case, that they would simply not be heard, and there are remnants of this attitude still at work. To overcome it, both communities need to acknowledge, rather than deny, that inter-communal tensions remain. And Protestants will have to master their reticence and accept the need to overcome the stereotype of standoffishness, however necessary their instinct for self-protection may have seemed in the past.

What, then, can be learned from highlighting how the legacy of the past irrupts into present-day life in the Republic, sustaining stereotypes that construct Protestants as 'other'? Firstly, that confessional difference, with its complex mix of cultural and ethnic elements, is emphatically not a thing of the past. Secondly, that a substantial minority of Irish people of all ages experience a continuing degree of alienation resulting from confessional marginalisation. Thirdly, that, whether unconscious or not, the ways the dominant construction of Irishness persists in Irish society need to be addressed not only in the interests of dealing with confessional difference but also successfully to negotiate multiculturalism in twenty-first century Irish society. Understanding the ways in which difference operates in the Irish context is essential for continuing to meet the challenges it raises. The successful integration of those not conforming to the dominant construction of Irishness, whoever they may be, requires not only consciousness of difference and the ways it manifests itself, but a respect for plurality, and it should not require the annihilation of minority individuality. Of course, minorities also need to consider the values of the society to which they are seeking entrance. All in all, a difficult balancing act – but one that is possible with mutual respect.

Notes

Introduction

1 Heather Kathleen Crawford, 'Protestants and Irishness in Independent Ireland: An Exploration', PhD thesis (NUI Maynooth, 2008).

2 Stephen Mennell, Mitchell Elliott, Paul Stokes, Aoife Rickard and Ellen O'Malley Dunlop, 'Protestants in a Catholic state – a silent minority in Ireland' in Tom Inglis, Zdzisław Mach and Rafał Mazanek (eds), *Religion and Politics: East–West Contrasts from Contemporary Europe* (Dublin, 2000), pp. 68–92.

3 For some of the memoirs read before embarking on this project, see bibliography, p. 221.

4 Robert Tobin, '"Tracing again the tiny snail track": southern Protestant memoir since 1950', *Year Book of English Studies Annual* (2005), p. 1.

5 Colin Murphy and Lynne Adair (eds), *Untold Stories: Protestants in the Republic of Ireland 1922–2002* (Dublin, 2002).

6 Stephen Amidon, 'A guide to Philip Roth', *Sunday Times Culture*, 23 Sept. 2007, p. 7.

7 Charles Flynn, 'Dundalk 1900–1960: an oral history', PhD thesis (NUIM, 2000), p. 68.

8 Dympna Devine and Mary Kelly, '"I just don't want to get picked on by anybody": dynamics of inclusion and exclusion in a newly ethnic Irish primary school', *Children and Society* XX (2006), p. 129; Fionnuala Waldron and Susan Pike, 'What does it mean to be Irish? Children's construction of national identity', *Irish Educational Studies* XXV: 2 (2006), p. 231.

9 R. V. Comerford, *Ireland* (London, 2003), p. 4.

10 Terence Brown, 'Religious minorities in the Irish Free State and the Republic of Ireland 1922–1995' in Forum for Peace and Reconciliation, *Building Trust in Ireland* (Belfast, 1996), p. 217.

11 Joseph Leichty and Cecelia Clegg, *Moving Beyond Sectarianism: Religion, Conflict and Reconciliation in Northern Ireland* (Dublin 2001), pp. 64–7.

12 Mennell et al., 'Protestants in a Catholic state', p. 79.

13 Comerford, *Ireland*, pp. 4–5.

14 Paul Ricoeur, 'Memory and forgetting' in Richard Kearney and Mark Dooley (eds), *Questioning Ethics: Contemporary Debates in Philosophy* (London and New York, 1999), p. 8.

15 Benedict Anderson, *Imagined Communities: Reflections on the Origin and Spread of Nationalism* (London, 1983), pp. 5–6.

16 Joseph Ruane, 'Majority–minority conflicts and their resolution: Protestant minorities in France and in Ireland', *Nationalism and Ethnic Politics*, XII: 3/4 (autumn/winter, 2006), p. 523.

17 Anderson, *Imagined Communities*, pp. 5–7.

18　H. K. Crawford, 'V. I. and I. D.: women's fractured subjectivity and the work of Sara Paretsky' (MA thesis, University of the West of England, 1996), p. 5.

19　Yvonne McKenna, *Made Holy: Irish Women Religious at Home and Abroad* (Dublin, 2006), p. 5.

20　Ibid., p. 5.

21　Paul Thompson, *The Voice of the Past: Oral History* (Oxford 2000), p. 129.

22　Paul Thompson, 'Problems of method in oral history', *Oral History Journal*, 1: 4 (1972), pp. 4–5.

23　Thompson, *The Voice of the Past*, p. 169.

24　Ibid., pp. 132–3.

25　Ibid., p. 172.

26　Ricoeur, 'Memory and forgetting', p. 5.

27　Joan Sangster, 'Telling our stories: feminist debates and the use of oral history', in Robert Perks and Alistair Thomson (eds), *The Oral History Reader* (London, 1998), p. 90.

28　Ibid., p. 94.

29　Personal narratives group, 'Truths', and Luisa Passerini, 'Women's personal narratives: myths, experiences, and emotions' in Personal Narratives Group (eds), *Interpreting Women's Lives: Feminist Theory and Personal Narratives* (Bloomington, 1989), pp. 261, 197, cited in Sangster, 'Telling our stories', p. 97.

30　McKenna, *Made Holy*, p. 3.

31　Ibid., p. 4.

Chapter One: The Background

1　*Church of Ireland Gazette*, 6 May 1949, p. 1.

2　For example, Daithí Ó Corráin, *Rendering to God and Caesar: The Irish Churches and the Two States in Ireland, 1949–73* (Manchester, 2006), p. 93 and Terence Brown, 'Religious minorities in the Irish Free State and the Republic of Ireland 1922-1995' in Forum for Peace and Reconciliation, *Building Trust in Ireland* (Belfast, 1996), pp. 226-7.

3　Eunan O'Halpin, 'Politics and the state' in J. R. Hill (ed.), *A New History of Ireland, vii: Ireland 1921–84* (Oxford, 2003), p. 119.

4　Kurt Bowen, *Protestants in a Catholic State: Ireland's Privileged Minority* (Dublin, 1983), p. 196.

5　Stephen Mennell, Mitchell Elliott, Paul Stokes, Aoife Rickard and Ellen O'Malley Dunlop, 'Protestants in a Catholic state – a silent minority in Ireland' in Tom Inglis, Zdzisław Mach and Rafał Mazanek (eds), *Religion and Politics: East–West Contrasts from Contemporary Europe* (Dublin 2000), pp. 68–92.

6　*Sunday Tribune*, 12 Oct. 2008.

7　*Irish Times*, Letters to the Editor, 26 Jan. 2007, p. 17.

8　Editorial, *Irish Times*, 26 Jan. 2007, p. 17.

9　Heather Kathleen Crawford, 'Protestants and Irishness in Independent Ireland: an exploration', PhD thesis (NUI Maynooth, 2008).

10　Michael Fogarty et al., *Irish Values and Attitudes: The Irish Report of the European Value Systems Study* (Dublin, 1984), p. 11.

11 Central Statistics Office, http://www.cso.ie/census2006results/volume_13_religion.pdf consulted 1 Feb. 2008.

12 Ibid.

13 George Hook, 'The Right Hook' on Newstalk 106FM, 6 Jan. 2006, 5.50 p.m., cited in Miriam Moffitt, 'The Society for Irish Christian Mission to the Roman Catholics, 1849–1950', PhD thesis (NUI Maynooth, 2006), p. 279.

14 J. H. Whyte, *Church and State in Modern Ireland 1923–1979* (London, 1980), pp. 24–61.

15 Tom Inglis, *Moral Monopoly: The Rise and Fall of the Catholic Church in Modern Ireland* (2nd edn; Dublin, 1998), pp. 2–3.

16 Patrick Cabanal et al., *Dire les Cévennes: mille ans de témoignages* (Montpellier, 1994), pp. 159–60. Grateful thanks to Joseph Ruane for assisting with the citation.

17 Paul Ricoeur, 'Memory and forgetting' in Richard Kearney and Mark Dooley (eds), *Questioning Ethics: Contemporary Debates in Philosophy* (London and New York, 1999), p. 8.

18 Crawford, 'Protestants and Irishness'.

19 Joseph Leichty and Cecelia Clegg, *Moving Beyond Sectarianism: Religion, Conflict and Reconciliation in Northern Ireland* (Dublin 2001), p. 71.

20 Joseph Ruane and Jennifer Todd, *The Dynamics of Conflict in Northern Ireland* (Cambridge, 1996), pp. 21–2.

21 Toby Barnard, *Irish Protestant Ascents and Descents, 1641–1770* (Dublin, 2004), pp. 1–2.

22 Ruane and Todd, *The Dynamics of Conflict*, p. 20.

23 Leichty and Clegg, *Moving Beyond Sectarianism*, pp. 71–2.

24 Nicholas Canny, *From Reformation to Restoration: Ireland 1534–1660* (Dublin, 1987), p. 10.

25 R. F. Foster, 'Ascendancy and union' in R. F. Foster (ed.), *The Oxford History of Ireland* (Oxford, 1992), pp. 164–6.

26 Terence Brown, *Ireland: A Social And Cultural History 1922–79* (Glasgow, 1981), pp. 19–20.

27 J. C. Beckett, *The Making of Modern Ireland* (London, 1981), p. 295.

28 Moffitt, 'Society for Irish Christian Mission', p. 1.

29 Alan Acheson, *A History of the Church of Ireland 1691–1996* (Dublin, 1997), p. 164

30 Ibid., pp. 191–2.

31 Moffitt, 'Society for Irish Christian Mission', pp. 279.

32 Miriam Moffitt, *The Society for Irish Church Missions to the Roman Catholics, 1850–1950* (Manchester, forthcoming).

33 Prunty, Jacinta, *Dublin Slums, 1800–1925: A Study in Urban Geography* (Dublin, 1998), pp. 238–9.

34 M. Creedon, 'Proselytism: its operations in Ireland', *Record of the Maynooth Union, 1926*, pp. 14–29.

35 Ibid., pp. 14–15, 21, 28–9.

36 June Cooper, 'The Protestant Orphan Society, Dublin, 1828–1928', PhD thesis (NUI Maynooth, 2009), p. 106.

37 Foster, 'Ascendancy and union', pp. 167–9.

38 R. V. Comerford, *Ireland* (London, 2003), p. 56.

39 Foster, 'Ascendancy and union', pp. 169-70.

40 Ibid., p. 161.

41 Brown, *Ireland*, p. 29.

42 Foster, 'Ascendancy and Union', p. 162.

43 Beckett, *Modern Ireland*, p. 417.

44 D. H. Akenson, *A Mirror to Kathleen's Face: Education in Independent Ireland, 1922–1960* (Montreal and London, 1975), pp. 118–19.

45 Beckett, *Modern Ireland*, pp. 416–17.

46 David Fitzpatrick, 'Ireland since 1870' in R. F. Foster (ed.), *The Oxford History of Ireland* (Oxford, 1992), pp. 198–9.

47 The *de facto* Sinn Féin parliament.

48 D. H. Akenson, *Small Differences: Irish Catholics and Irish Protestants, 1815–1922: An International Perspective* (Dublin, 1991), p. 4.

49 Leigh-Ann Coffey, *The Planters of Luggacurran, Co. Laois: A Protestant Community, 1879–1927* (Dublin, 2006), pp. 67–8.

50 Peter Hart, 'The Protestant experience of revolution in southern Ireland' in Richard English and Graham Walker (eds), *Unionism in Modern Ireland* (Basingstoke, 1996), pp. 89–90.

51 Ibid., p. 81.

52 Brown, *Ireland*, p. 107.

53 Bryan Fanning, *Racism and Social Change in the Republic of Ireland* (Manchester, 2002), p. 55.

54 Catherine O'Connor, 'Protestant women in Ferns, 1945–65: issues of gender, religious and social identity', paper delivered at interdisciplinary workshop on Protestants, University College Cork, 26 May 2006.

55 Martin Maguire, '"Our people": the Church of Ireland and the culture of community in Dublin since disestablishment' in Raymond Gillespie and W. G. Neely (eds), *The Laity and the Church of Ireland, 1000–2000: All Sorts and Conditions* (Dublin, 2002), p. 287.

56 Bowen, *Protestants in a Catholic State*, p. 16.

57 Ibid., pp. 94–103.

58 'Bishop refutes "widespread fantasy"', *Church of Ireland Gazette*, 14 Mar. 1975, pp. 1–2.

59 Ibid.

60 Acheson, *A History of the Church of Ireland*, p. 233.

61 Bowen, *Protestants in a Catholic State*, p. 174.

Chapter Two: Segregation and Education

1 Kevin Williams, 'Faith and the nation: education and religious identity in the Republic of Ireland', *British Journal of Educational Studies*, XLVIII: 4 (Dec. 1999), p. 318.

2 Adrian Kelly, *Compulsory Irish: Language and Education in Ireland 1870s–1970s* (Dublin, 2002), p. 15.

3 D. H. Akenson, *The Irish Education Experiment: The National System of Education in the Nineteenth Century* (London, 1970), p. 4.

4 Website of the Irish Government's Department of Foreign Affairs, http://www.citizens information.ie/categories/education/primary-and-post-primary-education/going-to-primary-school/ types_primary_school, consulted 12 Jan. 2009.

5 Dymphna Devine and Mary Kelly, '"I just don't want to get picked on by anybody": dynamics of inclusion and exclusion in a newly multi-ethnic Irish primary school', *Children and Society* xx (2006), pp. 133, 131.

6 Moira J. Maguire and Séamus Ó Cinnéide, '"A good beating never hurt anyone": the punishment and abuse of children in twentieth century Ireland', *Journal of Social History*, xxxviii: 3 (spring 2005), p. 649.

7 Ibid., pp. 635–6.

8 There were 12 Protestants over 60 in this category.

9 John McGahern, *Memoir* (London, 2005), p. 17.

10 Maguire and Ó Cinnéide, 'A good beating', p. 645.

11 Timothy Kelly, 'Education' in Michael Hurley (ed.), *Irish Anglicanism, 1870–1970* (Dublin, 1970), pp. 57–8.

12 The Revd E. C. Hodges, 'The future of primary education in the Free State in relation to the Church of Ireland', *Church of Ireland Gazette*, 12 Jan. 1934, p. 25.

13 D. H. Akenson et al., 'Pre-university education, 1921–84' in J. R. Hill (ed.), *A New History of Ireland, vii: Ireland 1921–84* (Oxford, 2003), p. 735.

14 Hodges, 'The future of primary education', p. 25.

15 Kurt Bowen, *Protestants in a Catholic State: Ireland's Privileged Minority* (Dublin, 1983), pp. 137–8.

16 Information supplied by Representative Church Body by email dated 2 Jan. 2008.

17 Information supplied by An Foras Pátrúnachta by email dated 2 Jan. 2008.

18 Prepared in consultation with An Foras Pátrúnachta by emails over the period 2–8 Jan. 2008.

19 Website of Educate Together Organisation, http://www.educatetogether.ie.html, consulted 10 Jan. 2009.

20 D. H. Akenson, *A Mirror to Kathleen's Face: Education in Independent Ireland, 1922–1960* (Montreal and London, 1975), p. 11.

21 Bowen, *Protestants in a Catholic State*, p. 141.

22 Akenson et al., 'Pre-university education', p. 726.

23 Bowen, *Protestants in a Catholic State*, p. 142.

24 Ibid., pp. 141–2.

25 R. V. Comerford, 'The British state and the education of Irish Catholics, 1850–1921' in Janusz Tomiak (ed.), *Comparative Studies on Governments and Non-Dominant Ethnic Groups in Europe, 1850–1940: Schooling, Educational Policy and Ethnic Identity* (Dartmouth, 1991), p. 21.

26 E. Brian Titley, *Church, State and the Controlling of Schooling in Ireland 1900–1944* (Dublin, 1983), p. 153–4.

27 Akenson et al, 'Pre-university education, 1921–84', p. 732.

28 Bowen, *Protestants in a Catholic State*, pp. 144–5.

29 Akenson et al., 'Pre-university education, 1921–84', p. 735.

30 Jack White, *Minority Report: The Protestant Community in the Irish Republic* (Dublin, 1975), p. 146.

31 Quoted in Bowen, *Protestants in a Catholic State*, p. 150.

32 Bowen, *Protestants in a Catholic State*, p. 150.

33 Ibid., pp. 147–51.

34 Akenson et al., 'Pre-university education, 1921–84', p. 722.

35 Bowen, *Protestants in a Catholic State*, p. 146.

36 Sean O'Connor, *A Troubled Sky: Reflections on the Irish Educational Scene 1957–68* (Dublin 1986), pp. 197–8.

37 Information supplied by Post Primary Administration, Department of Education by email on 17 Nov. 2008.

38 Comerford, 'The education of Irish Catholics', p. 22.

39 Website of Trinity College Dublin, http://www.tcd.ie/Visitors/tcd._hist.html, consulted 9 Feb. 2007.

40 Comerford, 'The education of Irish Catholics', p. 22.

41 F. S. L. Lyons, 'The minority problem in the 26 counties' in Francis MacManus (ed.), *The Years of the Great Test 1926–1939: The Thomas Davis Lectures* (Cork, 1967), p. 97.

42 Bowen, *Protestants in a Catholic State*, p. 154.

43 J. H. Whyte, 'The North erupts, and Ireland enters Europe, 1968–72', in Hill, *A New History of Ireland*, p. 325.

44 Diarmaid Ferriter, *The Transformation of Ireland 1900–2000* (London, 2004), pp. 598–9.

45 John Coolahan, 'Higher education 1908–1984' in Hill, *A New History of Ireland*, pp. 788–9.

46 Bowen, *Protestants in a Catholic State*, pp. 153–5.

47 Ibid., p. 134.

48 Ibid., p. 146.

49 Ibid., pp. 160–1.

50 Martin Maguire, '"Our people": the Church of Ireland and the culture of community in Dublin since disestablishment' in Raymond Gillespie and W. G. Neely (eds), *The Laity and the Church of Ireland, 1000–2000: All Sorts and Conditions* (Dublin, 2002), p. 287.

51 Ibid., p. 299.

Chapter Three: Education, Irish Language and Identity

1 Dymphna Devine and Mary Kelly, '"I just don't want to get picked on by anybody": dynamics of inclusion and exclusion in a newly multi-ethnic Irish primary school', *Children and Society* xx (2006), p. 136.

2 Tom Inglis, *Moral Monopoly: The Rise and Fall of the Catholic Church in Modern Ireland* (2nd edn; Dublin, 1998), pp. 7-8.

3 Jack White, *Minority Report: The Protestant Community in the Irish Republic* (Dublin, 1975), p. 139.

4 Diarmaid Ferriter, *The Transformation of Ireland 1900–2000* (London, 2004), p. 430

5 Inglis, *Moral Monopoly*, pp. 57, 60–1.

6 Kurt Bowen, *Protestants in a Catholic State: Ireland's Privileged Minority* (Dublin, 1983), pp. 156–7.

7 Inglis, *Moral Monopoly*, pp 2–3.

8 Revd Dr John MacNamara, *Bilingualism and Primary Education: A Study of Irish Experience* (Edinburgh, 1966).

9   D. H. Akenson, *A Mirror to Kathleen's Face: Education in Independent Ireland, 1922–1960* (Montreal and London, 1975), p. 58.

10   Ibid., pp 118–19.

11   Bowen, *Protestants in a Catholic State*, pp. 158–9.

12   Adrian Kelly, *Compulsory Irish: Language and Education in Ireland 1870s–1970s* (Dublin, 2002), pp. 20–1.

13   Bowen, *Protestants in a Catholic State*, p. 156.

14   Roland Tormey, 'The construction of national identity through primary school history: the Irish case', *British Journal of Sociology of Education* xxvii: 3 (July 2006), p. 314.

15   Bowen, *Protestants in a Catholic State*, p. 156.

16   Ferriter, *Transformation*, p. 430.

17   Department of Education, *Report of the Council of Education*, 1931, p. 98.

18   Ibid., p. 182.

19   Gabriel Doherty, 'National identity and the study of Irish history', *English Historical Review* cxi (Apr. 1996), p. 327.

20   Christian Brothers (eds), *The Higher Literary Reader* (Dublin, 1925).

21   The Very Revd T. O'Keeffe, 'The affection and reverence due to a mother' in The Christian Brothers (eds), *The Higher Literary Reader* (Dublin, 1925), pp. 29–30.

22   The Revd Joseph Farrell, two essays entitled 'About Books' in The Christian Brothers (eds), *The Higher Literary Reader* (Dublin, 1925), pp. 43–5.

23   Stephen J. Brown, SJ (ed.), *From the Realm of Poetry* (London, 1946).

24   The Revd Stopford A.Brooke, 'Introduction' in *A Treasury of Irish Poetry in the English Tongue* (London, 1900), p. xxi.

25   Website of Princess Grace Irish Library (Monaco) http://www.pgil-eirdata.org/html/pgil_datasets/authors/b/Brooke,SA/life.html, consulted 4 Jan. 2008.

26   D. J. Hickey and J. E. Doherty, *A New Dictionary of Irish History from 1800* (Dublin 2003), pp. 321–2.

27   A. C. Hepburn, 'Language, religion and national identity in Ireland since 1880' in *Perspectives on European Politics and Society* 11: 2 (Aug. 2001), pp. 204–5.

28   Keith C. Barton and Alan W. McCully, 'History, identity, and the school curriculum in Northern Ireland: an empirical study of secondary students' ideas and perspectives', *Journal of Curriculum Studies* xxvii: 1 (2005), p. 85.

29   Peter Sheridan, *44: A Dublin Memoir* (Basingstoke, 2000), p. 43.

30   John McGahern, *Memoir* (London, 2005), pp. 168–70.

31   Quoted in Ferriter, *Transformation*, p. 99.

32   Akenson, *A Mirror to Kathleen's Face*, pp. 122–3.

33   Ibid., pp. 125–6.

34   Ibid., p. 127.

35   Ibid., pp. 128–30.

36   Kelly, *Compulsory Irish*, pp. 29–30.

37   Akenson, *A Mirror to Kathleen's Face*, pp. 120–1.

38   Kelly, *Compulsory Irish*, p. 29.

39   Ferriter, *Transformation*, p. 351.

40   Government statement on the Irish language: 'Ireland is a bilingual state in which Irish is the first official language according to Article 8 of the Constitution of Ireland'. See website of Government of Ireland http://www.pobail.ie/en/IrishLanguage/StatementontheIrishLanguage2006/file,7802,en.pdf consulted 9 Jan. 2008. Also: Section 2 (1) of the Official Languages Act 2003 states that 'the official languages' means the Irish language (being the national language and the first official language) and the English language (being a second official language) as specified in Article 8 of the Constitution'. See website of the Office of the Attorney General, http://www.irishstatutebook.ie/2003/en/act/pub/0032/sec0002.html consulted on 9 Jan. 2008.

41   Liam Fay, 'More Irish than the Irish', *Sunday Times Culture*, 21 Jan. 2007, p. 32.

42   Ibid., p. 32.

43   The Irish-speaking Church of Ireland teacher training college.

44   Bowen, *Protestants in a Catholic State*, p. 165.

45   Akenson, *A Mirror to Kathleen's Face*, pp. 133–4.

46   Joseph Ruane and David Butler, 'Southern Irish Protestants: an example of de-ethnicisation?' *Nations and Nationalism* XII: 4 (winter, 2007), pp. 619–35.

47   Akenson, *A Mirror to Kathleen's Face*, p. 127.

48   Bowen, *Protestants in a Catholic State*, p. 200.

49   Alan Acheson, *A History of the Church of Ireland 1691–1996* (Dublin, 1997).

50   Bowen, *Protestants in a Catholic State*, p. 195.

51   Ibid., pp. 195–210.

52   Kevin Williams, 'Faith and the nation: education and religious identity in the Republic of Ireland', *British Journal of Educational Studies* XLVIII: 4 (Dec. 1999), p. 328.

Chapter Four: Protestants and Society

1   Kurt Bowen, *Protestants in a Catholic State: Ireland's Privileged Minority* (Dublin, 1983), p. 197.

2   Ibid., p. 195.

3   Ibid., p. 201.

4   Martin Maguire, '"Our people": the Church of Ireland and the culture of community in Dublin since disestablishment' in Raymond Gillespie and W. G. Neely (eds), *The Laity and the Church of Ireland, 1000–2000: All Sorts and Conditions* (Dublin, 2002), p. 278.

5   'Parish Week' in *Rathmines Parish Magazine*, Oct. 1934, p. 2.

6   Ibid., p. 2.

7   Ibid., pp. 3, 4–5.

8   Ibid., p. 6.

9   Revd J. McMurray Taylor, 'Editor's Letter', *Clogher Diocesan Magazine*, June 1960, p. 1.

10   Carole Holohan, '"Every generation has its task": Irish youth in the sixties', PhD thesis (University College Dublin, 2009), p. 7.

11   Ibid., p. 202.

12   Ibid., pp 234, 238.

13 Martin Maguire, 'Our people', p. 283.

14 Bowen, *Protestants in a Catholic State*, pp. 169–70.

15 Jack White, *Minority Report: The Protestant Community in the Irish Republic* (Dublin, 1975), p. 168.

16 Paul Anderson, 'Ulster Group confident about Dublin parade', *Irish Times*, 21 June 2007.

17 Bowen, *Protestants in a Catholic State*, pp. 187–8.

18 Ibid., pp. 189–91.

19 Ibid., p. 182.

20 Ibid., p. 176.

21 Ibid., pp. 175–81.

22 Desmond FitzGerald, the Knight of Glin, in Colin Murphy and Lynne Adair (eds), *Untold Stories: Protestants in the Republic of Ireland 1922–2002* (Dublin, 2002), pp. 80, 81.

23 Bowen, *Protestants in a Catholic State*, p. 166.

24 Martin Maguire, 'The Dublin Protestant working class, 1870–1932: economy, society, politics' (MA thesis, UCD, 1990), p. 17.

25 Bowen, *Protestants in a Catholic State*, p. 181.

26 John Crawford, *The Church of Ireland in Victorian Dublin* (Dublin, 2005), pp. 9–10.

27 Girls' Friendly Society.

28 Bowen, *Protestants in a Catholic State*, p. 171.

29 Grateful thanks to Dr Fergus O'Ferrall for providing this information by email dated 17 June 2009.

30 Bowen, *Protestants in a Catholic State*, p. 181.

31 Ibid., p. 194.

32 At diocesan level, this committee considered applications, which were subject to means testing, for financial assistance for educational purposes.

33 'Bishop refutes "widespread fantasy"', *Church of Ireland Gazette*, 14 Mar. 1975, pp. 1–2.

34 Catherine McGuinness, 'Being Protestant in the Republic of Ireland' in James McLoone (ed.), *Being Protestant in Ireland: Papers Presented at the 32nd Annual Summer School of the Social Study Conference* (Naas, 1985), p. 21.

35 Ibid., pp. 29–31.

36 R. V. Comerford, *Ireland* (London, 2003), p. 215.

37 D. J. Hickey and J. E. Doherty, *A New Dictionary of Irish History from 1800* (Dublin 2003), p. 162.

38 Diarmaid Ferriter, *The Transformation of Ireland, 1900–2000* (London, 2004), p. 36.

39 Comerford, *Ireland*, p. 214.

40 Ferriter, *Transformation*, p. 101.

41 'Leaping and vaulting', *Church of Ireland Gazette*, 6 Jan. 1978, p. 11.

42 Comerford, *Ireland*, p. 228.

43 Crawford, *Victorian Dublin*, p. 10.

44 Daithí Ó Corráin, *Rendering to God and Caesar: The Irish Churches and the Two States in Ireland, 1949–73* (Manchester, 2006), p. 199.

45 Rex Cathcart with Michael Muldoon, 'The mass media in twentieth-century Ireland' in J. R. Hill (ed.), *A New History of Ireland vii: Ireland 1921–84* (Oxford, 2003), pp. 693–4.

46 Ferriter, *Transformation*, p. 741.

47 Small chocolate biscuit with an orange jelly centre, hence Protestant.

48 'Slagged' = teased.

Chapter Five: Inter-Church Marriage

1 Richard O'Leary, 'Religious intermarriage in Dublin: the importance of status boundaries between religious groups', *Review of Religious Research* XLI (2000), p. 471.

2 Ibid., p. 474.

3 Ibid., p. 471.

4 J. H. Whyte, *Church and State in Modern Ireland 1923–1979* (London, 1980), pp. 24–61.

5 Jack White, *Minority Report: The Protestant Community in the Irish Republic* (Dublin, 1975), p. 114.

6 Tom Inglis, *Moral Monopoly: The Rise and Fall of the Catholic Church in Modern Ireland* (2nd edn; Dublin, 1998), pp. 2–3.

7 Bryan Fanning, *Racism and Social Change in the Republic of Ireland* (Manchester, 2002), p. 37.

8 Ibid., p. 32.

9 White, *Minority Report*, pp. 114, 115.

10 Diarmaid Ferriter, *The Transformation of Ireland 1900–2000* (London, 2004), p. 718

11 Ibid., pp. 716–20. See also: Patrick O'Mahony and Gerard Delanty, *Rethinking Irish History: Nationalism, Identity and Ideology* (Basingstoke, 2001), p. 179. 'The situation on abortion remains as laid down by the X case [in which a 14-year-old rape victim was prevented from travelling to seek an abortion outside the state.] 'The issues raised by [that] case led to a referendum on the constitution to allow women the right to travel and to allow information on abortion in certain circumstances, but the results have never been legislated as successive governments refused to address the issues.'

12 Ferriter, *Transformation*, p. 717.

13 Daithí Ó Corráin, *Rendering to God and Caesar: The Irish Churches and the Two States in Ireland, 1949–73* (Manchester, 2006), p. 182.

14 Ibid., p. 199.

15 Ibid., pp. 191–6.

16 Ibid., p. 208.

17 Ibid., p. 199.

18 Ibid. pp. 207–9.

19 Ibid., p. 208.

20 Ibid., pp. 213–14.

21 Thomas P. O'Neill, 'Political life in the South' in Michael Hurley (ed.), *Irish Anglicanism 1869–1969* (Dublin 1970), p. 105.

22 Ó Corráin, *Rendering to God*, pp. 184–5.

23 Raymond M. Lee, 'Intermarriage, conflict and social control in Ireland: the decree *Ne temere*', *Economic and Social Review* XVII: 1 (Oct. 1985), p. 14.

24 Ibid., pp. 16–25.

25 Ibid., pp. 24–5.

26 Ó Corráin, *Rendering to God*, p. 185.

27 Charles Flynn, 'Dundalk 1900–1960: an oral history' (PhD thesis, NUIM, 2000), p. 69.

28 Lee, 'The decree *Ne temere*', pp. 14–15.

29 Patrick Deignan, 'The Protestant community in Sligo, 1914–1949', PhD thesis (NUI, Maynooth, 2008), p. 49.

30 R. E. Bantry White, 'Church State and the Protestants since independence', *Church of Ireland Gazette*, 5 Nov. 1971, p. 3.

31 Kurt Bowen, *Protestants in a Catholic State: Ireland's Privileged Minority* (Dublin, 1983), p. 43.

32 J. H. Whyte, 'Economy, crisis and political cold war, 1949–57' in J. R. Hill (ed.), *A New History of Ireland, vii: Ireland 1921–84* (Oxford, 2003), p. 285.

33 Ó Corráin, *Rendering to God*, p. 189.

34 Paul Blanshard, *The Irish and Catholic Power: An American Interpretation* (London, 1954), p. 137.

35 Ó Corráin, *Rendering to God*, p. 189.

36 Ibid., p. 191.

37 Ibid., pp. 189–90.

38 *Church of Ireland Gazette*, 6 Sept. 1974, p. 1.

39 *Church of Ireland Gazette*, 13 Sept. 1974, p. 1.

40 In the 1975 Mixed Marriage Instruction it was stated that (i) there should be consultation with both intending partners, when the Church of Ireland doctrine of Holy Matrimony should be explained 'and it should be clearly indicated that the marriage can be solemnised in a Church of Ireland church according to the rites prescribed in the *Book of Common Prayer* with all legal and spiritual propriety' without any prior promises regarding children; (ii) if such a promise is made, it should not operate to exclude the other partner; (iii) arrangements should be made for joint pastoral care of the family; (iv) if the marriage is in a Church of Ireland church, the Roman Catholic priest be asked to assist, but he must be informed that the vows will be administered by the presiding cleric; if the marriage be in a Roman Catholic church, the Church of Ireland cleric may only assist if conditions (ii) and (iii) have been fulfilled; (v) finally, 'it is desirable that in all cases of mixed marriage the details should be sent to the Bishop in whose diocese the marriage shall take place, and that, on receiving an invitation to participate in a marriage ceremony in a Roman Catholic church where one partner is Church of Ireland, the clergy shall consult with the Bishop of the diocese before accepting the invitation.' *Church of Ireland Gazette*, 3 Jan. 1975.

41 Confirmed by Canon Victor Stacey in a telephone conversation on 22 January 2008.

42 Bowen, *Protestants in a Catholic State*, pp. 42–3.

43 John Fulton, *The Tragedy of Belief* (Oxford, 1991), p. 198.

44 Ferriter, *Transformation*, p. 582.

45 Ó Corráin, *Rendering to God*, p. 184.

46 Ferriter, *Transformation*, p. 582.

47 Bowen, *Protestants in a Catholic State*, pp. 193–4.

48 Desmond Connell, *A Survey into Some of the Needs and Attitudes of Young People in Church of Ireland Groups* (Dublin, 1975), pp. 29–30.

49 Carole Holohan, '"Every generation has its task": Irish youth in the Sixties', PhD thesis (University College Dublin, 2009), pp. 160, 167.

50 Ferriter, *Transformation*, p. 582.

51 The Revd Patrick Comerford in Colin Murphy and Lynne Adair (eds), *Untold Stories: Protestants in the Republic of Ireland 1922–2002* (Dublin, 2002), p. 61.

52 Explanations offered by Canon Victor Stacey in a telephone conversation on 22 January 2008.

53 Robert Armitage in Murphy and Adair (eds), *Untold Stories*, p. 23.

54 Phyllis Browne in Murphy and Adair (eds), *Untold Stories*, p. 35.

55 Patsy McGarry in Murphy and Adair (eds), *Untold Stories*, p. 127.

56 Bowen, *Protestants in a Catholic State*, p. 194.

57 Alan Acheson, *A History of the Church of Ireland 1691–1996* (Dublin, 1997), p. 233; Catherine O'Connor, 'Southern Protestantism: the interrelationship of religious, social and gender identity in the diocese of Ferns, 1945–65' (PhD thesis, University of Limerick, 2008).

58 White, *Minority Report*, p. 130.

59 Bowen, *Protestants in a Catholic State*, p. 181.

60 Ibid., p. 171.

61 Ibid., p. 209.

62 Ibid., pp. 219–20.

63 'Gazebo' in *Church of Ireland Gazette*, 22 Oct. 1971, p. 7.

64 Ibid., p. 7.

65 The Family Home Protection Act, 1976, No. 27/1976.

66 Nicola Yeates, 'Gender, familism and housing: matrimonial property rights in Ireland' in *Women's Studies International Forum* XXII: 6 (Nov.–Dec. 1999), p. 611.

67 Bowen, *Protestants in a Catholic State*, p. 169.

68 Richard O'Leary, 'Change in the rate and pattern of religious intermarriage in the Republic of Ireland', *Economic and Social Review*, XXX: 2 (Apr. 1999), pp. 119–20.

69 Terence Brown, 'Religious minorities in the Irish Free State and the Republic of Ireland 1922–1995' in Forum for Peace and Reconciliation, *Building Trust in Ireland* (Belfast, 1996), p. 233.

Chapter Six: 'There's no such thing as a poor Protestant'

1 Quoted in Alan Warner, *A Guide to Anglo-Irish Literature* (Dublin, 1981), p. 24.

2 Benjamin Black, *Christine Falls* (London, 2006), pp. 23, 24, 26.

3 Stephen Mennell, Mitchell Elliott, Paul Stokes, Aoife Rickard and Ellen O'Malley Dunlop, 'Protestants in a Catholic state – a silent minority in Ireland' in Tom Inglis, Zdzisław Mach and Rafał Mazanek (eds), *Religion and Politics: East–West Contrasts from Contemporary Europe* (Dublin, 2000), pp. 90–1.

4 Kurt Bowen, *Protestants in a Catholic State: Ireland's Privileged Minority* (Dublin, 1983), pp. 97–8.

5 Terence Dooley, *'The Land for the People': The Land Question in Independent Ireland* (Dublin, 2004), pp. 1–2.

6 R. V. Comerford, *Ireland* (Dublin, 2003), p. 9.

7 Dooley, *'The Land for the People'*, p. 89.

8 Lindsay Proudfoot, in S. J. Connolly, *The Oxford Companion to Irish History* (Oxford, 1998), p. 297.

9 Terence Dooley, *The Decline of the Big House in Ireland: A Study of Irish Landed Families 1860–1960* (Dublin, 2001), p. 272.

10 Ibid., p. 11.

11 Quoted in Dooley, *'The Land for the People'*, p. 81.

12 R. V. Comerford in Connolly, *The Oxford Companion*, pp. 300–1.

13 Bowen, *Protestants in a Catholic State*, p. 15.

14 J. C. Beckett, *The Making of Modern Ireland 1603–1923* (2nd edn, London, 1981), p. 352; Bowen, *Protestants in a Catholic State*, p. 16.

15 Roy Foster, 'Ascendancy and Union' in Roy Foster (ed.), *The Oxford History of Ireland* (Oxford, 1992), p. 169.

16 Bowen, *Protestants in a Catholic State*, p. 16.

17 Diarmaid Ferriter, *The Transformation of Ireland 1900–2000* (London, 2004), p. 313.

18 Eunan O'Halpin, 'Politics and the state, 1922–32' in J. R. Hill (ed.), *A New History of Ireland vii: Ireland 1921–84* (Oxford, 2003), p. 113.

19 Dooley, *'The Land for the People'*, p. 57.

20 Ibid., p. 66.

21 Quoted in Ferriter, *Transformation*, p. 315.

22 Dooley, *'The Land for the People'*, pp. 3–4.

23 Ibid., p. 2.

24 Ibid., p. 66.

25 Ferriter, *Transformation*, p. 315.

26 'The week: cattle bounty', *Church of Ireland Gazette*, 7 Oct. 1932, p. 574.

27 'The future', *Church of Ireland Gazette*, 22 July 1932, p. 426.

28 For example, Letters to the Editor, *Church of Ireland Gazette*, 14 Oct. 1932.

29 Brian Girvin, 'The republicanisation of Irish society, 1932–48' in Hill, *A New History of Ireland*, pp. 130, 137.

30 Bowen, *Protestants in a Catholic State*, p. 83.

31 Ibid., p. 85.

32 White, *Minority Report*, p. 159.

33 Terence Dooley, *The Plight of Monaghan Protestants, 1912–1926* (Dublin, 2000), p. 9.

34 Ferriter, *Transformation*, pp. 371–2.

35 Dooley, *Monaghan Protestants*, p. 11.

36 Bowen, *Protestants in a Catholic State*, p. 95.

37 Comerford, *Ireland*, p. 266.

38 Dooley, *'The Land for the People'*, pp. 12–13.

39 White, *Minority Report*, p. 159.

40 Bowen, *Protestants in a Catholic State*, p. 15.

41 White, *Minority Report*, p. 85.

42 Ibid., p. 163.

43 Ruth Barrington, 'Catholic influence on the health service 1830–2000' in James P. Mackey and Enda McDonagh (eds), *Religion and Politics in Ireland at the Turn of the Millennium* (Dublin, 2003), p. 152.

44 Jacinta Prunty, *Dublin Slums, 1800–1925: A Study in Urban Geography* (Dublin, 1998), pp. 237–8.

45 Barrington, 'Catholic influence', p. 152.

46 White, *Minority Report*, p. 164.

47 Barrington, 'Catholic influence', p. 152.

48 Ibid., pp. 153–5.

49 Correspondence in *Church of Ireland Gazette*, 2 Dec. 1932, p. 708.

50 Barrington, 'Catholic influence', p. 157.

51 Tom Garvin, *Preventing the Future: Why was Ireland So Poor For So Long?* (Dublin, 2005), p. 90.

52 Ibid., pp. 91–4.

53 Daithí Ó Corráin, *Rendering to God and Caesar: The Irish Churches and the Two States in Ireland, 1949–73* (Manchester, 2006), p. 93.

54 Website of the Order of the Knights of St Columbanus, http://www.knightsofstcolumbanus.ie/home.php.html, consulted 3 July 2008.

55 Ó Corráin, *Rendering unto God*, pp. 93–4.

56 Barrington, 'Catholic influence', p. 159.

57 Ibid., pp. 159–65.

58 Rosemary French in Murphy and Adair (eds), *Untold Stories*, p. 83. She was Chairman of the Board of the Adelaide Hospital/Adelaide Hospital Society 1995–8, and of the Adelaide and Meath Hospital, Dublin, incorporating the National Children's Hospital, 1996–9.

59 Bowen, *Protestants in a Catholic State*, p. 94.

60 White, *Minority Report*, p. 158.

61 Bowen, *Protestants in a Catholic State*, pp. 96–7.

62 White, *Minority Report*, pp. 159–60.

63 W. B. Stanford, *Faith and Faction in Ireland Now* (Dublin, 1946), pp. 19–20.

64 Patrick O'Mahony and Gerard Delanty, *Rethinking Irish History: Nationalism, Identity and Ideology* (Basingstoke, 2001), p. 43.

65 White, *Minority Report*, p. 159.

66 Fergus Campbell, 'Who ruled Ireland? The Irish administration 1879–14', *Historical Journal* l: 3 (Sept. 2007), p. 623.

67 White, *Minority Report*, p. 162.

68 Bowen, *Protestants in a Catholic State*, p. 99.

69 Ibid., p. 102.

70 Michael Fogarty et al., *Irish Values and Attitudes: The Irish Report of the European Value Systems Study* (Dublin, 1984), p. 11.

71 Bowen, *Protestants in a Catholic State*, p. 96.

72 Ibid., p. 100.

Chapter Seven: Protestants and Irishness

1 Dymphna Devine and Mary Kelly, '"I just don't want to get picked on by anybody": dynamics of inclusion and exclusion in a newly multi-ethnic Irish primary school', *Children and Society* xx (2006), pp. 129, 131.

2 R. V. Comerford, *Ireland* (London, 2003), pp. 51–84.

3 D. H. Akenson, *A Mirror to Kathleen's Face: Education in Independent Ireland 1922–1960* (London and Montreal, 1975), p. 119.

4 Bruce Stewart, 'Inside nationalism: a meditation upon inventing Ireland', *Irish Studies Review*, VI: 1 (1998), p. 6.

5 Ruth Barrington, 'Catholic influence on the health service 1830–2000' in James P. Mackey and Enda McDonagh (eds), *Religion and Politics in Ireland at the Turn of the Millennium* (Dublin, 2003), p. 157.

6 Alan Acheson, *A History of the Church of Ireland 1691–1996* (Dublin, 1997), p. 233; Catherine O'Connor, 'Protestant women in Ferns, 1945–65: issues of gender, religious and social identity', paper delivered at an interdisciplinary workshop on Protestants at UCC, 26 May 2006, p. 1.

7 Stephen Mennell, 'Introduction' in Colin Murphy and Lynne Adair (eds), *Untold Stories: Protestants in the Republic of Ireland 1922–2002* (Dublin, 2002), p. 6.

8 Judith Butler, *Gender Trouble: Feminism and the Subversion of Identity* (New York, 1990), p. 25.

9 Joseph Ruane, 'Majority–minority conflicts and their resolution: Protestant minorities in France and in Ireland', *Nationalism and Ethnic Politics* XII: 3–4 (autumn/winter, 2006), p. 523.

10 Paul Ricoeur, 'Memory and forgetting' in Richard Kearney and Mark Dooley (eds), *Questioning Ethics: Contemporary Debates in Philosophy* (London and New York, 1999), pp. 6–7.

11 H. K. Crawford, 'V. I. and I. D: women's fractured subjectivity and the work of Sara Paretsky' (MA thesis, UWE at Bristol, 1996), pp. 71–2.

12 Joseph Ruane and David Butler, 'Southern Irish Protestants: an example of de-ethnicisation?' *Nations and Nationalism* XIII: 4 (winter, 2007), p. 633.

13 Ian Beamish, 'Protestants in the Republic' in Letters to the Editor, *Irish Times*, 2 Nov. 2005. Grateful thanks to R. V. Comerford for drawing attention to this letter.

14 Crawford, 'Protestants and Irishness in Independent Ireland: An Exploration', PhD thesis (NUI Maynooth), pp. 283–4, p. 408.

15 Fionnuala Waldron and Susan Pike, 'What does it mean to be Irish? Children's construction of national identity', *Irish Educational Studies* XXV: 2, pp. 248–9.

Bibliography

PRIMARY SOURCES

PERSONAL TESTIMONY
The archive of oral evidence consisted of 100 anonymised transcripts of taped interviews. The interviews were carried out over the period April 2004 to July 2005 in counties Cork, Dublin, Kildare, Mayo, Sligo, Tipperary and Wicklow and in Dublin city and suburbs. The places of birth of the interviewees included counties Antrim, Carlow, Cavan, Clare, Cork, Donegal, Down, Dublin, Galway, Kildare, Limerick, Longford, Mayo, Monaghan, Sligo, Tipperary, Westmeath, Wexford, Wicklow, and Dublin and Cork cities, as well as England and Canada.

WRITTEN MEMOIR
Beattie, Geoffrey, *Protestant Boy* (London, 2004).
Dalton, Kevin, '*That Could Never Be*' (Dublin, 2003).
Griffin, Victor, *Mark of Protest: An Autobiography* (Dublin 1993).
Hamilton, Hugo, *The Speckled People* (London, 2003).
Hyndman, Marilyn, *Further Afield: Journeys from a Protestant Past* (Belfast, 1996).
Kearns, Kevin C., *Dublin's Lost Heroines: Mammies and Grannies in a Vanished City* (Dublin, 2004).
Lander, Ben, *Irish Voices Irish lLves* (Dingle, 1997).
Murphy, Colin and Adair, Lynne (eds), *Untold Stories: Protestants in the Republic of Ireland 1922–2002* (Dublin, 2003).
Murphy, Maura, *Don't Wake Me at Doyle's* (Dublin, 2005).
O'Connor, Lily, *Can Lily O'Shea Come Out to Play?* (Dingle, 2000).
Potterton, Homan, *Rathcormick: A Childhood Recalled* (London, 2004).
Semple, Patrick, *Believe or Not: A Memoir* (Dublin, 2002).
Sheridan, Peter, *44: A Dublin Memoir* (London, 2000).
Stanley, Alan, *I Met Murder on the Way: The Story of the Pearsons of Coolacrease* (Carlow, 2005).
McGahern, John, *Memoir* (London, 2005).

PARLIAMENTARY MATERIAL AND OFFICIAL PUBLICATIONS
Website of the Central Statistics Office, www.census.ie
Website of the Irish Government, www.pobail.ie

Bibliography

Website of the Irish Government's Department of Foreign Affairs, http://foreign affairs.gov.ie
Website of the Office of the Attorney General, www.irishstatute book.ie
Senate Reports online: Website of the Houses of the Oireachtas, http://historical-debates.oireachtas.ie
Department of Education, *Report of the Council of Education, 1931*, held in Allen Library, Dublin.

CONTEMPORARY NEWSPAPERS AND PERIODICALS
Irish Times. Online archive, from 1859, http://Irishtimes.com
Sunday Times Culture.
Observer Review.

LIBRARIES
Representative Church Body Library, Dublin (RCBL) http://www.citc.ie/library.html
Church of Ireland Gazette.
Clogher Diocesan Magazine.
Rathmines Parish Magazine.

National Archives of Ireland *http://www.nationalarchives.ie/html*
DE/1 – DE/4, Cabinet papers, Dáil Éireann Secretariat, 1919–24.
    Department of Education:
Annual Reports, 1930–2.
ED/2: Registers, 1832–1963.
ED/7: Newspaper cuttings 1854–1923.
        Teachers' Notes, 1931.

National Library of Ireland http://webdev.eircom.net/nci2005_beta/site/library/Default.asp
Newspapers' archives.

Allen Library, Dublin
Curriculum materials from Christian Brothers' schools, mid-1920s.

WEBSITES
Website of the Educate Together Organisation, http://www.educatetogether.ie
Website of EduNet, Irish schools on the internet, http://www.EduNet.ie/links/ireland/html
Website of International Constitutional Law, http://www.servat.unibe.ch/icl/ei00000.html
Website of Ireland Now, http://irelandnow.com/marriage.html
Website of Irish language, created by Paulo Ferreira of Salamanca, http://www.irishlanguage.net/irish/history.asp.html
Website of Marriage Matters, the Church of Ireland Marriage Council, http://www.marriagematters.ireland.anglican.org/service/documents/Inter-churchMarriage-AGuide.doc.html
Website of the Mater Hospital, Dublin, http://www.mater.ie/aboutus/mmcuh.html

Website of the Order of the Knights of St Columbanus, http://www.knightsofst
    columbanus.ie/home.php.html
Website of Princess Grace Irish Library (Monaco)
http://www.pgil-eirdata.org/html/pgil_datasets/authors/b/Brooke,SA/life.html
Website of St Vincent's Hospital, Dublin, http://www.stvincents.ie/About_Us/Governance_
    &_Management_Structure.htm
Website of Trinity College Dublin, html://www.tcd.ie/Visitors/tcd_hist.html

REFERENCE BOOKS
Connolly, S. J. (ed), *The Oxford Companion to Irish History* (Oxford, 1998).
Hickey, D. J. and Doherty, J. E., *A New Dictionary of Irish History from 1800* (Dublin, 2003).
Hill, J. R. (ed), *A New History of Ireland, vii: Ireland 1921–1984* (Oxford, 2003).
Hanks, Patrick and Pearsall, Judy, *The New Oxford Dictionary of English* (Oxford, 1998).

RADIO PROGRAMME
George Hook, 'The Right Hook', Newstalk 106FM, 6 Jan. 2006, 5.50 p.m.

SECONDARY SOURCES

BOOKS
Acheson, Alan, *A History of the Church of Ireland 1669–1997* (Dublin 1997).
Akenson, D. H. *The Irish Education Experiment: The National System of Education in the
    Nineteenth Century* (London, 1970).
Akenson, D. H. *A Mirror to Kathleen's Face: Education in Independent Ireland, 1922–1960*
    (Montreal and London, 1975).
Akenson, D. H. *Small Differences, Irish Catholics and Irish Protestants, 1815–1922* (Dublin, 1988).
Anderson, Benedict, *Imagined Communities: Reflections on the Origin and Spread of
    Nationalism* (London and New York, 1983).
Barnard, T. C., *A New Anatomy of Ireland: the Irish Protestants, 1649–1770* (New Haven and
    London, 2003).
Barnard, T. C., *The Kingdom of Ireland, 1641–1760* (London, 2004).
Barnard, T. C., *Irish Protestant Ascents and Descents, 1641–1779* (Dublin, 2004).
Barrington, Ruth, *Health, Medicine and Politics in Ireland 1900–1970* (Dublin, 1987).
Beckett, J. C., *The Making of Modern Ireland 1603–1923* (London, 1966).
Beckett, J. C., *A Short History of Ireland* (London, 1952, reprint 1981).
Black, Benjamin, *Christine Falls* (London, 2006).
Blanshard, Paul, *The Irish and Catholic Power: An American Interpretation* (London, 1954).
Bourdieu, Pierre, *Language and Symbolic Power* (Cambridge, 1972).
Bowen, Desmond, *The Protestant Crusade in Ireland, 1800–70: A Study of Protestant-Catholic
    Relations Between the Act of Union and Disestablishment* (Dublin and Montreal, 1987).
Bowen, Kurt, *Protestants in a Catholic State: Ireland's Privileged Minority* (Dublin, 1983).
Boyce, D. George, *Nationalism in Ireland* (3rd edn, London and New York, 1995).

Boyce, D. George (ed.), *The Revolution in Ireland, 1879–1923* (Dublin, 1988).

Boyce, D. George, *Ireland 1828–1923: From Ascendancy to Democracy* (Oxford, 1992).

Boyce, D. George and O'Day, Alan (eds), *The Making of Modern Irish History: Revisionism and the Revisionist Controversy* (London, 1996).

Boyce, D. G. and O'Day, Alan (eds), *Ireland in Transition, 1867–1921* (London and New York, 2004).

Boyce, D. George and Swift, Roger (eds), *Problems and Perspectives in Irish History since 1800* (Dublin, 2004).

British Academy, *Ireland after the Union* (Oxford, 1989).

Brooke, Revd Stopford A., *A Treasury of Irish Poetry in the English Tongue* (London, 1900).

Brown, Stephen J., SJ (ed.), *From the Realm of Poetry* (London, 1946).

Brown, Terence, *Ireland: A Social and Cultural History, 1922–79* (Glasgow, 1981).

Brown, Terence, *Ireland: A Social and Cultural History, 1922–2002* (London, 2004).

Bryson, Valerie, *Feminist Political Theory: An Introduction* (London, 1992).

Butler, Hubert, 'Boycott village' in *Escape from the Anthill* (Dublin 1986).

Butler, Judith, *Gender Trouble: Feminism and the Subversion of Identity* (New York, 1990).

Cabanal, Patrick, Chabrol, Jean-Paul, Pelen, Jean-Noel, Poujol, Olivier and Travier, Daniel, *Dire les Cévennes: mille ans de témoignages* (Montpellier, 1994).

Canny, Nicholas, *Making Irish British, 1580–1650* (Oxford, 2001).

Canny, Nicholas, *From Reformation to Restoration: Ireland 1534–1660* (Dublin, 1987).

Christian Brothers (eds), *The Higher Literary Reader* (Dublin, 1925).

Clarke, Desmond, *Church and State* (Cork, 1984).

Coffey, Leigh-Ann, *The planters of Luggacurran, County Laois: A Protestant community, 1879–1927* (Dublin, 2006).

Collins, Stephen, *The Power Game: Fianna Fáil since Lemass* (Dublin, 2000).

Comerford, R. V., *Ireland* (London, 2003).

Coogan, T. P., *Ireland in the Twentieth Century* (London, 2003).

Crawford, John, *The Church of Ireland in Victorian Dublin* (Dublin, 2005).

Cullen, Mary and Luddy, Maria (eds), *Women, Power and Consciousness in Nineteenth Century Ireland* (Dublin, 1995).

Cullingford, Elizabeth Butler, *Ireland's Others: Gender and Ethnicity in Irish Literature and Popular Culture* (Cork, 2001).

Crotty, William and David E. Schmitt (eds), *Ireland and the Politics of Change* (London and New York, 1998).

Crowley, Tony, *The Politics of Language in Ireland 1366–1922: A Sourcebook* (London, 1999).

d'Alton, Ian, *Protestant Society and Politics in Cork 1812–1844* (Cork, 1980).

de Paor, Liam, *The Peoples of Ireland: From Prehistory to Modern Times* (London, 1986).

Dooley, Terence, *The Decline of the Big House in Ireland: A Study of Irish Landed Families 1860–1960* (Dublin, 2001).

Dooley, Terence, *The Plight of Monaghan Protestants, 1912–1926* (Dublin 2000).

Dooley, Terence, *'The Land for the People': The Land Question in Independent Ireland* (Dublin, 2004).

Duerst-Lahti, Georgia and Kelly, Rita Mae, *Gender Power, Leadership, and Governance* (Ann Arbor, 1995).

Dunaway, David K., and Baum, Willa K., *Oral History: An Interdisciplinary Anthology* (California, 1996).

English, Richard and Walker, Graham (eds), *Unionism in Modern Ireland: New Perspectives on Politics and Culture* (Dublin 1996).

Fanning, Bryan, *Racism and Social Change in the Republic of Ireland* (Manchester, 2002).

Farmar, Tony, *Ordinary Lives: Three Generations of Irish Middle Class Experience* (Dublin, 1991).

Fennell, Desmond, *The Revision of Irish Nationalism* (Dublin, 1989).

Ferriter, Diarmaid, *The Transformation of Ireland 1900–2000* (London, 2004).

Fogarty, Michael, Ryan, Liam and Lee, Joseph, *Irish Values and Attitudes: The Irish Report of the European Value Systems Study* (Dublin, 1984).

Foster, R. F., *Modern Ireland, 1600–1972* (London, 1988).

Foster, R. F. (ed.), *The Oxford History of Ireland* (Oxford, 1992).

Fuller, Louise, *Irish Catholicism since 1950: The Undoing of a Culture* (Dublin, 2002).

Fulton, John, *The Tragedy of Belief: Division, Politics and Religion in Ireland* (Oxford, 1991).

Garvin, Tom, *Preventing the Future: Why Was Ireland so Poor for so Long?* (Dublin, 2004).

Geary, Laurence M., *Medicine and Charity in Ireland 1718–1815* (Dublin, 2004).

Gluck, S. B. and Patai, Daphne (eds), *Women's Words: The Feminist Practice of Oral History* (New York, 1991).

Griffin, Victor, *Enough Religion to Make Us Hate: Reflections on Religion and Politics* (Dublin, 2002).

Griffith, Kenneth and O'Grady, Timothy, *Curious Journeys: An Oral History of Ireland's Unfinished Revolution* (Cork, 1998).

Harkness, D. W., *The Restless Dominion: The Irish Free State and the British Commonwealth of Nations 1921–31* (London, 1969).

Hart, Peter, *The IRA and its Enemies: Violence and Community in Cork, 1916–1923* (Oxford, 1998).

Hickey, D. J. and Doherty, J. E., *A New Dictionary of Irish History from 1800* (Dublin, 2003).

Hoppen, K. Theodore, *Ireland Since 1800: Conflict and Conformity* (London, 1989).

Inglis, Tom, *Moral Monopoly: The Rise and Fall of the Catholic Church in Modern Ireland* (2nd edn; Dublin, 1998)

Inglis, Tom, Mach, Zdisław and Mazanek, Rafał (eds), *Religion and Politics: East-West Contrasts from Contemporary Europe* (Dublin, 2000).

Jordan, Glenn, *Not of this world? Evangelising Protestants in Northern Ireland* (Belfast, 2001).

Kelly, Adrian, *Compulsory Irish: Language and Education in Ireland 1870s–1970s* (Dublin, 2002).

Kiberd, Declan, *Inventing Ireland: The Literature of the Modern Nation* (London, 1996).

Lee, J. J., *The Modernisation of Irish Society, 1848–1918* (Dublin 1973).

Lee, J. J. *Ireland, 1912–1985: Politics and Society* (Cambridge, 1989).

Lennon, Colm, *Sixteenth-Century Ireland: The Incomplete Conquest* (Dublin, 1994).

Lyons, F. S. L. *Ireland Since the Famine* (London, 1971).

Leichty, Joseph and Clegg, Cecelia, *Moving Beyond Sectarianism: Religion, Conflict and Reconciliation in Northern Ireland* (Dublin, 2001).

Logue, Paddy, *Being Irish: Personal Reflections on Irish Identity Today* (Dublin, 2000).

Mac Gréil, Míchéal, *Prejudice and Tolerance in Ireland* (Dublin, 1977).

Mac Gréil, Míchéal, *Prejudice in Ireland Revisited* (Maynooth, 1996).

McElligott, T. J., *Secondary Education in Ireland 1870–1921* (Dublin, 1981).

McKenna, Yvonne, *Made Holy: Irish Women Religious at Home and Abroad* (Dublin, 2006).

Mackey, J. P. and McDonagh, Enda (eds), *Religion and Politics in Ireland at the Turn of the Millennium* (Dublin 2003).

MacManus, Francis (ed.), *The Years of the Great Test 1926–39: The Thomas Davis Lectures* (Cork, 1967).

Malik, Kenan, *The Meaning of Race, History and Culture in Western Society* (London, 1996).

Mistry, Rohinton, *A Fine Balance* (London, 1996).

Moffitt, Miriam, *The Church of Ireland Community of Killala and Achonry 1870–1940* (Dublin, 1999).

Munro, Hector Hugh, 'Reginald on house parties' in *Collected Short Stories of Saki* (Hertfordshire, 1993).

Moody, T. W. and Martin, F. X., *The Course of Irish History* (Cork, 2001).

Murphy, J. A., *Ireland in the Twentieth Century* (Dublin, 1975).

O'Connor, Pat, *Emerging Voices: Women in Contemporary Irish Society* (Dublin, 1998).

O'Connor, Sean, *A Troubled Sky: Reflections on the Irish Education Scene 1957–1968* (Dublin, 1986).

Ó Corráin, Daithí, *Rendering to God and Caesar: The Irish Churches and the Two States in Ireland, 1949–73* (Manchester, 2006).

Ó Duigneáin, Proinnsíos, *The Priest and the Protestant Woman: The Trial of Revd Thomas Maguire, P.P., December, 1827* (Dublin, 1997).

Ó Gráda, Cormac, *A New Economic History of Ireland, 1780–1939* (Oxford, 1994).

Ó Gráda, Cormac, *A Rocky Road: The Irish Economy Since the 1920s* (Manchester, 1997).

O'Mahoney, Patrick and Delanty, Gerard, *Rethinking Irish History: Nationalism, Identity and Ideology* (Basingstoke, 1998).

Owens, Rosemary Cullen, *A Social History of Women in Ireland 1870–1970* (Dublin, 2005).

Patterson, Henry, *The Politics of Illusion: A Political History of the IRA* (London, 1997).

Perks, Robert, *Oral History: Talking About the Past* (London, 1992).

Perks, Robert and Thomson, Alistair (eds), *The Oral History Reader* (London, 1998).

Prunty, Jacinta, *Dublin Slums, 1800–1925: A Study in Urban Geography* (Dublin, 1998).

Refaussé, Raymond, *Church of Ireland Records* (Dublin, 2000).

Ritchie, Donald A., *Doing Oral History* (New York, 1995).

Ruane, Joseph and Todd, Jennifer, *The Dynamics of Conflict in Northern Ireland* (Cambridge, 1996).

Selden, Raman and Widdowson, Peter, *A Reader's Guide to Contemporary Literary Theory* (Hemel Hempstead, 1993).

Skeggs, Beverley (ed.), *Feminist Cultural Theory: Process and Production* (Manchester, 1995).

Stanford, W. B., *A Recognised Church: The Church of Ireland in Eire* (Dublin, 1944).

Stanford, W. B., *Faith and Faction in Ireland Now* (Dublin, 1946).

Stanley, Alan, *I Met Murder on the Way: The Story of the Pearsons of Coolacrease* (Carlow, 2005).

Thompson, Paul, *The Voice of the Past: Oral History* (3rd edn, Oxford, 1978).

Thompson, Paul, *The Edwardians: The Remaking of British Society* (London, 1975).

Titley, E. Brian, *Church, State and the Control of Schooling in Ireland 1900–1984* (Dublin, 1983.

Ward, Alan J., *The Irish Constitutional Tradition: Responsible Government and Modern Ireland, 1782–1992* (Dublin, 1994).

Ward, Margaret, *Unmanageable Revolutionaries: Women and Irish Nationalism* (Dingle, 1989).

Warner, Alan, *A Guide to Anglo-Irish Literature* (Dublin, 1981).

Webster, Jason, *Guerra* (London, 2006).

Whelan, Gerard and Swift, Carolyn, *Spiked: Church-State Intrigue and the Rose Tattoo* (Dublin, 2002).

White, G. K., *A History of St Columba's College, 1843–1974* (Dublin, 1980).

White, Jack, *Minority Report: The Protestant Community in the Irish Republic* (Dublin, 1975).

Whyte, J. H., *Church and State in Modern Ireland 1923–1979* (2nd edn, London, 1980).

Young, Iris Marion, *Justice and the Politics of Difference* (Princeton, 1990).

CHAPTERS FROM BOOKS

Akenson, D. H., with Farren, S. and Coolahan, J., 'Pre-university education, 1921–84' in Hill, J. R. (ed.), *A New History of Ireland, vii: Ireland 1921–84* (Oxford, 2003), pp. 711–55.

Barrington, Ruth, 'Catholic influence on the health service 1830–2000' in Mackey, James P. and McDonagh, Enda (eds), *Religion and Politics in Ireland at the Turn of the Millennium* (Dublin, 2003), pp. 152–65.

Barnard, T. C., 'Improving Clergymen' in McGuire, James, Ford, Alan, and Milne, Kenneth (eds), *As by Law Established: The Church of Ireland since the Reformation* (Dublin, 1995), pp. 136–51.

Barnard, T. C., 'Protestantism, ethnicity and Irish identities' in Claydon, Tony, and McBride, Ian (eds), *Protestantism and National Identity: Britain and Ireland, c.1650–c.1850* (Cambridge, 1998), pp. 206–35.

Brown, Terence, 'Religious minorities in the Irish Free State and the Republic of Ireland 1922–1995' in Forum for Peace and Reconciliation, *Building Trust in Ireland* (Belfast, 1996), pp. 216–53.

Buttimer, Neil, 'The Irish language' in Hill, J. R. (ed.), *A New History of Ireland, vii: Ireland 1921–84* (Oxford, 2003), pp. 538–73.

Canny, Nicholas, 'Early modern Ireland, c.1500–1700' in Foster, R. F. (ed.), *The Oxford History of Ireland* (Oxford, 1992), pp. 104–60.

Canny, Nicholas, 'Foreword' in Kenny, Kevin (ed.), *Ireland and the British Empire* (Oxford, 2004), pp. ix–xviii.

Cathcart, Rex with Muldoon, Michael, 'The mass media in twentieth-century Ireland' in Hill, J. R. (ed.), *A New History of Ireland, vii: Ireland 1921–84* (Oxford, 2003), pp. 671–710.

Coakley, John, 'Religion, ethnic identity and the protestant minority in the Republic' in Crotty, William and Schmitt, David (eds), *Ireland and the Politics of Change* (London and New York, 1998), pp. 86–106.

Comerford, R. V., 'The British state and the education of Irish Catholics, 1850–1921' in Tomiak, Janusz (ed.), *Comparative Studies on Governments and Non-Dominant Ethnic Groups In Europe, 1850–1940, i: Schooling, Educational Policy and Ethnic Identity* (Dartmouth, 1991), pp. 13–33.

Comerford, R. V., 'Nation, nationalism, and the Irish language' in Hachey, Thomas E. and McCaffrey, Lawrence, J. (eds), *Perspectives on Irish Nationalism* (Lexington, 1989), pp. 20–41.

Coolahan, John, 'Higher Education 1908–1984,' in Hill, J. R. (ed.), *A New History of Ireland, vii: Ireland, 1921–84* (Oxford, 2003), pp. 757–95.

English, Richard, 'The same people with different relatives? modern scholarship, Unionists and the Irish nation' in English, Richard and Walker, Graham (eds), *Unionism in Modern Ireland: New Perspectives on Politics and Culture* (Basingstoke, 1996), pp. 220–35.

Graham, Brian. 'Ireland and Irishness: place, culture and identity' in Graham, Brian (ed.), *In Search of Ireland: A Cultural Geography* (London and New York, 1997), pp. 1–15.

Grele, R. J., 'Directions for oral history in the United States' in Dunaway, D. K. and Baum, W. K. (eds), *Oral History: An Interdisciplinary Anthology* (Walnut Creek, 1996), pp. 62–84.

Farrell, Revd Joseph, two essays 'About Books' in Christian Brothers (eds), *The Higher Literary Reader* (Dublin, 1925), pp. 43–5.

Fitzpatrick, David, 'Ireland since 1870' in Foster, R. F. (ed.), *The Oxford History of Ireland* (Oxford, 1992), pp. 174–226.

Fulton, John, 'The religious boundaries of group reproduction: Catholic-Protestant marriages north and south' in Fulton, John, *The Tragedy of Belief: Division, Politics and Religion in Ireland* (Oxford, 1991), pp. 159–75.

Girvin, Brian, 'The republicanisation of Irish society, 1932–48' in Hill, J. R. (ed.), *A New History of Ireland vii: Ireland 1921–84* (Oxford, 2003), pp. 127–60.

Hart, Peter, 'The Protestant experience of revolution in southern Ireland' in English, Richard and Walker, Gerard (eds), *Unionism in Modern Ireland* (Basingstoke, 1996), pp. 81–98.

Heron, Alasdair, 'The ecclesiological problems of inter-church marriage' in Hurley, Michael (ed.), *Beyond Tolerance: The Challenge of Mixed Marriage* (Aylesbury, 1975), pp. 73–103.

Hill, Jacqueline R., 'Dublin after the Union: the age of the ultra Protestants, 1801–22' in Brown, Michael, Geoghegan, Patrick and Kelly, James (eds), *The Irish Act of Union, 1800: Bicentennial Essays* (Dublin, 2003), pp. 144–56.

Lyons, F. S. L., 'The minority problem in the 26 counties' in MacManus, Francis (ed.), *The Years of the Great Test 1926–39: The Thomas Davis lectures* (Cork, 1967), pp. 92–103.

Lyons, John B., 'Irish medical historiography' in O'Brien, Eoin (ed.), *Essays in honour of J. D. H. Widdess* (Dublin, 1978), pp. 89–111.

McBride, Ian, 'Memory and national identity in modern Ireland' in McBride, Ian (ed.), *History and Memory in Modern Ireland* (Cambridge, 2001), pp. 1–42.

McGuinness, Catherine, 'Being Protestant in the Republic of Ireland' in McLoone, James (ed.), *Being Protestant in Ireland: Papers Presented at the 32nd Annual Summer School of the Social Study Conference* (Naas, 1985), pp. 20–33.

Maguire, Martin, 'The Church of Ireland and the problem of the Protestant working class of Dublin' in Ford, Alan, McGuire, James and Milne, Kenneth (eds), *As by Law Established: The Church of Ireland Since the Reformation* (Dublin, 1995), pp. 195–203.

Maguire, Martin, '"Our people": the Church of Ireland and the culture of community in Dublin since disestablishment,' in Gillespie, Raymond and Neely, W. G. (eds), *The laity and the Church of Ireland, 1000–2000: All Sorts and Conditions* (Dublin, 2002), pp. 277–303.

Megahey, Alan, 'God will defend the right': the Protestant churches and opposition to home rule' in Boyce, D. G. and O'Day, Alan (eds), *Defenders of the Union* (London, 2001), pp. 159–75.

Mennell, Stephen, Elliott, Mitchell, Stokes, Paul, Rickard Aoife and O'Malley Dunlop, Ellen, 'Protestants in a Catholic state – a silent minority in Ireland' in Inglis, Tom et al., *Religion and Politics: East-West Contrasts from Contemporary Europe* (Dublin, 2000), pp. 68–92.

Milne, Kenneth, 'The Protestant churches in independent Ireland' in Mackay, James P. and McDonagh, Enda (eds), *Religion and Politics in Ireland at the Turn of the Millennium* (Dublin, 2003), pp. 64–83.

Ó Catháin, Seán, 'Education in the new Ireland' in MacManus, Francis (ed.), *The Years of the Great Test 1926–39: The Thomas Davis Lectures* (Cork, 1967), pp. 104–14.

O'Halpin, Eunan, 'Politics and the state' in Hill, J. R. (ed.), *A New History of Ireland, vii: Ireland 1921–84* (Oxford, 2003), pp. 86–126.

O'Keeffe, Very Revd T., 'The affection and reverence due to a mother' in Christian Brothers (eds), *The Higher Literary Reader* (Dublin, 1925), pp. 29–30.

O'Leary, Richard, 'The President's communion' in Slater, Eamon (ed.), *Memories of the present: A sociological chronicle 1997–98* (Dublin, 2000), pp. 145–52.

O'Neill, Thomas P., 'Political life: 1870–1921' in Hurley, Michael (ed.), *Irish Anglicanism, 1870–1970* (Dublin, 1970), pp. 101–10.

Passerini, Luisa, 'Work ideology and consensus under Italian fascism' in *History Workshop: 8*, 1979, pp. 84–92, in Perks, Robert, and Thomson, Alistair (eds), *The Oral History Reader* (London, 1998), pp. 53–62.

Poole, Michael A., 'In search of ethnicity in Ireland' in Graham, Brian (ed.), *In Search of Ireland: A Cultural Geography* (London and New York, 1997), 128–47.

Ricoeur, Paul, 'Memory and forgetting' in Kearney, Richard and Dooley, Mark (eds), *Questioning Ethics: Contemporary Debates in Philosophy* (London and New York, 1999).

Sangster, Joan, 'Telling our stories: feminist debates and the use of oral history' in Perks, Robert and Thomson, Alistair (eds), *The Oral History Reader* (London, 1998), pp. 87–100.

Sexton, J. J. and O'Leary, Richard, 'Factors affecting population decline in minority religious communities in the Republic of Ireland' in Forum for Peace and Reconciliation, *Building Trust in Ireland* (Belfast, 1996), pp. 257–332.

Whyte, J. H., 'Political life in the South' in Hurley, Michael (ed.), *Irish Anglicanism 1869–1969* (Dublin, 1970), pp. 143–53.

Williams, T. Desmond, 'Conclusion' in MacManus, Francis (ed.), *The Years of the Great Test, 1926–39: The Thomas Davis Lectures* (Cork, 1967), pp. 173–83.

ARTICLES

Amidon, Stephen, 'A guide to Philip Roth', *Sunday Times Culture*, 23 Sept. 2007, p. 7.

Barnard, T. C., 'Crises of identity among Irish Protestants 1641–1685', *Past and Present*: 127 (May 1990), pp. 39–83.

Bibliography

Barton, Keith C. and McCully, Alan W., 'History, identity and the school curriculum in Northern Ireland: an empirical study of secondary students' ideas and perspectives', *Journal of Curriculum Studies* XXXVII: 1 (2005), pp. 85–116.

Campbell, Fergus, 'Who ruled Ireland? The Irish administration 1879–14', *The Historical Journal*, l: 3 (Sept. 2007), pp. 623–44.

Considere-Charon, Marie-Claire, 'The Church of Ireland: continuity and change', *Studies* XCVII: 386 (summer 1998)

Curtis, L. P. Jr, 'The greening of Irish history', *Éire–Ireland* XXIX: 1 (1994), pp. 7–28.

Devine, Dymphna and Kelly, Mary, '"I just don't want to get picked on by anybody": dynamics of inclusion and exclusion in a newly multi-ethnic Irish primary school', *Children and Society* XX (2006), pp. 128–39.

Doherty, Gabriel, 'National identity and the study of Irish history', *English Historical Review*, CXI (Apr. 1996), pp. 324–49.

Fay, Liam, 'More Irish than the Irish', *Sunday Times Culture*, 21 Jan. 2007.

Garvin, Tom, 'The return of history: collective myths and modern nationalisms', *Irish Review* IX (1990), pp. 16–30.

Hepburn, A. C., 'Language, religion and national identity in Ireland since 1880', *Perspectives on European Politics and Society* II: 2 (Aug. 2001), pp. 197–220.

Lee, R. M., 'Intermarriage, conflict and social control in Ireland: the decree "*Ne temere*"' *Economic and Social Review* XVII: 1 (Oct. 1985), pp. 11–27.

Loughlin, James, 'Allegiance and illusion: Queen Victoria's Irish visit of 1849', *History* LXXXVII: 288 (Oct. 2002), pp. 491–513.

Maguire, Moira J. and O Cinneide, Seamas, 'A good beating never hurt anyone': the punishment and abuse of children in twentieth century Ireland', *Journal of Social History* XXXVIII: 3 (spring 2005), pp. 635–52.

Nelsen, Hart M., 'The religious identification of children of interfaith marriages', *Review of Religious Research* XXXII: 2 (Dec. 1990), pp. 122–34.

Nutt, Kathleen, 'Irish identity and the writing of history', *Éire–Ireland* XXIX: 2 (1994), pp. 160–72.

O'Leary, Richard, 'Modernisation and religious intermarriage in the Republic of Ireland', *British Journal of Sociology* 52: 4 (Dec. 2001), pp. 647–65.

O'Leary, Richard, 'Change in the rate and pattern of religious intermarriage in the Republic of Ireland', *Economic and Social Review* XXX: 2 (Apr. 1999), pp. 119–32.

O'Leary, Richard and Finnäs, Fjalar, 'Education, social integration and minority–majority group intermarriage', *Sociology* XXXVI: 2 (2002), pp. 235–54.

O'Reilly, Clodagh, 'Psychiatry and Irish culture: interview with Anthony Clare', *The Crane Bag* VII: 2 (1983), pp. 172–6.

Ruane, Joseph, 'Majority–minority conflicts and their resolution: Protestant minorities in France and Ireland', *Nationalism and Ethnic Politics* XII: 3–4 (autumn/winter, 2006), pp. 509–32.

Ruane, Joseph and Butler, David, 'Southern Irish Protestants: an example of de-ethnicisation?', *Nations and Nationalism* XIII: 4 (winter, 2007), pp. 619–35.

Ruane, Joseph and Todd, Jennifer, 'The roots of intense conflict may not in fact be ethnic …
categories, communities and path dependence', *European Journal of Sociology* XLV: 2,
pp. 209–32.

Stewart, Bruce, 'Inside nationalism: a meditation upon inventing Ireland', *Irish Studies Review*
VI: 1 (1998), pp. 5–16.

Thompson, Paul, 'Problems of method in oral history', *Oral History Journal* 1: 4 (1972),
pp. 4–5.

Tobin, Robert, 'Tracing again the tiny snail track': southern Protestant memoir since 1950',
The Yearbook of English Studies XXXV: 1 (Jan. 2005), pp. 171–85.

Tormey, Roland, 'The construction of national identity through primary school history: the
Irish case', *British Journal of Sociology of Education* XXVII: 3 (July 2006), pp. 311–32.

Waldron, Fionnuala and Pike, Susan, 'What does it mean to be Irish? Children's construction
of national identity', *Irish Educational Studies* XXV: 2 (June 2006), pp. 231–51.

Williams, Kevin, 'Faith and the nation: education and religious identity in the Republic of
Ireland', *British Journal of Educational Studies* XLVIII: 4 (Dec. 1999), pp. 317–44.

Yeates, Nicola, 'Gender, familism and housing: matrimonial property rights in Ireland',
Women's Studies International Forum XXII: 6 (Nov.–Dec., 1999), pp. 607–18.

THESES AND PAPERS
Crawford, H. K., 'V. I. and I. D: women's fractured subjectivity and the work of Sara Paretsky'
(MA thesis, University of the West of England at Bristol, 1996).

Creedon, M., 'Proselytism: its operations in Ireland', *Record of the Maynooth Union, 1926,*
pp. 14–29.

Deignan, Patrick, 'The Protestant community in Sligo, 1914–1949', PhD thesis (National
University of Ireland, Maynooth, 2008).

Flynn, Charles, 'Dundalk 1900–1960: an oral history', PhD thesis (National University of
Ireland, Maynooth, 2000).

Holohan, Carole, '"Every generation has its task": Irish youth in the sixties', PhD thesis
(University College Dublin, 2009).

Maguire, Martin, 'The Dublin Protestant Working Class 1870–1932: Economy Society
Politics', MA thesis (University College Dublin, 1990).

Moffitt, Miriam, 'The Society for Irish Christian Mission to the Roman Catholics,
1849–1950', PhD thesis (National University of Ireland, Maynooth, 2006).

O'Connor, Catherine, 'Protestant women in Ferns, 1945–65: Issues, of gender, religious and
social identity', paper delivered at interdisciplinary workshop on Protestants, University
College Cork, 26 May 2006.

O'Connor, Catherine, 'Southern Protestantism: the inter-relationship of religious, social and
gender identity in the diocese of Ferns 1945–65', PhD thesis (University College
Limerick, 2008).

'New School Kilternan Parish', pamphlet, unnumbered pages, undated, but letter affixed to
inside back cover from Rector dated October 1981. Held in RCB.

Index